MW00872581

KEYS TO SUCCESS

Credit Counselor Certification

Exam Study Guide

info@acecertificate.com

www.acecertificate.com

Table of Contents

Introduction

The Academy for Credit Education (ACE) offers the fifth edition of the nationally recognized Credit Counselor Certification Program, *Keys to Success*. This new edition is offered in three formats: a free online course, a mobile-ready ebook and a hard copy text. Certification candidates are strongly encouraged to visit www.acecertificate.com to view the slide presentations that cover each of the five modules and to complete the self-scoring practice exam. Candidates can also request the certification exam at the ACE website.

Keys to Success has prepared thousands of credit counselors, debt settlement specialists and other financial-based counseling professionals for certification. Curriculum is based on a formal job/needs analysis of the debt management and debt settlement industries conducted by ACE affiliate, Center for Financial Literacy(CFL) and Florida Institute of Technology's Center for Professional Development.

FIFTH EDITION DEVELOPMENT

The fifth edition includes a new module, *Setting Standards* which examines the role of the credit counselor. It surveys the history and trends of debt management and debt settlement services in the United States and provides a summary of the Uniform Debt-Management Services Act (UDMSA). Included in Module 1 curriculum is the *Code of Ethics* which previously appeared in an appendix.

The glossary is now segmented into *Counseling Key Words* and *Credit Key Words.* Generally, words pertaining to counseling appear in the first three modules while words pertaining to credit appear in the last two modules.

Appendix B: Consumer Protection Legislation is expanded, most notably, with the CARD Act of 2009. Active links for further reading are provided for each law.

Appendix C: Consumer Resources is updated and expanded with links to consumer information and financial tools.

Statistics and facts throughout the text have been checked for accuracy and updated where necessary.

Budget worksheets and other interactive features of the previous hard copy editions are replaced with suggested links to online consumer tools. These links also appear in *Appendix C*. Most graphics and images have been removed in favor of the simple format of headings, sub-headings and content text. Visual learners will benefit from the Review Presentations at the ACE website.

Finally, the term *credit counselor* is used instead of *financial-based counselor*. The later term was adopted as a way to address the readership which includes debt negotiators as well as budget counselors who may or may not offer debt management plans. The fifth edition reverts to the original *credit counselor* for simplicity's sake and to avoid confusion with the terms *financial counselor* and *financial planner*. It is to be understood, however, that *credit counselor*, as it appears here, refers to any professional who offers services regarding consumer debt and education.

OBJECTIVES

Objectives are to deliver the knowledge, skills and abilities to:

Promote financial literacy. Participants become resources of timely information about money management, credit use, and options for resolving debt.

Implement financial action plans. Participants will understand the "how-to" of the personal financial tasks essential to financial well-being.

Provide support and resources. Participants learn essential counseling techniques and give referrals when necessary to ensure client success.

CONTENT & FORMAT

Program curriculum is designed for independent study and is organized into five content areas. Each module is comprised of four to five units which include a preview, a summary and a short-answer quiz. There are five modules:

Module 1: Setting Standards examines the role of credit counseling today from professional ethics to industry standards.

Module 2: Communicating with Clients explores the counseling process and the essential skills necessary for affecting positive change.

Module 3: Taking Control of Finances analyzes the problem-solving process from the client's presenting concern to creation of the action plan.

Module 4: Demystifying Credit provides a timely knowledge base about choosing and using credit cards to optimize financial well-being. Credit reports and credit scoring are also examined.

Module 5: Understanding and Resolving Debt considers the many sources of debt, debt collection practices and consequences of unpaid debt. Options for resolving debt are then surveyed from budget counseling to bankruptcy.

APPROACH TO COUNSELING

This program recognizes there is a difference between counseling provided by licensed professionals and the application of counseling skills and processes as they apply to credit counseling or any type of financial-based counseling.

Clients who initiate credit or debt counseling may exhibit levels of emotional duress that may be inappropriate for the financial-based counselor to address. Mental health issues should be referred to licensed professionals; financial-based counselors do not provide therapy.

Financial-based counselors, however, can and should familiarize themselves with counseling techniques that facilitate positive change for the client. The counseling methods and models presented in this program are:

- Solution-Focused Counseling
- The Problem-Management/Opportunity-Development Model
- The Human/Business Model
- Bandura's Theory of Self-Efficacy
- Rotter's Locus of Control Theory
- Ellis' Cognitive Theory
- Maslow's Hierarchy of Needs

APPROACH TO LEGAL ISSUES

Financial-based counselors refrain from dispensing legal advice to their clients although they should know and understand the important consumer protection legislation that applies to credit and debt issues. A specific law can be sited but not interpreted by a financial-based counselor. Clients with specific legal questions are to be referred to licensed attorneys -- especially questions relating to bankruptcy, foreclosure and workman's compensation.

TESTING

The Certification Exam consists of 100 multiple-choice items. A passing score is 70% or higher. Candidates who do not pass the first time can retest after 30 days. The test is written in accordance with current measurement standards and is monitored for validity, reliability and fairness.

Testing is administered by qualified proctors through our website. Candidates fill out the Request Exam Form located at the bottom center of the homepage and receive an Authorization to Test. Candidates can then schedule their exam and will have the option of completing it online or in person. There is a two-hour time limit to complete the test.

CERTIFICATION

Successful candidates earn a two-year, renewable certificate with the designation Certified Credit Counselor. Certification begins on the date a candidate passes the exam.

THE ASSOCIATION OF DEBT COUNSELORS

Successful candidates become members of the Association of Debt Counselors (ADC). ADC sets and monitors standards for counselor training and certification. Member benefits include access to a password protected MyACE dashboard, automated alerts to certification time lines and preferred rates for the Academy's continuing education offerings.

RENEWAL

Counselors renew their certificates by completing a total of 16 continuing education units (CEUs) for each two-year period. Like other professions such as medicine, law, and education, financial-based counseling is a dynamic field that requires continued training and access to new information for optimal job effectiveness.

The Academy for Credit Education offers a variety of CEU programs that can be accessed and completed at its website. Counselors also have the option to submit a course or seminar for CEU approval.

Certification is renewed by completing the Certification Renewal Form located at the bottom right of the ACE homepage. Counselors will list their completed CEUs (no less than 16) and include a $50.00 renewal fee.

CODE OF ETHICS

Module I, Unit 4 contains the *Code of Ethics* developed for credit counselors. It is based on professional counseling ethics modified to the industry standards specific to credit counseling.

STUDY TIPS

For independent study, candidates are encouraged to utilize the SQ3R method. SQ3R stands for Survey, Question, Read, Recite and Review.

S = Survey

Gives you a preview of what you are about to read.

Helps you determine how long it will take.

Helps you relate what you are about to read with what you already know.

This means reading through the Introduction, the Table of Contents, the Unit Previews, and the Summaries.

Q = Question

Ask yourself questions about what you are about to read.

Questions help you study - you are looking for the answers.

Questions provide a personal purpose for reading.

For example: What does the unit title mean? What do I want to learn from this unit? How is the material related to what I already know?

You will read with more understanding if you do the SQ activities first. As you read, answer the questions you raised in SQ. that will give your reading a sense of purpose. Read carefully any italicized/bold printed words. If you do not know the meaning of a word, click on the hyperlink provided.

R2 = Recite

Go over what you read in R1 by either orally summarizing it or by making notes. We tend to forget 80% of what we read after two weeks. If we recite it, we forget only 20%.

R3 = Review

Review each unit after reading it.

Read any notes you have jotted down.

Review periodically.

The Academy for Credit Education wishes you success in pursuing your certification, continued education and professional endeavors.

Module I: Setting Standards

The relationship between credit counselor and client is unique. In what other exchange does one stranger tell another the intricate details of his/her financial dilemma? In what other interpersonal communication is trust so critical? Clients who seek out credit counseling do so under the assumption that credit counselors are professionals who will help them. If that trust is broken, there is no turning back. Trust is earned by adhering to a code, a standard of doing things that provides a necessary measure of consistency.

The credit counseling and debt settlement industries share a dynamic history punctuated by economic ups and downs and consumer protection legislation, the most comprehensive legislation being the Uniform Debt Management Services Act (USDMA). The USDMA is an attempt to establish federal standards for agencies working with consumers in debt. Prior to this law, agencies had to contend with different state laws that often were at odds with each other.

Industry standards, however, begin with the development and implementation of workplace ethics. Unit 4 of this module includes our industry-specific *Code of Ethics*. Counselors are the ones on the front lines interacting with a wide array of clients in debt. Counselors -- credit counselors and debt negotiators -- are the representatives of their profession and it is through them that standards are established and upheld.

After completing this module, you will:

- gain insight into the history of the credit card.
- understand the need for intervention concerning debt.
- be able to identify various causes of debt.
- be able to give an example of an insolvency event.
- determine the proper role of the credit counselor.
- understand how to avoid the unauthorized practice of law.
- understand the definition of therapy.
- become familiar with the main provisions of the UDMSA.
- gain insight into the importance of ethics.
- become familiar with the *Code of Ethics*.

Unit 1: From Credit Cards to Credit Counseling

OBJECTIVES
- To gain a historical perspective on credit cards.
- To explore how an insolvency event can trigger severe debt issues.
- To identify destructive behaviors that fuel debt.

According to the Federal Reserve, credit-card debt is the third largest source of debt after mortgage debt and student loan debt. The average credit-card debt per household in the United States is $7,281. It is estimated that over half of American households with credit cards carry a credit-card balance from month to month.

Other sources report that Americans spend over one trillion dollars every year with their credit cards. They owe more than $700 billion of it. Fifteen percent of the disposable income of Americans goes to paying credit card debt.

With these statistics, it may be hard to believe that the credit card as we know it today has only been around for a little more than fifty years. Within that short amount of time, however, it has made a tremendous, and often devastating, impact on personal finances. How did this explosion in credit use get started and why are so many Americans finding themselves in the credit trap?

A SHORT HISTORY OF THE CREDIT CARD

Although the idea of "have now, pay later" has been around in one form or another as far back as the 1700s, the use of a credit card originated in the United States in the 1920s when oil companies and hotel chains issued them to their customers. These types of cards and the ones to follow were created for convenience while on the road.

In 1946, John Biggins of the Flatbush National Bank of Brooklyn invented the "Charge-It" card. It was the first bank-issued credit card. Merchants could deposit sales slips in the bank after which the bank billed the customer who used the card.

Then, in 1951, a fateful event occurred. Frank McNamara had dinner at a restaurant but when he went to pay his bill, he realized he had forgotten his wallet. This embarrassing situation propelled him to invent the Diners Club Card. Initially, 200 of these cards were issued for use in 27 New York restaurants. Technically, they were "charge cards" in that the entire amount had to be repaid in one payment.

American Express, which began with traveler's checks, issued its first card in 1958. As with earlier cards, it was primarily designed for on-the-road convenience. During this period, the traveling salesman was an integral part of the American business landscape.

Later in 1958, Bank of America offered the Bank Americard within the state of California. Shortly thereafter, the name of this card was changed to VISA.

The early 1960s saw more companies entering the credit card arena. They were still advertised primarily as time-saving rather than as a form of credit. By 1966, American Express and MasterCard became huge overnight successes marketing mainly to the traveling salesman.

In 1970, the use of credit cards increased dramatically due to the establishment of standards for the magnetic strip. The system of a magnetic strip, originally called a *stripe*, had been used first by the London Transit Authority in the early 1960s.

The United States Congress began regulating the credit-card industry in the mid 1970s. Practices such as mass mailing active cards to people who never requested them were banned.

The pendulum swung the other way in the 1990s, however, when many restrictions on creditors were lifted. This deregulation allowed creditors to charge high late fees as well as some very high interest rates.

In 1987, American Express offered its first card that could be paid off over time. The Discover Card, part of Sears Corporation, came after that.

Today, it is hard to imagine life without credit cards. They provide us with convenience and a way to get what we want today and pay for it later. Merchants readily accept credit cards because they know consumers buy more on credit. In fact, the average credit-card purchase is 12 -- 18% higher than if cash was used. Also, bank cards are welcomed because they are less expensive than merchant-specific cards and safer than accepting cash.

CREDIT COUNSELING
The same year that Frank McNamara invented the first Diners Club Card, the first credit counseling agencies were established. They began as face-to-face counseling services designed to increase consumer financial literacy and help those in debt avoid bankruptcy.

By the early 1990s, many agencies favored over-the-phone counseling that could reach people nationwide. Debt management plans could effectively be set up and administered through telephone, fax and email technology. Today, there are a wide array of credit counseling agencies in the United States from local independent operators to national corporate organizations.

DEBT SETTLEMENT

Debt settlement offers a way to avoid bankruptcy for people with significant debt issues who may not qualify for a debt management plan.

A debt settlement is an agreement between a creditor and a debtor to satisfy a debt for a reduced payoff amount. Since the debtor is unable to fully meet his/her debt obligations, the creditor agrees to reduce the debt and accept the agreed upon sum as a settlement.

Although the practice of settling debts through a third party began soon after the invention of money, debt settlement as a business service is less than thirty years old. Debt settlement developed in the late 1980s and early 1990s as bank deregulation, coupled with an economic recession, left many consumers facing severe financial hardships. In the late 1980s, banks set up debt settlement departments to address the high number of charge-offs generated from cardholders defaulting on loans. Bank personnel were authorized to negotiate with consumers and settle outstanding balances for payments that ranged from 25% to 65% of the amount owed. From their standpoint, something was better than nothing.

By the early 1990s, independent agencies were established for the negotiation and settlement of consumer debt. Today, the debt settlement industry continues to grow as individuals and families find themselves in unresolved debt dilemmas.

THE NEED FOR INTERVENTION

Why is there such a need for credit counselors and debt settlement specialists? Why do consumers need counseling about their use of credit? Why are consumers getting into so much trouble with their credit cards?

One of the major debates prior to the passage of the Bankruptcy Abuse Prevention and Consumer Protection Act of 2005 was the question of who is to blame for the high levels of consumer debt one sees today. On the one hand are those who accuse consumers of spending beyond their means and not fully understanding how credit and interest works. On the other hand are those who accuse the creditors for aggressively soliciting credit to consumers who easily become trapped by excessive finance charges and late fees.

INSOLVENCY EVENTS

More often than not, it is an insolvency event that starts a downward spiral toward debt. These often tragic but common life events include:

- Job loss
- Medical emergency
- Divorce
- Death in the family

The insolvency event often creates a panicked reaction in which credit is used as a short-term solution. As an example, let's consider Ted.

Ted, like many Americans, has little or no savings in case of an emergency. Then, the emergency occurs; he looses his job due to corporate downsizing. With nothing to fall back on, he starts using more and more of his available credit on essentials such as groceries and car repairs. The credit-card statements start coming but he can't pay the bills. He's still out of work. Now the interest starts to compound and the late fees pile up. In a few more weeks, he's considering bankruptcy.

It does no good to assign blame. Ted may even consider himself to be credit savvy. He would never have dreamed of using credit to buy groceries. But what choice did he have? Plus, his available credit at the time was quite extensive. After all, he was granted credit back when he was employed. The fact that he has no income now is of little concern to the creditors.

Suddenly, Ted finds himself with a mountain of unpaid debt. The financial strain causes marital fighting. His self esteem plummets and he finds it hard to be upbeat at job interviews.

ECONOMIC FACTORS

Ted's case is typical in that he had no emergency fund to fall back on when his income stopped. Like many people, he lived paycheck to paycheck. The average percent of consumer income that goes to personal savings in the United States is somewhere below 5% (June 2012). Why is it so hard for people to save money today?

Consider the following: Housing and health care costs have increased substantially in the last fifteen years while real incomes for the vast majority of Americans have remained stagnant or have declined. According to State of Working America, the median income for 2011 was $50,054 -- down from a high of $54,841 back in 2000.

Meanwhile, the number of families spending more than 50% of their income on housing expenses grew drastically during the period from the late 1990s to the present.

Add to this the issue of health care. According to the 2004 report of the Commonwealth Fund, 40% of Americans reported that they have gone without needed medical care due to prohibitive costs. Sixteen percent or 45.8 million people have no health care coverage whatsoever. When a medical emergency occurs, the medical bills may go unpaid for months damaging the credit rating and making any use of credit all the more costly.

Rising housing and medical costs plus sinking incomes equal a potentially disastrous debt situation. A job loss, a mortgage payment you just can't make, or unpaid medical bills could all spark an unhealthy use of credit. For example, if you pay a medical bill you cannot afford with a credit card, you have created new debt but unlike the medical bill, the credit card bill will increase substantially over time.

DEREGULATION

Since the late 1970s, state usury laws prohibiting high interest rates and fees have been relaxed. Two Supreme Court rulings -- one in 1978 and one in 1996 -- permitted banks to charge the highest interest rate allowed in the bank's home state. Previously, the highest interest rate was based on the highest rate allowed in the state where the consumer lives.

Other lender practices that some contend keep consumers in debt are:

Aggressive marketing. According to statistics published by CreditCards.com, credit-card companies mailed over 6 billion credit card offers in 2005. That's an average of 6 offers per household per month.

Higher credit limits. The average credit-card balance was $4,617 in 2004. Average credit lines were $3,500 on each card with an average of six cards for a total of $21,000 in available credit.

Low minimum payments. Minimum payments have been as low as 2% of the balance on an account. Currently, they are twice that but at 4%, minimum payments are a sure way to grow your debt. Paying the minimum payment on a balance of $5000 with a 15% interest rate would take thirty-two years to pay off. In other words, you could be paying for a dinner out long into the future. Forty-five percent of American cardholders were only making the minimum payments in 2004.

Penalties and fees. Late fees are the fastest growing source of revenue for creditors. Along with over-the-limit fees and balance transfer fees, this brought the industry 43 billion in income in 2004. Perhaps the most controversial creditor practice was universal default. Pay late on one card and your interest rate can skyrocket on all your cards. Forty-four percent of credit cards in circulation carried universal default provisions in 2004.

THE BEHAVIORAL DEBTOR

Given the economic landscape and current lending trends, it is easy to see how well-intentioned consumers can get into insolvent situations. Yet, there is another force at work that contributes to delinquent consumer debt. It is how an individual behaves with his or her money. In many cases, personal financial well-being is compromised by poor money management. Here's a short list of the common negative behaviors consumers engage in when it comes to money:

- spending too much
- saving too little
- not keeping track of bills
- not balancing the checkbook
- not talking about spending decisions with spouse
- not setting financial goals
- refusing to acknowledge a need to budget
- using credit cards to buy essentials
- only paying the minimum on credit card balances
- ignoring bill collectors
- spending to alleviate stress
- spending on impulse
- rationalizing destructive spending
- blaming others for financial problems

Often these behaviors occur in conjunction with an insolvency event. For example, an individual who has just lost a job may fail to adjust his or her spending habits even though there is no longer any money coming in.

Divorce is another life event that can propel someone into irresponsible financial behavior. When two people living in one house split, there is literally a doubling of expenses. This includes mortgage or rent, household items, furniture, groceries, separate cars, insurance, and medical plans.

Many people will try and maintain the lifestyle they have grown accustomed to and continue to spend as they did before their financial circumstance changed. More often than not, the power of credit is abused. When cash is short, the credit card carries on the grand illusion of financial security.

SUMMARY

1. For all its convenience and benefits, the credit card has the potential to do real damage to personal finances.

2. In a climate of deregulation in lending coupled with an economic downturn, consumers increasingly use credit for essential expenses.

3. Severe debt issues are caused by insolvency events, the debtor's behavior or a combination of both.

4. The growth of credit counseling and debt settlement is a direct response to increased consumer debt.

REVIEW QUESTIONS

1. Describe some of the early types of credit cards.

2. List the common insolvency events that often trigger debt issues.

3. Identify consumer behaviors that often contribute to excessive debt.

Unit 2: Between Legal Advice and Therapy

OBJECTIVES
- To identify the proper role of the credit counselor.
- To determine the components of financial literacy

If someone asks, "What do credit counselors do?", you could tell them
The "7 Cs" -- Credit Counselors Counsel Consumers Concerning
Credit Cards.

However, more explanation may be required. Whereas *consumer* and *credit card*
may be well-known terms, what exactly does it mean *to counsel*?

According to the American Heritage Dictionary, *counsel* has the following
meanings: "To give counsel; advise, to recommend."

In its noun form, counsel means "advice or guidance, especially as solicited from
a knowledgeable person." It can also mean "a plan of action."

So we have an idea now that credit counselors advise or give guidance to
consumers about their use of credit and help in devising a plan of action to
address problems resulting from credit card use -- namely, debt.

CREDIT COUNSELORS DO NOT PROVIDE THERAPY
However, a clear distinction must be made between credit counselors and other
types of counselors who provide assistance that goes beyond giving advice. As
we know, there are several varieties of counseling requiring licensure. Mental
health counseling, marriage counseling, substance abuse counseling, and anger
management counseling are just a few. These types of counseling often involve
the diagnosis of a psychological condition or a certain interpersonal dynamic and
various forms of therapy to address the condition or dynamic.

 The word therapy comes from the Greek *therapeia* meaning "healing" or
"curing." Credit counselors do not offer their clients therapy. If a client might
benefit from therapy or a specialized form of counseling, the credit counselor
refers that client to information that will point them in the right direction.

UNIVERSAL COUNSELING SKILLS
The credit counselor's expertise lies primarily with consumer debt issues. What
credit counselors do have in common with other forms of counseling is the use
and practice of specific communication skills that serve to facilitate the

counseling process. These essential counseling skills include:

Rapport building skills. Techniques for creating a bond of trust include conveying positive regard to the client, demonstrating empathy, and being genuine and open to self disclosure.

Listening skills. These skills involve attentiveness and interest in what the client is saying. Responses to client talk are non-judgmental. Specific questions are designed to ensure the accurate transmission of information.

Interviewing skills. Although the client directs the desired outcomes of the counseling session, the counselor remains in control of the flow and direction of the interview. Techniques include the use of open and closed-ended questions.

Problem solving skills. Counseling helps to fast-forward problem solving by following specific steps designed to gather accurate data, consider the options, and work toward a chosen plan of action.

Doctors, lawyers, teachers, real estate agents, bankers, accountants, and marketers utilize these skills every day. They are universally beneficial even when applied to personal and social situations.

CREDIT COUNSELORS DO NOT GIVE LEGAL ADVICE
The other side of credit counseling - the "credit" side, however, opens up another issue. Consumer credit, lending, debt, and collections by their very nature all have a legal dimension to them. Clients in debt may be facing court judgments involving garnishments or seizures. Some are being harassed by collection agencies. Others are unsure about the new bankruptcy laws. How far can a credit counselor go as they advise their clients?

Consider the following from Jeffrey S. Tenebaum and Jonathan L. Pompan from their article, Credit Counseling and Avoiding the Unauthorized Practice of Law: Suggestions for Minimizing Risk:

"For those who work in the credit counseling industry, an issue often forgotten in the midst of counseling sessions is that the credit counseling agency (CCA) is not a law firm and that its counselors are not lawyers." Their September 19, 2006 article appearing in the trade publication *Venable*, examines ways to ensure that credit counselors do not engage in the potentially liable unauthorized practice of law (UPL). First, they define legal advice:

"Legal advice is the application of legal principles and judgment to the circumstances or objectives of another person or entity. In other words, under most state laws, a non-lawyer cannot tell a client anything that, if acted upon, would change the client's legal rights or legal status."

Concerns arise primarily with regards to bankruptcy counseling. Examples of UPL in the context of bankruptcy include:

- Determining when and whether to file bankruptcy
- Deciding whether to file a Chapter 7 or a Chapter 13 petition
- Filling out or helping a client complete court documents or schedules
- Providing clients with definitions of legal terms
- Advising clients which exemptions they should claim
- Advising clients about whether or not certain debts are dischargeable
- Speculating on how a bankruptcy might affect a foreclosure
- Speculating on the tax consequences of filing for bankruptcy

STATE LAWS

Some states such as Rhode Island and Massachusetts have specifically authorized credit counseling agencies to engage in certain services without being subject to UPL liabilities. These services include the primary job of the credit counselor:

- giving financial and budgetary advice
- helping create a spending plan
- administering a repayment plan
- providing education about the use of credit.

In this way, some states provide protection to CCAs from ambiguous interpretations of what constitutes an unauthorized practice of law. In fact, there is no universally accepted definition of UPL. Furthermore, the various state laws regulating UPL are not preempted by the state laws that regulate credit counseling agencies. In other words, a CCAs compliance with state credit counseling regulations does not guarantee immunity from UPL liability.

Recommendations for Minimizing Risk of UPL Liability

It is then up to the CCA to implement steps to help avoid UPL. Tenebaum and Pompon recommend the following safeguards that pertain to individual credit counselors:

Avoid definitive statements regarding a course of action. A counselor should not say, "You are ineligible for Chapter 7 Bankruptcy" or "Bankruptcy is your best option." The counselor should instead say, "You might be ineligible for Chapter 7" or "Bankruptcy might be your best option." The counselor should then recommend that the client consult an attorney for a definitive answer.

Discuss bankruptcy in general terms. Avoid any discussion of how bankruptcy could affect a particular client. If and when the subject of bankruptcy comes up, focus on general, factual information without relating it to the specifics of the client's situation. Primary attention should go to financial/budgetary analysis.

CONSUMER PROTECTION LEGISLATION

This is not to say that credit counselors should avoid the topic of legislation completely. Several laws are important for clients to be aware of. These include:

- The Equal Credit Opportunity Act
- The Truth in Lending Act
- The Fair Credit Billing Act
- The Fair Credit Reporting Act
- The Fair Debt Collection Practices Act

These important acts are summarized in *Appendix B*. General discussion of these laws should not constitute UPL unless they are interpreted in light of a client's specific case.

ROLES OF THE CREDIT COUNSELOR

Effective counselors:

Affect positive change. The premise of all counseling is to help clients resolve problems and manage their resources more efficiently. Credit counselors guide clients through the problem-solving process.

Promote financial literacy. Credit counselors teach their clients about the proper use of credit, budgeting, and the consequences of unpaid debt.

Provide support. Being in debt can present many challenges for clients. Counselors are non judgmental and supportive toward clients expressing fear and frustration over their debt.

Link clients to resources. Counselors anticipate the needs of the clients and provide them with any resources they may need to ensure the successful resolution of their debt issue.

A primary role of the credit counselor is to help clients develop financial literacy. But what exactly is financial literacy?

Let's examine the components that make up financially literate consumers:

- They understand basic money management principles such as budgeting resources, saving, investing, and balancing a checking account.
- They read and understand credit and loan agreements.
- They use credit wisely by avoiding high interest rates and paying bills on time.
- They make short and long-term goals with their money.
- They understand their consumer rights with regards to getting credit, disputing billing statements, and fixing credit reporting errors.
- They check their credit report at least once a year for accuracy.
- They check their credit reports prior to making a major purchase.
- They know their rights concerning debt collectors.
- They understand that a reduction in income calls for adjusting spending.
- They communicate with their spouses' or family members regarding financial goals and substantial purchases.
- They avoid impulse buying; they can delay gratification and adhere to financial goals.

In 2003, FleetBoston Financial sponsored a national survey of consumer knowledge on basic financial issues. Nearly, three-fours of the respondents (73%) said that parents should be the ones primarily responsible for teaching children about basic finances. However, less than half of the parents participating in the survey believed themselves to be competent to teach basic finances. Also, only about one-third of the respondents described themselves as in control of their own finances.

1. Credit counselors utilize counseling skills but refrain from entering into a therapeutic relationship with their clients.

2. Credit counselors are well-informed about consumer legislation but they refrain from interpreting laws with regards to the specific circumstances of the client.

REVIEW QUESTIONS

1. Identify counseling skills that effective credit counselors use when helping clients.

2. Give three examples of the unauthorized practice of law (UPL) that credit counselors are prohibited from engaging in.

3. How do credit counselors avoid or minimize the unauthorized practice of law?

4. List five behaviors of the financially literate consumer.

Unit 3: The Uniform Debt-Management Services Act

OBJECTIVES
- To survey the evolution of credit and debt counseling services.
- To appraise the main provisions of the UDMSA.

In July 2005, the National Conference of Commissioners on Uniform State Laws finalized and issued the Uniform Debt-Management Services Act (UDMSA). It is the first effort on the federal level to provide a uniform set of rules to govern the two primary services available for consumers in debt -- credit counseling and debt settlement.

Issues such as debt adjusting, debt management, debt pooling, debt settlement and consumer credit counseling have already been addressed by nearly every state but the scope and content of this state legislation varies considerably.

What follows is a short summary of the rise and development of debt management services in the United States.

FOUR GENERATIONS OF DEBT MANAGEMENT

1. Debt Adjusters
Consumer credit counseling originated in the early 1900s in the form of debt adjusters. Also known as debt poolers, debt consolidators, debt managers and debt pro-raters, they represent the first generation of debt management services and operated as for-profit agencies. These early debt managers communicated with the consumer's creditors to negotiate a partial payment of the debtor's obligation. Once a settlement amount was agreed upon, the debt manager would collect monthly payments from the consumer and forward portions of it to each of the creditors.

These early for-profit entities came under scrutiny by legislators due to instances involving exorbitant fees, deception and, in some cases, outright theft of the payments collected from consumers. By the 1950s, more than half of the United States outlawed the operation of these companies. Approximately two-thirds of the remaining states imposed requirements and restrictions. Meanwhile, many states exempted non profit agencies from these statutes.

2. Non profits
This led to the growth of the second generation of debt management services - non profit entities. The 1950s saw a dramatic growth of these agencies in part due to the formation of the National Foundation of Consumer Credit (later called

the National Foundation for Credit Counseling). Created by retailers and banks that issued credit cards, the objectives set forth were:

- to enable consumers to repay their debts in full
- to help consumers avoid bankruptcy
- to provide education and budget counseling
- to enroll consumers in debt management plans when appropriate.

A consumer enrolled in a debt management plan received concessions from the creditors which may have included elimination of late fees or reduction of interest. The agencies received a "fair share" contribution from the creditors amounting to 15% of the payments received. This second generation continues to operate today.

3. Trade Organizations
The third generation arose during the late 1980s and 1990s, a time when consumer debt was skyrocketing. It was also a time when consumer income increased and standards for creditworthiness decreased. New agencies were formed that were unaffiliated with NFCC. The Association of Independent Consumer Credit Counseling Agencies (AICCCA) and the American Association of Debt Management Organizations (AADMO) formed as new trade organizations whose affiliates saw dramatic growth in the late 1990s. Their share in the debt management industry grew from 20% in 1996 to 80% by 2001 (NCCUSL). At the same time, services were increasingly conducted offered over the phone and on the Internet as opposed to in person.

4. Debt Settlement
Another segment of the debt management industry formed during this time thus creating the fourth generation -- debt settlement agencies. In 2004, trade organizations merged into the United States Organization for Bankruptcy Alternatives (USOBA). In a sense, this fourth generation represents a return to the first generation of debt managers whose goal it was to negotiate to settle a consumer's debt for less than the full amount. However, unlike their predecessors, this new generation of debt negotiators work with consumers first to set up a savings account and once there is a target amount saved, the debt counselor will then negotiate with the consumer's creditors.

FEDERAL STANDARDS
The draft committee of the UDMSA characterize the history of debt management as "somewhat checkered." While there have been benefits to consumers including education, assistance with budget creation and relief from debts involving multiple fees and high interest rates, both the Consumer Federation of America and the National Consumer Law Center have sited deceptive practices

and excessive costs to the consumer.

By January 2003, a drafting committee was authorized to develop the UDMSA. It became an increasingly important initiative since the majority of debt management agencies operate in multiple states and were subject to multiple and sometimes conflicting requirements.

The UDMSA defines "debt management services" as encompassing both credit counseling agencies and debt settlement agencies. With very few exceptions, the provisions of the Act apply equally to both types of services.

The UDMSA is neutral on the question of whether for profit entities should be permitted to provide services to the consumer and leaves that up to individual states.

Bankruptcy reform in 2005 has only increased the need for both credit counseling and debt negotiation. For a consumer to file a Chapter 7 bankruptcy, the consumer must, in most cases, show that credit counseling and debt education has been sought and attempted. Since the bankruptcy reform legislation is federal, this creates yet another reason why a uniform set of guidelines and restrictions are necessary for agencies that, for the most part, operate nationwide.

SUMMARY OF THE UDMSA*

Purpose
This Act provides guidance and regulation to the consumer credit counseling and debt settlement industries. The Act applies to both consumer credit counseling services and debt settlement services. The Act is a comprehensive statute that provides rules for, among other things, registration requirements, bond requirements, certification requirements, disclosure requirements and penalties for non-compliance.

UDMSA may be divided into three basic parts: registration of services, service-debtor agreements and enforcement. Each part contributes to the comprehensive quality of the Uniform Act.

Registration
No service may enter into an agreement with any debtor in a state without registering as a consumer debt-management service in that state. Registration requires submission of detailed information concerning the service, including its financial condition, the identity of principals, locations at which service will be

offered, form for agreements with debtors and business history in other jurisdictions.

To register, a service must have an effective insurance policy against fraud, dishonesty, theft and the like in an amount no less than $250,000.00. It must also provide a security bond of a minimum of $50,000.00 which has the state administrator as a beneficiary. If a registration substantially duplicates one in another state, the service may offer proof of registration in that other state to satisfy the registration requirements in a state. A satisfactory application will result in a certificate to do business from the administrator. A yearly renewal is required.

Agreements

In order to enter into agreements with debtors, there is a disclosure requirement respecting fees and services to be offered, and the risks and benefits of entering into such a contract. The service must offer counseling services from a certified counselor or certified debt specialist and a plan must be created in consultation by the counselor for debt-management service to commence. The contents of the agreements and fees that may be charged are set by the statute. There is a penalty-free three-day right of rescission on the part of the debtor. The debtor may cancel the agreement also after 30 days, but may be subject to fees if that occurs. The service may terminate the agreement if required payments are delinquent for at least 60 days.

Any payments for creditors received from a debtor must be kept in a trust account that may not be used to hold any other funds of the service. There are strict accounting requirements and periodic reporting requirements respecting funds held.

Enforcement

The Act prohibits specific acts on the part of a service including: misappropriation of funds in trust; settlement for more than 50% of a debt with a creditor without a debtor's consent; gifts or premiums to enter into an agreement; and representation that settlement has occurred without certification from a creditor. Enforcement of the Uniform Act occurs at two levels, the administrator and the individual level. The administrator has investigative powers, power to order an individual to cease and desist; power to assess a civil penalty up to $10,000.00, and the power to bring a civil action. An individual may bring a civil action for compensatory damages, including triple damages if a service obtains payments not authorized in the Uniform Act, and may seek punitive damages and attorney's fees. A service has a good faith mistake defense against liability. The statute of limitations pertaining to an action by the administrator is four years, and two years for a private right of action.

Banks as regulated entities under other law are not subject to the Uniform Act, as are other kinds of activities that are incidental to other functions performed. For example, a title insurer that provides bill-paying service that is incidental to title insurance is not subject to it.

*From the National Conference of Commissioners on Uniform State Laws

SUMMARY

1. The Uniform Debt Management Services Act addresses both the credit counseling and debt settlement industries.

2. These industries are closely related in that they both provide services to consumers in debt but differ in the processes by which consumer debt is resolved.

3. The UDMSA represents a set of standards on the national level under which these two industries continue to operate.

REVIEW QUESTIONS

1. Debt management has been described in terms of consisting of four generations. Identify these four generations.

2. What are the three areas that the main provisions of the UDMSA address?

Unit 4: Ethics in Financial-based Counseling

OBJECTIVES

- To understand the importance of ethics in the workplace.
- To determine the difference between credit counseling and providing therapy.
- To identify the two types of crisis situations that can occur in the workplace.
- To identify behaviors that may indicate the need for intervention.
- To establish a Code of Ethics.

WHAT EXACTLY ARE ETHICS?

Ethics are quality control for people. People do not become professionals because they wear business suits, have offices, drive company automobiles or possess the keys to the executive washroom. People become professionals when they understand and follow a standard of intention and behavior.

Human beings have survived thus far as a direct result of our ability to cooperate with one other. The common good has been proved, again and again, to benefit the individual. Generally, ethics are based on the values (innate and/or instilled) of honesty and fairness. We treat others as we would like to be treated, we do not lie, or cheat, or steal.

Certain parameters of ethics remain constant through the ages. They stand as permanent laws that describe honorable conduct -- DO NOT DECEIVE, DO NOT TAKE ADVANTAGE OF SOMEONE, TELL THE TRUTH, etc. Other aspects of ethics are in a constant state of change and growth. For example, RESPECT DIVERSITY is a relatively new idea that author Rene Dubois characterizes as, not only a virtue, but a "requirement."

For this reason, ethics need to be, on the one hand, preserved and adopted from the past and, on the other hand, discussed and debated, changed, and amended as times and conditions warrant. The formation of ethics literally requires full participation from the individual. The individual needs to own his/her ethics and the only way to truly own something is to help create it.

BUSINESS ETHICS ARE BASED ON PERSONAL ETHICS

We all create our version of personal ethics. These personal ethics in turn become the basis for good business ethics. Whenever we are selling hamburgers, computers, or legal services, we are operating in the world of commerce.

In this special environment of doing business and exchanging goods, we take on new roles that require that we expand the guidelines of our personal ethics. Now that you have taken on the responsibility to provide a product or service to a customer, you must deliver. Thus, DO NOT PROMISE WHAT YOU MAY NOT DELIVER might be one of the first laws carved in the pedestal of your business enterprise.

Business ethics provide guidelines regarding two groups of people who depend on the quality, viability, and growth of your organization:

Customers. You have heard the well-worn phrase, "The customer is always right." That may be true some of the time or even most of the time but what do you do when the customer is not right? Maybe the customer does not understand, is overreacting, or even suicidal (see Crisis Intervention). Successful organizations build specific guidelines for serving customers and accommodating to their needs.

Employees. Employees have certain ethical obligations to their employers. ADHERE TO COMPANY POLICY and GIVE TWO WEEKS NOTICE IF YOU QUIT are two that come to mind. Likewise, employers have certain obligations to their employees - none more important than to ensure the continued success of the organization. The bottom line requires a profit and so does ethics. Without profits and a plan for future profits, there can be no ethics.

PROFESSIONAL ETHICS

The development and implementation of professional ethics comes into play with the idea of the client. The client is not just a customer seeking a product or service but an individual seeking specialized assistance. He/she seeks assistance from what are assumed to be experts whether they are lawyers, doctors, or financial analysts. Professional ethics ensures that a special relationship is preserved in which the client is attended to, accepted, and shown respect.

Ethics in business and in the professions have two primary benefits:

- Ethics provide guidelines for negotiating the often tough decisions that arise in the workplace.
- The establishment of ethics enhance professional status.

Ethics Start from the Top

Without leadership, ethics is just an idea. Successful implementation of ethics relies on Team Leaders to initiate the standard. They set the tone of the entire organization. Either there are clear values that are upheld or corners get cut and a slippery slope of deceit ensues.

Managers and supervisors will rise or sink to the level of behavior that is modeled by the leader of the organization. This, in turn, is transferred to everyone in the workplace. Leadership is all about motivation and ethics is an easy sell. Without ethics, there is no product or service to sell; there are no guarantees. Ethics provides for a way of doing things that are grounded in values.

COUNSELING VS. THERAPY

It is important to differentiate counseling from the practice of therapy. Credit counselors are not licensed therapists. They need to know where to draw the line in their relationship with clients.

They need to know when it is appropriate to refer clients who may be experiencing emotional distress over their outstanding debt.

Credit counselors assess client debt, client resources, and client attitudes and emotions. Attending to clients is a special way of giving undivided attention and assistance. However, credit counselors do not diagnose clients as suffering from specific psychological problems. Also, credit counselors seek to facilitate solutions. They do not, in any way, attempt to cure clients.

Therapy is a form of treatment. The word *therapy* originally meant "to heal." Credit counselors do not heal patients; they attend to clients.

CRISIS INTERVENTION

Effective organizations prepare for crisis situations through the establishment of specific guidelines. Emergencies involving imminent danger require the notification of 911 dispatchers, emergency medical services (EMS) and/or the police. How crisis situations are handled is a direct reflection of the professionalism of the organization.

As you know, financial distress is a major reason for depression and stress in our society. Those working in the debt management industry are bound to interact, sooner or later, with individuals who exhibit behavior that may require referral - sometimes immediate referral. Practitioners of crisis intervention must undergo special training that enables them to effectively stop or de-escalate life-threatening emergencies. Our purpose here is to give an overview of the signs that should cause concern and/or require action. There are two types of crisis situations -- imminent danger emergencies and non-imminent danger emergencies.

Imminent danger emergencies override guidelines of client/counselor confidentiality and require the involvement of a 911 dispatcher, police, or EMS. In these cases, behavior is exhibited that is dangerous, threatening, violent, self-harming, destructive, or suicidal.

Non-imminent danger emergencies that make up the vast majority of crisis situations require appropriate referrals for effective interventions. These cases involve signs of depression, severe stress, on-going spousal abuse, child abuse, and anger management problems. Again, credit counselors are not licensed therapists and cannot diagnose depression, stress overload, or rage disorders. They can, however, learn to understand some common behaviors associated with these conditions and provide clients with the resources that can help them find solutions to these problems.

What follows is a list of some of the common signs that a client may be potentially violent or suicidal:

- The client expects, without sufficient basis, to be exploited or taken advantage of.
- The client reads hidden demeaning or threatening meanings into benign remarks or events.
- The client is reluctant to confide in others.
- The client is easily slighted or quick to react with anger.
- The client rarely reciprocates gestures of facial expressions.
- The client relates odd or strange beliefs.
- The client is unable to sustain consistent employment due to job abandonment, repeated absences, or conflict.
- The client repeatedly fails to honor financial responsibilities.
- The client exhibits reckless behavior.
- The client lacks remorse or feels justified to mistreat others.
- The client has unstable and/or intense relationships. The client exhibits rapidly shifting moods.
- The client exhibits frequent displays of temper.
- The client's style of speech is excessively impressionistic and lacking in detail to support impressions.
- The client exhibits a grandiose sense of importance. The client is unable to see other perspectives.

Many of these client behaviors do not, in and of themselves, signify a serious problem that must be addressed. However, it is important to keep the above list in mind when communicating to clients. Financial dilemmas do cause stress and, in some cases, desperation.

CALLING 911

We have all seen 911 dispatchers on T.V. shows that dramatize emergency situations. Few of us, however, appreciate that the individuals who respond to 911 calls perform a very demanding and complex job. Personalities, attitudes, and professionalism of 911 dispatchers vary considerably. Keep in mind that 911 calls are recorded to ensure that dispatchers follow prescribed guidelines. However, a significant number of dispatchers are overworked or severely distressed by their jobs. They must manage the powerful emotions that go with any crisis situation while performing multiple tasks simultaneously.

Here are tips when calling 911:

- Answer all questions of the dispatcher.
- Do not argue or disagree with the dispatcher.
- Always request the incident number of your 911 call. This makes call backs and follow ups much easier.
- Always remember 911 calls are NOT confidential. They are a matter of public record.

Individuals resort to violent acts including suicide for many reasons. One of these reasons is the loss or potential loss of the ability to meet financial obligations. It is important for credit counselors to be aware of and sensitive to the potentially volatile nature of credit problems and financial distress in general.

CODE OF ETHICS

Preamble
The code of ethics developed specifically for the debt management and debt settlement industries is based on the professional ethics and standards of counseling. It seeks to promote and maintain the idea that the client/counselor relationship is founded on trust, respect, and acceptance. Any code of ethics in no way supersedes the policies of an organization. Rather, they stand as a framework for the basis of true professionalism.

SECTION I: THE CLIENT/COUNSELOR RELATIONSHIP

A. CLIENT WELFARE

1. Prime directive. The primary directive of credit counselors is to assist clients in the successful management of their debt.

2. Respect. Counselors respect clients and attend to all issues relating to personal finance.

3. Fostering independence. Counselors encourage client growth and development; counselors avoid promoting a client/counselor relationship of dependency.

B. RESPECT FOR DIVERSITY

1. Non-discrimination. Counselors do not engage in or promote in any way discrimination based on age, color, culture, disability, ethnic group, gender, race, religion, sexual orientation, marital status, or socioeconomic stature.

2. Value differences. Counselors actively accept and attempt to understand the diverse cultures represented by clients.

3. Identity impact. Counselors actively seek to understand and take into account their own cultural/ethnic/racial identity and how it may influence their values and beliefs related to the counseling process.

C. RIGHTS OF THE CLIENT

1. Full disclosure. Counselors inform clients truthfully and accurately concerning the goals, procedures, and expected outcomes of the counseling process. Likewise, the client is privy to billing procedures and documentation regarding the client.

2. Freedom of choice. Counselors understand that clients enter the counseling process through their own informed decision. They are in no way coerced by counselors or third parties to enter into the counseling process.

D. DUAL RELATIONSHIP

Whenever possible, counselors avoid dual relationships with clients that may compromise professional judgment. Examples of such relationships include, but are not limited to, familial, social, financial, business or close personal relationships with clients. Whenever a dual relationship cannot be avoided,

31

counselors take the necessary precautions to ensure that judgment is not impaired and no exploitation occurs. Such precautions include, but are not limited to, informed consent, consultation, supervision and documentation.

E. CLIENT NEGLECT

1. Abandonment prohibited. Counselors do not abandon or neglect clients in counseling.

2. Inability to assist client. If a client does not qualify for credit counseling or the counselor is unable to assist the client, the counselor provides information, referrals, resources and suggests appropriate alternatives.

SECTION II: CONFIDENTIALITY

A. RIGHT TO PRIVACY

1. Respect for privacy. Counselors avoid illegal and unwarranted disclosures of confidential information. Counselors respect their clients' rights to privacy.

2. Exception. Confidentiality does not apply when disclosure is necessary to prevent clear and imminent danger to the client or others or when legal requirements necessitate that confidential information be disclosed. Exceptions are determined through consultation with other counselors or professionals. Examples of exceptions include, but are not limited to, threats of suicide, threats to inflict bodily harm or property damage and revelation of contagious, fatal diseases.

B. RECORDS

1. Maintenance of records. Counselors keep and maintain client records as required by the counseling organization.

2. Confidentiality of records. In the creation, maintenance, transfer, or destruction of client records, counselors understand that a client's right to privacy extends to client/counselor documentation.

3. Client access. Clients have the right to request records relating to their debt management or settlement agreement.

SECTION III: PROFESSIONAL RESPONSIBILITY

A. Knowledge of Ethics. Counselors are responsible for reading, and adhering to the Code of Ethics.

B. Competency. Counselors understand and are aware of their limitations concerning knowledge and competency based on education, training, and credentials. Counselors refer clients to other counselors or supervisors when uncertainties arise or knowledge is insufficient to answer to client circumstances. Counselors do not improvise or infer information.

C. Review Effectiveness. Counselors consistently evaluate the performance and outcome gains of their counseling. When necessary, counselors seek to improve their performance through continuing education, peer evaluation and supervision.

D. Continuing Education. Counselors understand the importance of continuing education in a dynamic field that is affected by new developments in counseling, consumer rights, the economy, current legislation and current lending trends.

SECTION IV: EMPLOYEE RELATIONS

A. Reporting Problems. It is of universal interest that conditions or behaviors that may be disruptive, damaging or illegal are brought to the attention of a supervisor.

B. Professionalism. It is of universal interest that counselors display and maintain high standards of professional conduct.

C. Employee Policies. Accepting employment with an organization infers that counselors are in agreement with the organization's policies and objectives.

SUMMARY

1. Ethics is a necessary part of conducting business.

2. Effective counselors who interact with consumers in debt recognize crisis situations and provide referrals when appropriate.

3. The Code of Ethics developed for credit counselors is based on professional counseling ethics.

REVIEW QUESTIONS

1. Business ethics address what two groups of people?

2. Describe the difference between counseling and therapy.

3. Identify five behaviors that may indicate suicidal or violent tendencies.

4. In the *Code of Ethics*, what is meant by "dual relationship"?

Module II: Communicating with Clients

PREVIEW

This module explores the counseling process and the essential skills used to facilitate communication and problem solving between you and your clients. What is the premise of counseling? What is the process? What are the specific techniques counselors use that transform a conversation into a catalyst for positive change?

You will find that the skills you learn about in this module can be applied, not only to the counseling session, but to your daily life. Do you want to know how to establish great rapport, increase you listening abilities, understand how to go about tackling problems? You will learn about these skills and more in the units that follow.

By completing this module, you will:

- understand the premise and process of counseling.
- be able to differentiate between process goals and outcome goals.
- become familiar with the Human/Business Model.
- be able to identify the 5 stages of counseling.
- be able to identify the 5 types of communication.
- gain techniques for building rapport.
- learn specific active listening techniques.
- be able to differentiate between open-ended and closed-ended questions.

Unit 5: The Premise & Process of Counseling

OBJECTIVES:

- To understand the premise behind counseling.
- To determine the five stages of counseling.
- To know the difference between process goals and   outcome goals.
- To correlate these goals to The Human/Business Model.
- To define Solution-Focused Counseling.

The Problem-Management/Opportunity-Development Model

Gerard Egan, author of *The Skilled Helper*, says:

"Helpers are effective to the degree that their clients, through client-helper interactions, are in better positions to manage their problem situations and/or develop the unused resources and opportunities of their lives more effectively."

The premise of counseling is to help clients manage problems and utilize resources more effectively. In the case of credit counseling, the problems center around unpaid debt. To resolve debt issues, the client and the counselor collaborate to manage repayment and, at the same time, find ways to optimize the resources available to the client.

The model that describes the overall premise of counseling is The Problem-Management/Opportunity-Development Model. The client presents a problem and the counselor is there to facilitate a solution. However, the problem will not actually be solved by the counselor. The counselor helps the client to discover the opportunities and resources available to deal with the problem.

**The Problem-Management/Opportunity-Development Model
Applied to Credit Counseling**

Manage Problem	Develop Opportunities
Unresolved Debt	Optimize Income, Cut Spending

FIVE STAGES OF COUNSELING

Counseling is a process that moves through a series of stages toward a desired outcome. There are five stages:

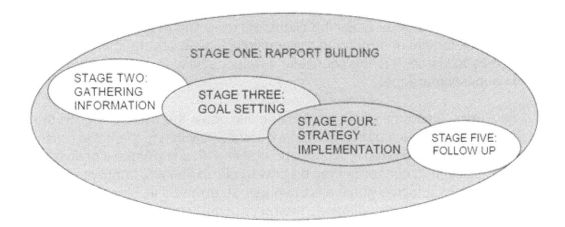

1. Rapport Building. This first step actually encompasses the entire counseling process. Rapport is the essential vehicle for effective communication.

2. Gathering Information. The counselor assesses the client's current situation by asking questions and listening actively.

3. Goal Setting. Now the counselor helps the client determine the desired scenario. What do you want to accomplish?

4. Strategy Implementation. Implementing the plan of action is often the most challenging stage of counseling because it requires commitment on the part of the client.

5. Follow Up. Is the plan working? Were goals accomplished? You will never know unless there is follow up communication.

Rapport building encompasses the entire counseling process from the initial interview to the final follow up. The other stages overlap each other. For example, during strategy implementation, goals may be changed. While gathering information, rapport is being established.

PROCESS GOALS AND OUTCOME GOALS

Process Goals. Credit counseling shares goals universal to all types of counseling. These are called *process goals*. Process goals work to ensure that the counseling process is a positive experience for the client. Are the client's concerns being addressed? Does the client feel trust and respect? Is there a sense of completeness at the end of the session? These are the things that process goals focus on. It is the counselor's responsibility to see that the process goals of counseling are met.

Outcome Goals. Outcome goals are the specific goals the client brings to the table. The client communicates a *presenting concern* which is the initial reason for the consultation. In the case of credit counseling, this is primarily delinquent debt. Other presenting concerns may be how to cut expenses, improve credit, or avoid bankruptcy. Outcome goals are the goals determined in Stage 3 of the counseling process and it is ultimately the responsibility of the client to follow through with the necessary steps to implement those goals.

The Human/Business Model

A valuable perspective is gained when everyday interactions are seen as operating on two levels. One is the business level where tasks are completed and objectives are met. The other is the human level where an individual's needs for attention, respect and acceptance are met. For any interaction to be positive, both levels must be addressed.

For example, the mechanic where you took your car was very friendly and courteous toward you but failed to fix the problem. He met your human needs but not your business needs. Conversely, the mechanic down the street fixed the problem at a reasonable price but was rude and disrespectful. He took care of your business needs but not your human needs. The next time your car needs repairs, you will most likely try yet another mechanic because neither one so far has satisfied both levels of need.

The Human/Business Model

Human Level Needs	Attention, Respect, Caring
Business Level Needs	Product Delivery, Services Rendered

5 TYPES OF COMMUNICATION

Understanding the five types of communication helps counselors become aware of and monitor the messages and information they give and receive during client/counselor interaction.

1. Social Communication is used in getting to know individuals on a superficial level or to simply acknowledge their presence. Social communication involves many common types of questions and responses that are non-threatening. Examples of this casual small talk are "How was your weekend?" or "It's a beautiful day!" Social communication avoids revealing anything personal.

2. Persuasive Communication is used when attempting to influence others. Counselors need to be assertive while at the same time avoiding an aggressive delivery that may make clients feel pressured. Effective counselors refrain from overtly persuasive language. Instead, they work to affect positive change for the client by objectively exploring all available options.

3. Non-verbal Communication occurs through gestures, body language, and facial expressions. Our eyes, mouth, hands and posture are all conductors of non-verbal communication. For this reason, in-person contact is highly advantageous. Through face-to-face contact, non-verbal signs provide cues that permit better understanding of clients and their particular needs.

4. Expressive Communication is used when individuals express attitudes, feelings, values, morals, as well as many other traits that reveal personality. At times, it is difficult or inappropriate to express our innermost feelings, judgments, or needs about sensitive issues.

5. Cognitive communication is used to transmit content or information. It may involve simple messages such as confirming an appointment or giving someone your address. Cognitive communication also includes messages that impart complex instructions and knowledge.

Human interaction consists of a mixture of the different types of communication. For example, simple social communication like "How are you today?" can reveal information that is cognitive in nature. The client may reveal discouragement by responding, "Same as always -- behind the eight ball." This response then provides information which is cognitively processed by the counselor who then adjusts his/her response to be more affirming and motivational.

COMMON BARRIERS TO COMMUNICATION

At times, the communication process may be hindered by various negative attitudes or inappropriate emotional states. Below is a list of the most common ways that communication is compromised.

1. Anxiety/Preoccupation. Counselors who are preoccupied, anxious, agitated, or self-centered do not communicate well. Communication is a two-way process. A counselor must be attentive and focused on what is being said. Failure to respond to key words or phrases could result in loss of confidence by clients, or cause them to become irritated with the counselor. A counselor who is distracted by personal issues may react from his/her own experience rather than the professional training he/she has received, thereby giving poor and inappropriate information.

2. Needless Interruption. Besides being rude and inconsiderate, needless interruptions distract the client, resulting in repetition and frustration. Professional counselors need not exhibit their knowledge to impress the client. Rather, they should allow the client to talk, responding only when necessary. Ask questions in a manner that will help the client feel at ease. Clients need the opportunity to finish their thoughts completely. Often, it is appropriate to wait 3 - 5 seconds before responding to the client. This wait time provides the client with a window of opportunity to elaborate or offer additional information without being prompted with further questioning. Once the counselor has processed that information, he/she can interject whatever pertinent responses or questions are necessary.

3. Hidden Agenda. When counselors enter a conversation or meeting with special interests or attitudes not evident on the surface, the resulting communication is distorted by a hidden agenda. That's why it is so important for counselors to maintain objectivity. Effective counselors work to develop an open and inquisitive mind -- not one that's already made up.

4. Overreacting to Emotional Words. Overreaction to emotional or derogatory words can often derail effective communication. Counselors avoid using labels, slang, biased phrases, and furthermore avoid reacting to the use of such language. Clients who are upset may be very dramatic or accusatory while describing their situations. Maintaining a professional attitude while assessing the actual facts can help avoid escalation of emotions which can lead to offensive or defensive reactions on the part of the client.

5. Passing Judgments. Skilled counselors assess client messages without judging, condemning, or disagreeing with them. A counselor should not use his/her position to make a value judgment about the client. Any impulse to pass judgments will derail positive communication.

6. Stereotyping. Stereotyping is the unjustified placement of people in categories based on broad, misinformed generalizations. Professional counselors do not base decisions on preconceived notions or stereotyped profiles.

11 WAYS TO IMPROVE COMMUNICATION

1. Adopt an Accepting Attitude. Unconditional acceptance is critical for creating a positive climate for communication. The term acceptance refers to a basic attitude of trust and positive regard toward others. Clients are more likely to express themselves openly and honestly, thus creating a better counselor/client relationship. The client will also listen more attentively to advice being given. In contrast, negative attitudes such as distrust and suspicion put the client on the defensive, making for limited and guarded communication.

2. Express Yourself Clearly. Counselors need to speak clearly and articulate in a manner that makes others want to listen. Being expressive, using voice inflection, and being specific and direct in the information presented will assure accurate interpretation by the listener.

3. Listen for the Total Meaning. Individuals communicate to express their attitudes and emotions as well as factual information. Listening for and interpreting the total meaning of client messages means attending to not only WHAT they say but HOW they say it.

4. Be Physically Attentive. Whether speaking or listening, a counselor must focus to communicate effectively. Being completely alert when discussing a situation with a client whether it is in person or by telephone is important. If the client is physically present in the office, a counselor must demonstrate attentive behaviors such as maintaining eye contact, sitting or standing at a comfortable distance, and making certain that posture and gestures appropriately support information. Avoid anything that distracts away from client/counselor talk.

5. Observe Non-verbal Communication. Body language is often a key to success with a client. Observing facial expressions, eye contact, attentiveness, the inflection in the clients voice, how close or distant the person stands or sits, are all factors which can be considered in determining whether the body language confirms or contradicts what is being communicated.

6. Share Responsibility for the Communication. A counselor, whether speaking or listening, should be an active participant. If uncertain about information, he/she need not be apprehensive about asking the client to

explain details more clearly. Never presume understanding, but ask the client to clarify the entire meaning and to provide more active feedback. An example would be when a client says, "I will get back to you soon." A counselor, rather than assuming follow-up, might suggest, "When is the best time I can reach you?" Persistence in assigning shared responsibilities for specific follow-up will ensure continued sharing of information with little or no misunderstanding.

7. Be Expressive, Be Yourself. Don't feel that it is inappropriate to use your personality in business related communication. Being expressive facilitates all types of communication by building rapport and making those human connections that are a necessary part of any problem solving relationship.

8. Be Assertive, Not Aggressive. When counselors project assertiveness, clients gain confidence in their abilities and knowledge. Assertive counselors easily control the pace and direction of the interview. On the other hand, counselors who project aggressiveness may seem pushy, hostile or threatening to clients. The difference is putting the needs of the client first and foremost in mind.

9. Avoid "You Should" Messages. Skilled counselors avoid "you should" messages. Such messages tend to put people on the defensive and make them more apt to disagree or want to argue with you rather than consider your suggestion.

10. Use "I" Messages. "I" messages are a more effective way to express ideas and options. As a counselor, you want to be able to communicate in an honest manner as to how you feel but in a way that makes the client want to listen to you. "I" messages are helpful in expressing opinions and alternatives.

"I" messages have four components:

1. They contain suggestions which are expressed in an objective, non-judgmental way.
2. They include tangible outcomes or consequences of an action taken.
3. They communicate how the speaker feels.
4. They include a positive solution or alternative.

11. Show Empathy. It is important for the client to feel that the counselor cares about their situation, feels for their circumstance, and wants to help by providing solutions. Showing empathy means listening to information the client offers voluntarily and expressing interest. This does not mean saying, "I know what you're going through." Rather, it entails being in emotional agreement with the client. Effective counselors acknowledge and validate the way their clients feel.

SUMMARY

1. Counseling is a process that moves through five stages toward a desired outcome.

2. Stage One, rapport building, encompasses the other four stages and is focused on the process goals of counseling.

3. Process goals work to ensure that clients experience counseling as positive and affirming.

4. Outcomes goals are the specific goals clients bring to the table.

5. Understanding the five different types of communication helps counselors to monitor the messages they give and receive.

6. Being judgmental, self-centered or overly emotional greatly hinders effective communication.

7. Being accepting, attentive, and observant of non-verbal cues helps to improve communication.

8. Effective counselors use "I" messages and avoid "you should" messages.

REVIEW QUESTIONS

1. Describe how process goals differ from outcome goals.

2. According to the Human/Business Model, what do clients need at the human level?

3. List the five stages of counseling.

4. Name the five types of communication.

5. List at least five ways counselors can improve communication with their clients.

6. Look over the six different barriers to communication described in this chapter. Which one(s) do you feel you need to pay attention to ?

Unit 6: Establishing Rapport

OBJECTIVES:

- To recognize the importance of trust as the foundation for positive interaction.
- To determine the three essential elements for building rapport.
- To explore ways to convey empathy, genuineness, and positive regard.

Establishing a positive relationship with the client is a necessary prerequisite for viable problem solving and decision making to take place. Counselors act as a bridge between client dilemmas and workable solutions if and only if the necessary conditions exist that serve to create rapport and confidence between people. Effective counselors apply skills that help clients feel comfortable, attended to, and in control.

All positive interpersonal relationships begin when a bond of trust and acceptance is established. Without this bond, the relationship cannot move forward. Just how is trust established between two people who have no prior knowledge of each other? How are reluctant clients put at ease? What do counselors do that allows for positive interpersonal communication to take place? This unit will explore these counseling issues as well as specific techniques for building viable relationships with clients.

BUILDING TRUST

Have you ever met someone who won your trust right away? If you think about it, it was probably because the person seemed genuine, respectful, and caring. These are the qualities counselors strive to convey to their clients right from the start. In the initial interview, effective counselors communicate empathy, genuineness, and positive regard to clients who are often uneasy or inexperienced with the counseling process.

Skilled helpers work to establish a bond of trust between themselves and their clients by understanding the three elements that go into rapport development:

Empathy. Empathy is the ability to understand what another individual is going through. You relate to their situation as if it were your own. However, you never loose sight of the "as if." You remain objective and professional while showing the client that you care about the problem being presented and you want to help solve the problem. You convey that you are involved with helping the client in human terms. There is debate as to whether empathy is something that can be learned or if it is simply a personality trait. It is possible, nonetheless, to increase one's level of sensitivity and awareness about another person's circumstance.

44

Genuineness. Genuineness is the quality of being yourself with the client beyond your role as a skilled helper. It's easy to forget that you can and should use your personality in professional interactions. Clients need to know they are talking to another human being -- not just an efficient, knowledgeable professional. Effective counselors convey spontaneity and honesty that go beyond a business-like facade.

Positive Regard. Counselors convey positive regard by showing respect for the client as an individual with inherent value and dignity regardless of any external factors the client may demonstrate. Positive regard is giving affirmation to the client. Counselors strive to remain non-judgmental. They work to encourage the client through an often difficult situation by demonstrating respect and acceptance.

DEVELOPING EMPATHY

Empathy is a communication skill that can be developed and increased by considering the following two points:

1. Understand the Effects of Counseling on Clients. Increasing empathy begins by increasing your awareness and understanding of who the client is and how he/she relates to the counseling process. Let's begin by recognizing that counseling is not always an easy process for clients. Clients who seek out counseling may feel defeated or embarrassed. Many contact a counselor as a last resort when the effects of severe outstanding debt can no longer be ignored. Others are in crisis situations regarding money and inter-family conflict.

Yet, they face a daunting challenge. Some face the stigma that going through-any form of counseling is a sign of weakness or inadequacy. They feel as though they are relinquishing their sense of independence and self-reliance. Humbled and uneasy, they must search for someone they can trust with their finances, someone who has their best interest in mind, who possesses the competencies and expertise to assist them.

Clients straddle an emotional fence between hope and doubt. During the assessment stage of the interview, clients experience a range of both positive and negative effects. On the positive side, they may feel a sense of relief as they disclose their situation to someone else. Finally, someone is listening! Finally, I am doing something about this problem! Psychologically, they are removing debt from their lives as they give it (accounts and amounts) to the counselor.

On the negative side, clients may feel anxious and vulnerable during the interview. If the questioning is too rapid or if the counselor exhibits aggressiveness, the client may feel interrogated and evaluated. Clients come to counseling with conflicting emotions. It is important to remain aware of the difficult challenge they face in counseling. Be sensitive to their circumstances.

2. Increase Awareness and Sensitivity of Cultural Differences. When we think of culture, we usually confine its meaning to differences in race and/or ethnicity. However, the word culture conveys a much broader meaning as it relates to counseling. Culture includes:

- Demographic variables -- age, sex, and place of residence
- Status variables -- level of education, income bracket
- Ethnographic variables -- race, nationality, language, religion

With this view of culture, all counseling is multicultural. It crosses parameters of different, sometimes opposing, worldviews, values, attitudes, and expectations. Even if the client and counselor are both Hispanic, for example, one may be a middle-aged female and the other one a male in his early twenties. Or, you and your client may be of the same sex and age group but your level of education is different. It is important for counselors to be aware of all these differences and the impact they have on how clients see problems, make decisions, set goals, and accomplish tasks.

Effective counselors strive to avoid what is referred to as cultural encapsulation which is perceiving reality through only one set of cultural assumptions. Someone who is culturally encapsulated is insensitive to cultural differences and sees the values and perceptions of their culture as the only true and legitimate one. Acceptance of client diversity is an essential ingredient for productive client/counselor interaction to take place.

It's important that counselors understand who they are in the cultural mix. Who are you and how does your identity impact how you see the world around you? Accepting others begins by accepting the fact that you represent just one variation in a world of cultural possibilities.

CONVEYING GENUINENESS

Counselors convey that they are genuine by making sure that what they say and how they feel are the same. This is known as congruence. Your statements and actions reflect how you truly feel. Counselors who demonstrate congruence are aware that clients are sensitive to mixed messages. It is important for counselors to be able to evaluate their own feelings and behaviors during the counseling session.

Genuineness is also demonstrated through openness to self-disclosure. Though the focus of the interview is on the client, sometimes the tables get turned when the client asks personal questions of the counselor. This is a natural part of the process as clients seek to find out to whom they are talking. For example, a client may ask, "Are you married?", "Do you go to school?" or "How long have you been counseling?" It is best to answer such direct questions with a direct answer. All self-disclosure should be brief and honest. Providing clients with a little personal information (when they ask) serves to increase the comfort level of the session.

Finally, counselors convey genuineness through immediacy. Immediacy is a special kind of spontaneous communication. Counselors use immediacy to respond to events as they occur in the helping process. In other words, the process of counseling -- following the prescribed steps -- can and should be interrupted to allow the counselor to communicate what is observed at the moment. Phrases that contain counselor immediacy begin with "I see that you are..." or "I get the feeling that...". Immediacy in the counseling session works to overcome feelings of distance, guardedness, or hesitancy in client/counselor communication.

SHOWING POSITIVE REGARD
Counselors demonstrate positive regard by attending to the client through both verbal and non-verbal behaviors. Non-verbal behaviors are associated with a smiling or interested facial expression, relaxed posture, and good eye contact. Surprisingly, these elements of communication can be transmitted during telephone contact.

Verbal behaviors that convey positive regard are the use of a soft or soothing tone of voice as well as the use of enhancing statements. Enhancing statements serve to provide what all clients need from a skilled helper - - acceptance. Often a client may communicate information that prompts disapproval. However, the counselor avoids making judgments concerning client values and attitudes since this would be counter-productive to a positive change. Instead, effective counselors give enhancing statements that focus on the positive and affirming aspects of the client. The goal is always to provide encouragement and support to the client. Counselors refrain from instructing, correcting, or chastising clients.

Let's review the counselor actions that help create positive and productive relationships with clients:

1. **Establish trust.** Trust is the foundation on which the client/counselor relationship is built. Trust is established when:

- the counselor communicates to the client that he/she has the client's best interests in mind.
- the client feels confident that the counselor has the expertise and knowledge necessary to help with their dilemma.

2. **Show empathy.** Professional counselors strive to:

- understand how the counseling process affects clients.
- gain awareness and sensitivity about client cultural differences.
- gain understanding of themselves among diverse groups.

3. **Be genuine.** It is important for counselors to meet the human needs of the client as well as the business needs. Effective counselors:

- convey openness and spontaneity.
- avoid hesitancy, inconsistency, and defensiveness.
- are comfortable expressing their personality with clients.

4. **Demonstrate positive regard.** Effective counselors:

- avoid making judgments about clients
- convey acceptance toward clients
- focus on the positive aspects of the client

When the human needs of the client are attended to, a positive relationship is created. The client becomes a willing participant in the counseling process.

SUMMARY

1. Effective counselors exhibit empathy, genuineness and positive regard to establish rapport and trust with their clients.

2. Clients may experience a range of emotions during the counseling session from anxiety and doubt to relief and hopefulness.

3. Counseling is multicultural in that counselors often cross parameters of different worldviews, values and attitudes by interacting with diverse clients.

REVIEW QUESTIONS

1. Describe how effective counselors establish rapport with their clients.

2. Explain how counselors show positive regard to their clients.

3. How do counselors convey genuineness?

4. Suggest ways counselors can increase empathy toward their clients.

Unit 7: Active Listening

OBJECTIVES:
- To understand the importance of being an active listener.
- To determine the three components of active listening.
- To explore the listening techniques of reflective and non-reflective listening.
- To assess your current level of listening skills.

There is no better way to communicate empathy, genuineness, and positive regard than to *actively* listen to the client. All the techniques utilized by counselors hinge upon your ability to give this form of undivided attention to the individual seeking help. What is active listening and how does it work?

Active listening is showing respect and demonstrating interest. It is the process by which the human needs of the client are met. It allows the client to relax and therefore, communicate more information more accurately. This, in turn, benefits the counseling process as client situations, obstacles, and needs become better understood. Through the process of active listening, the barriers of communication that often cause clients to withhold crucial information are removed.

Everyone loves a good listener. In a world where we are constantly bombarded by outside messages, the good listener is like an island of tranquility. Someone is listening to you! They are attentive and interested in what you have to say. They do not interrupt you even as you pause to form your thoughts. For many people, being attended to by a good listener is a rare experience.

Counselors take good listening to the next level. They do this by incorporating specific techniques that serve to ensure total and accurate transmission of their clients' messages. We will learn these essential techniques as we explore the components of active listening.

THE 3 COMPONENTS OF ACTIVE LISTENING

There are three components to active listening: what you do, what you say, and what you observe during the counseling session. Let's look at the specific strategies for each of these processes.

WHAT YOU DO

This component consists of four things that effective counselors do to create a caring and respectful communicative environment for the client:

1. Maintain an upright, relaxed posture. Turn so you are completely facing the client. This demonstrates that he/she has your undivided attention. Avoid crossing your arms in front of you as this suggests an aloof, judgmental attitude. Also, avoid propping your head up with your hand. This is a sure indication of either boredom or tiredness.

2. Establish eye contact. Always look directly into the clients eyes whenever you are speaking to the client or he/she is speaking to you. However, you will want to avoid a cold, unwavering stare.

3. Use appropriate facial expressions. Smile during social communication. Show seriousness (usually mouth closed and eyebrows slightly squeezed together) when the topic is of a serious nature.

4. Provide non-verbal feedback. This includes nodding your head to acknowledge what the client is saying. It communicates that you are paying close attention and that you fully understand what is being related.

How Does What You Do Apply to Telecommunications?

You may be wondering how the physical actions of counselors have any effect during telephone communication. Surprisingly, what you can't see, you can often hear.

Vocal tone and delivery can alter dramatically depending on posture and facial expression. Have you ever answered the phone while lying in bed? An observant caller will notice a change in your voice and may comment, "You sound funny" or "Did I wake you?" Similarly, clients who need your energized assistance will pick up on clues that you are not sufficiently engaged should you be slouched over your desk or leaning back in your chair with your feet up.

And is it not possible to hear a smile over the telephone? Try this simple experiment: Say, "Hello, how are you" – first while frowning and then while smiling broadly. The words are the same but the effect is completely different.

But how can I make eye contact with someone on the phone?

Here, it's a matter of focus. Keep a small pad next to the telephone and write out the client's name. This provides a visual aid that keeps your eyes from wandering around the room. By focusing on something visual that relates to the client, you can avoid becoming distracted.

What about the use of non-verbal feedback?

Who does not make use of visual signals such as nodding and hand gestures while on the telephone? These physical movements help with the flow and effectiveness of your vocal delivery. Words that require emphasis get a boost from talking hands.

One final point on the doing component of active listening. Today we often find ourselves doing more than one thing at a time. We read the paper while eating breakfast, shave or apply make up while driving, and go through our mail while watching television. While multitasking saves time in our busy schedules, it really has no place in the realm of counseling. Counseling requires that you give clients YOUR FULL ATTENTION.

WHAT YOU SAY

The saying component of active listening can be divided into reflective and non-reflective listening techniques. With reflective listening, counselors reflect back the content as well as the feelings of client messages.

Example 1

Al: I've always worked for myself, but now the cost of the medical care my daughter needshas got me thinking about a job that provides benefits. Still, I can't stand the idea of working 9 to 5.

Counselor: It sounds like you're torn between the freedom of working for yourself and the security that a benefits package can offer.

Example 2

Sarah: Right now, I'm receiving child support payments which just barely cover the monthly cost of day care. But there's still all the other expenses of running a family. I mean, I have to work long hours every day.

Counselor: So, you're concerned you still have to work so much even though you are receiving child support.

In both examples, the counselor reflected back to the client the content and emotion of the message. Using this technique facilitates communication in two ways:

1. It assures the client that you received the correct message.
2. It shows empathy and caring while avoiding any judgmental comments.

When counselors use reflective listening, they make reflecting statements. Reflecting statements often begin with the following phrases:

"It sounds like..."
"I noticed that you..."

"You sound like you feel..."
"I sense that you are feeling..."

Read the following client statements. Then, create a reflecting statement in the space provided. Remember to share what you are observing about what the client is communicating. Avoid judgmental comments.

1. Sarah: I went through so much to get them to garnish his wages so I'd get the child support on time. Now, it's just a joke how little it really helps. Like I say, it barely takes care of what I'm paying for childcare.

Counselor:

_____
_____
_____

2. Al: My wife offered to go back to work but for me that's just not an option. Besides, she's busy enough with our daughters. I'm supposed to be the one taking care of things.

Counselor:

_____
_____
_____

3. Amy: I wish someone had been there to tell me about all these finance charges and late fees. I mean, I guess I knew about them but I thought I could manage it. It's amazing how fast it all adds up!

Counselor:

_____
_____
_____

4. Ray: The lay-off came as quite a shock. I worked there for seven years doing pretty much what I like to do -- designing software. I didn't think I would need a back up plan.

Counselor:

_____
_____
_____

4 TYPES OF REFLECTING STATEMENTS

There are many obstacles in the encoding process. Because of this, the client may fail to communicate clearly what he/she actually means. At times, the client may not be sure what he/she is trying to say, let alone communicate the thought properly.

To avoid misinterpreting what the client is saying, the counselor must decode the client's message through non-judgmental feedback. The client then has the opportunity to clarify his/her statement so that it more closely coincides with the intended message. Reflective listening consists of a give and take between client and counselor.

Reflective listening involves the following 4 techniques:

1. Clarifying. This technique helps to gather accurate data, facts, or additional meanings. Asking clients to clarify a statement will alert them to the fact that they need to explain details more clearly. Encourage clients to say or do more to clarify communication:

"Would you please clarify that?"
"I'm not sure I understand what you just said."

2. Paraphrasing. When counselors paraphrase client responses, clients gain assurance that what they said was communicated accurately. This does not mean parroting the client. Counselors communicate back client messages in their own words preceded by phrases such as:

"As I understand you..."
"Correct me if I'm wrong..."
"In other words ..."

3. Summarizing. Summing up client responses helps to connect various segments of the conversation into a meaningful whole. Effective counselors determine the main point behind the details of client talk and give back a statement that puts it in a nutshell. Summarizing gives a sense of closure to a conversation:

"The point is..."
"In general, what you're saying is..."
"Summing up what you said..."

4. Reflecting Feelings. The focus of this method is on the tone of the client's message. What the counselor now wants to do is reflect or mirror back the client's feelings, attitudes, and personal meanings. In effect, the counselor tries to get emotionally in tune with the client. Avoid attempts to pamper or sympathize with the client by saying "I know what you are going through." This is a sure way to alienate or frustrate the client. The client should sense that the counselor understands by reflective expression. Show empathy without patronizing the client:

"It appears that you feel..."
"It sounds like you feel..."

When you begin listening reflectively, you may feel that you are not being yourself or you are being artificial. This is a natural response. As you acquire any new skill, you will experience an initial stage of awkwardness. This is true with reflective listening. Integrating these new techniques into your everyday communication takes time and practice. Remember that acquiring good listening skills is not only important in counseling but extremely useful for all types of interpersonal communication.

Non-Reflective Listening consists of verbal affirmations that encourage the client to continue communicating. These include short phrases such as "I see", "Yes", "Go on", and "Mm-mm." It is important to avoid any verbal phrase that is negative or judgmental like "Ugh!", "That's terrible!" or "Are you kidding?"

Non-reflective listening is particularly useful when a client appears hesitant during communication. Simple verbal encouragements go a long way toward helping a client relax and feel assured that what he/she has to say is important for the counselor to hear. Remember, you are gathering information. Being nonjudgmental and affirming are key ingredients for allowing the client to open up with the genuine and accurate information you will need to facilitate solutions.

Example 1
Ray: My wife used to do our finances, but... (sighs)

Counselor: Go on.

Ray: Well, now that she's working and I'm not, the responsibility falls on me to keep track of the bills.

Counselor: I see.

Ray: But, I guess I haven't done such a good job. I mean...

Counselor: Yes.

Ray: I'm just not a detail-orientated guy.

Notice how the use of non-reflective listening helped the counselor to uncover a potentially useful bit of information, namely, the client's belief that he's not good with details.

Example 2
Amy: Basically, my parents have cut me off financially.

Counselor: I see.

Amy: But...

Counselor: Please continue.

Amy: They said I could move back with them until I get this straightened out, but that's... I don't know.

Counselor: Go on.

Amy: I really want to stay where I am. I've got a really fun job at a great restaurant and all my friends live around here and...

Counselor: Yes.

Amy: The money's supposed to be really good.

Here again, the counselor uncovers some key information about the client's situation using non-reflective listening. Specifically, her job as a waitress is supposed to bring in good money.

Both reflective and non-reflective listening are excellent techniques for achieving the process goals of counseling. They both work to establish a non-threatening environment where interest and acceptance are expressed. Consider how the negative, judgmental phrases "Ugh!", "Gee!", or "That's crazy!" could inhibit genuine and accurate communication.

REFLECTIVE & NON-REFLECTIVE LISTENING
The two most important counseling techniques that optimize listening are reflective and non-reflective listening. These two techniques provide specific ways that counselors respond to clients as they speak.

Reflective listening is giving back to the client the messages received by the counselor. It involves reflecting statements that paraphrase, clarify, or summarize what the client has communicated. Reflective listening also involves responding to the client's emotional state. Most importantly, reflective listening is a way of responding to client talk in a non-judgmental and accepting way. Instead of saying "Calm down" to an irate client, effective counselors say, "It sounds like you're really upset about this." Instead of trying to change a client's behavior, the emotional state of the client is acknowledged.

Non-reflective listening is the simplest form of listening. This type of listening involves attentive silence with minimal vocal response. Appropriate nodding, verbal affirmation, and facial expressions encourage the client to continue talking. When possible, counselors should use encouraging responses that are nonjudgmental in nature. Examples of these short responses include "Please continue", "All right" and "Yes."

Many times the client will render cues which suggest serious hidden details. Non-reflective listening can also be utilized to draw out information which the client is hesitant to disclose. It is an important strategy for prompting the client forward with sometimes sensitive details. Money is a sensitive issue. Remember to be non-judgmental!

WHAT YOU OBSERVE

The third component of active listening is what you observe. During active listening, the effective counselor observes two interrelated aspects of client talk:

- what they are saying and
- how they are saying it.

In other words, the counselor receives the client's verbal content *and* the client's emotions regarding the content they communicate.

EXERCISE: CLIENT EMOTIONS

Client emotions can be identified through verbal statements (what is said) and verbal behavior (how it is said). Let's start by identifying client emotions from what is said. Our four clients will each make a verbal statement. In the space provided, write down a word to describe the emotion communicated. It is helpful to ask yourself "How would I feel in a similar circumstance?" You may use words from the list below that describe common emotions or use your own descriptive words.

Words to Describe Emotions

Happy Fearful Unsure Confused Conflicted Troubled Undecided
Lost Mixed up Content Elated Delighted Glad Satisfied
Sad Dejected Despondent Glum Hurt Angry Furious, Nervous
Irate Agitated Dismayed Fuming Afraid Scared Insecure

1. Sarah: My ex-husband thinks I'm living high off the hog. Boy, if he only knew!

Emotions:

_____

2. Al: I never thought I would even consider bankruptcy, but my credit is such a mess now anyway. What difference does it make?

Emotions:

_____

3. Amy: Right now, I'm working a lot of lunch shifts but I should get some weekend nights soon. There are people there that make two or three hundred dollars in a night!

Emotions:

_____

4. Ray: Sometimes I think I'm just not with it. Ever hear of the absent-minded professor?

Emotions:

_____

LISTENING BETWEEN THE LINES

The second way to identify client emotions is to pay attention to the verbal behavior of the client. This consists of how words are spoken, tone of voice, pace, pauses, sighs, laughing, and sobbing. For example, a loud voice usually indicates anger while a soft voice can mean the client is sad or fearful. A client who talks very quickly might be nervous whereas a client who talks slowly could be depressed.

It is important to keep in mind that emotions are complex. Laughter can indicate nervousness as well as delight. Crying could be a sign of joyous relief as well as sadness. Sighs and silences may well be signs of depression, or they may just indicate a client who is exhausted. Remember to relate verbal behavior to what the client is saying.

In some cases, verbal behavior will match verbal content. In other cases, it will seem to contradict what the client is saying. For example, a client may announce that he/she just landed a new job and then begin sobbing. But it makes perfect sense if getting the job was extremely important to that person. Similarly, a client may mention with a chuckle that he/she just got laid-off. This may indicate a client who was less than thrilled with his/her former employment or it may be a way for the client to cope with yet another setback.

Considering what the client is saying and how they are saying it will help you get the complete picture of the clients state of mind. The three components of active listening -- what you do, what you say, and what you observe -- go a long way toward establishing a relationship of trust and respect with your clients.

Listening skills are indispensable in the counseling process. Counselors who are good listeners build solid rapport with their clients. Good listeners also are able to gather accurate and complete information about their clients which serves as the essential starting point for finding solutions. Are you a good listener? Complete the following self-assessment to find out!

SELF-ASSESSMENT: LISTENING SKILLS

Never - 1 / Rarely - 2 / Sometimes - 3 / Often - 4 / Very Often - 5

1. I avoid staying on any one subject with others.
   1   2   3   4   5
2. I make assumptions about other's feelings or thoughts.
     1   2   3   4   5
3. I ignore another's view if I feel my way is the right way.
     1   2   3   4   5
4. I bring up past issues during current disagreements.
     1   2   3   4   5
5. I interrupt others' conversations.
     1   2   3   4   5
6. I use sarcasm or jokes to respond when others talk.
     1   2   3   4   5
7. I respond to a complaint with a complaint.
     1   2   3   4   5

8. I insult and criticize those I communicate with.

      1   2   3   4   5

9. I can be very opinionated and defensive.

      1   2   3   4   5

10. I see only my point of view.

      1   2   3   4   5

If you scored in the range of 10 - 25 you are usually a very effective listener. If you scored in the range of 26 - 50 you need to improve on your skills and be aware where your weaknesses may lie.

SUMMARY

1. There are three components to active listening -- what you do, what you say, and what you observe.

2. Non-reflective listening serves to encourage client communication.

3. Reflective listening serves to assure the client that you receive and understand what the client is trying to say.

4. Effective counselors listen not only to what is said but also to *how* it is said.

REVIEW QUESTIONS

1. Define active listening.

2. What are the three components of active listening?

3. How do counselors physically demonstrate interest and caring?

4. What do counselors observe about client messages?

5. List the four specific techniques used during reflective listening.

6. How does non-reflective listening help client/counselor communication?

Unit 8: Interviewing Skills

OBJECTIVES:
- To learn ways to interview effectively.
- To know when to use open-ended and closed-ended questions.

Good interviewers:

1. ask short, direct questions.
2. ask only one question at a time.
3. ask questions that do not need to be explained.
4. wait for the client to answer.
5. do not answer their own questions.

Numbers 4 and 5 can be hard to remember especially for those of us who like a fast-paced exchange of information. However, some clients require several seconds to respond to a question. They are more deliberate and thoughtful and need that extra time to consider their answer. For these clients, silence can indeed be golden.

OPEN-ENDED AND CLOSED-ENDED QUESTIONS

There are two types of questions: Open-ended questions and closed-ended questions. Each has its particular use during the interview.

Open-Ended Questions encourage clients to explore their thoughts and feelings. Often they involve getting clients to analyze their situation or evaluate options or courses of action to be taken.

Open-ended questions usually require an answer longer than just a word or two. Open-ended questions are used for the following reasons:

1. To ask for a statement of the problem. For example:

   "How can I help you?"

   "Can you describe the trouble you're having?"

2. To explore alternatives to solving the problem. For example:

   "How have you dealt with this before?"

"Have you thought about keeping a spending record?"

3. To refocus the client back to the topic at hand. For example:

"Let's get back to your unsecured debt. What solutions have you sought out before?"

4. To ask the client's opinion concerning an option or course of action. For example:

"How does that sound to you?"

"What do you think about this idea?"

Closed-Ended Questions, on the other hand, are used to get factual information from the client. They can often be answered with a "yes", a "no" or one or two words. Closed-ended questions are asked for the following reasons:

1. To obtain specific information. For example:

"Did you sign a lease?"

"Who is your employer?"

2. To ask the client to clarify a statement you did not fully understand. For example:

"I'm not sure I understand. Are you saying you co-signed on the loan?"

3. To coordinate or schedule future plans. For example:

"Can you send me your last billing statement?"

"Do you think you can call tomorrow with that information?"

ASKING OPEN-ENDED QUESTIONS

Asking open-ended questions requires that you begin with an initial phrase that invites the client to speak freely and openly. Examples of initial phrases for open-ended questions are:

"How do you feel about..."
"Could you tell me about..."
"What do you think..."

Notice that the phrases above cannot be answered with a simple "yes" or "no."

Since open-ended questions may require extended answers from clients, it is important to provide verbal encouragement through non-reflective listening as the client speaks. This will help the client answer open-ended questions more completely.

After asking an open-ended question, wait for the client to respond. Avoid rephrasing the question, explaining the question or answering the question yourself. Give the client those five (or even ten) seconds necessary to answer these sometimes difficult questions.

EXERCISE: OPEN-ENDED QUESTIONS

Read the client statements below. Then, create your own open-ended questions to obtain more information or a better understanding about the situation.

1. Al: My security business requires that I travel quite a bit and I tend to use my credit cards when I'm on the road. Trouble is, I lose track of all my expenses. When I get home, I try to play catch up but before you know it, I'm staring at late charges.

Counselor:

_____

2. Amy: I was studying marine biology. I guess I thought I could work at Sea World you know, training dolphins or something. I'm just trying to be more realistic now. I know I need to make money to get out of this debt.

Counselor:

_____

3. Sarah: My ex-husband gets the kids every other weekend that's the arrangement we worked out with the judge. Anyway, that's my time to take care of all the things I have no time for. It just seems like the bills always get pushed to the end of my to do list.

Counselor:

_____

4. Ray: Not working is actually harder than working. At my old job, I got to put together my own projects at a pace that was right for me. That's what was so great about that company.

Counselor:

_____

ASKING CLOSED-ENDED QUESTIONS
Closed-ended questions need to begin with an initial phrase that requires a short answer or a "yes" or "no" response. Examples of initial phrases that begin a closed-ended question are:

"When..."
"Where..."
"Who..."
"Are you..."
"How much..."
"Is it..."

Notice that the answers to questions that begin with the phrases above can consist of a word or two. If you were to ask "How much credit debt do you have?", the question could be answered by disclosing an amount – $5,000, for example. If you were to ask "Where do you work?", the answer would be nothing more than the name of the employer or the location.

Read the client statements below and write either a closed-ended or an open-ended question in the space provided. Indicate whether it is closed-ended or open-ended.

1. Sarah: This is the first time I've ever called a counselor but I've got to do something about this debt.

Counselor:

_____

2. Ray: Even though I'm unemployed now, I never seem to have enough time.

Counselor:

_____

3. Amy: I just got another billing statement from Big Chain Department Store and more late charges have been added.

Counselor:

_____

4. Al: My wife is the homemaker. I really don't want her working outside the home. She has enough to do taking care of our two daughters.

Counselor:

_____

SUMMARY

1. Good interviewers ask short, direct questions.

2. Good interviewers wait for clients to respond to their questions.

3. Open-ended questions solicit longer answers concerning ideas, feelings, and opinions.

4. Closed-ended questions seek factual information and can be answered with a "yes" or "no" response or a short phrase.

REVIEW QUESTIONS

1. List the five things good interviewers do.

2. Give three examples of closed-ended questions.

3. Give three examples of open-ended questions.

Module III: Solving Financial Problems

PREVIEW

The framework of this module is based on the problem-solving process that is at the core of all counseling. It consists of three primary steps:

1. assessing the client's current situation
2. determining the client's goals
3. helping the client actualize those goals

Finding solutions is a combination of art and science. Problem solving follows a series of logical steps but the destination and the options for getting there require an informed imagination.

The Problem Solving Process examines problem solving as it occurs naturally and within the context of counseling. Principles of the Problem-Management/ Opportunity-Development Model are related specifically to financial problem solving.

Where the Client is Now introduces several assessments to determine the client's current financial situation. These include the net worth statement, debt-to-income ratio, and budget analysis. Money relationships are also explored.

Where the Client Wants to Go takes the next step by exploring the processes of goal setting and decision making. Financial goals arising naturally through the life-cycle are surveyed; personal financial goals are explored by assessing our values.

How the Client Will Get There examines the third step in the problem-solving process. Following through with action plans, over-coming inertia and increasing client motivation and confidence are some of the topics discussed here.

Throughout this module, the facts-and-figures dimension of personal finances is presented side by side with the cognitive/emotional dimension of money relationships and money-related behavior. These two dimensions are inter-related and they are of equal importance for getting a clear picture of the client's financial situation.

By completing this module, you will:

- be able to identify ways to assess a client's current financial scenario.
- understand how to calculate net worth.
- understand how to calculate debt-to-income ratio.
- know how to analyze a budget using a spending percentage guideline.
- gain insight into the problem-solving process.
- learn about various spending personalities.
- gain awareness about money relationships.
- learn about the goal-setting process.
- become familiar with Maslow's Hierarchy of Needs.
- become introduced to Solution-Focused Counseling.
- learn about the four ways to economize.

Unit 9: The Problem-Solving Process

- To understand how the Problem-Management/Opportunity-Development Model relates to financial counseling.
- To examine the problem-solving process that occurs naturally.
- To explore the problem-solving process facilitated through counseling.

The Problem-Management/Opportunity-Development Model

The Problem-Management/Opportunity-Development Model describes the underlying process utilized by helpers to address client needs. It is based on the idea that the helping process involves the inter-related goals of managing problems more effectively and developing opportunities more fully. Financial counselors can benefit from this approach for three main reasons:

1. **It is client-centered.** The client is situated squarely at the center of the helping process. Clients communicate their particular financial scenarios, provide critical information, offer resources, establish objectives, and ultimately take the actions necessary to improve their financial situation. Ultimately, it is the client who pays down his/her debt and nobody else. Counselors act to facilitate and support client-directed outcomes.

2. **It is an open-systems model.** The Problem-Management/Opportunity-Development Model is inclusive of any approach that adds success in the helping process. Simply put, the philosophy behind this approach is one size does NOT fit all. Different approaches are necessary for different clients. Each client brings a new situation to the table ‑new obstacles and dilemmas as well as new strengths and resources. There is no attachment to a particular theory or model. The rules are simple: If it works, do it. If it doesn't work, stop doing it and try something else.

3. **It specifically compliments financial problem solving.** People experiencing unresolved debt usually have this core problem: a negative debt-to-income ratio. Reversing this insolvency depends on two complimentary actions: (1) decreasing expenses (managing the problem) and (2) increasing income (developing opportunities). These two processes work hand in hand to pay down debt.

Because this model views the client as the ultimate source of the solution, we will now explore how individuals naturally face and address dilemmas. We will see that people are intrinsically motivated through progressive steps toward the resolution of conflict. It is this dynamic that client-centered helpers acknowledge and work with to generate solutions.

PROBLEM SOLVING: A NATURAL PROCESS

People are naturally motivated to resolve the problems in their lives. According to Aristotle, we are all hardwired to seek pleasure and avoid pain. Some more recent observers of human nature theorize that people naturally seek to resolve conflict.

In *The Social Brain*, M.S. Gazzaniga contends that the human mind is designed specifically to seek harmony and consistency between what we believe about the world around us and what we actually experience. People naturally feel discomfort and anxiety when they have accumulated debt that they cannot seem to pay back. This situation causes tension because the individual's belief that he or she is honest and responsible is challenged by the reality that products and services have been rendered without payment in full. This tension creates a natural motivation to set things straight.

When clients seek out counseling, they are somewhere along a natural progression of steps from an awareness of the problem to finding a solution to the problem. However, the problem still exists. Somewhere in the process, the client got stuck.

THE SEVEN STEPS TO PROBLEM SOLVING

1. **Awareness of the problem.** The first step involves an awareness of the problem -- namely, the client is in a financially unhealthy situation.

2. **Problem creates urgency.** Next, the client begins to feel a sense of urgency about the problem. For example, debt creates annoyance or interference in the client's personal and business life.

3. **The search begins.** In the third step, the client begins to search for a solution. This may be the point a which the client initiates counseling. However, at this stage, the client is merely exploring the options.

4. **Decisions, decisions.** By the fourth step, the client weighs the consequences of the different options explored. For example, the client may weigh the option of bankruptcy against what that would do to his or her long term credit rating.

5. **What if I did nothing?** Now the client seriously considers his/her options against the cost of simply ignoring the problem. This is often hard to do in the case of credit debt since the amount owed continues to grow.

6. **I've made a decision!** An intellectual decision is made to follow a particular course of action. "I'm going to sell some of my assets" or "I'm going to get a

home-equity loan." However, a decision made only by the head is insufficient to cause action. In reality, the client does not sell his powerboat. The client does not even apply for a home-equity loan.

7. C is for commitment. Then a decision involving the heart is made. With the client's head and heart involved, the commitment needed to solve the problem is in place.

EXERCISE: NATURAL PROBLEM-SOLVING PROCESS
For the following exercise, see if you can identify the stage each client is at in the natural problem-solving process. Refer to steps 1 - 7 to designate the number. For the purposes of this exercise, we will include the option of Step 0 which is denial of the problem.

1. Al: My main concern is my credit rating. That's what I used to start my business. Look, I'm a finagler. I've been robbing Peter to pay Paul for years. I mean, I could wiggle my way out of this really, but that involves taking more chances and, you know, I've got my family to think about. It's not just me anymore.

   STEP _____

2. Amy:I kept getting these notices in the mail but, like, it didn't seem like anything to worry about. I mean it's all just paper, right? I guess somewhere in the back of my mind I'm thinking somebody's going to bail me out, you know, or maybe six months from now I'll be a millionaire. Who knows?

   STEP_____

3. Ray: I just need some more time to think this through and go over the numbers. Based on the interest rates, I know my debt is just going to increase but my income -- that's a variable I'm not comfortable with. My unemployment benefits won't last indefinitely. Of course, I will get a job. Heck, software designers are supposed to be in demand.

   STEP_____

4. Sarah: If I had all the child support due to me, I could pay off my debt and then some. You know, they started to garnish his wages and then guess what? He got fired! Anyway, I've got to do something and stop waiting around for what's not coming.

   STEP_____

PROBLEM SOLVING THROUGH COUNSELING

Effective counselors follow steps that serve to compliment, as opposed to replace, the natural process we outlined. This process assists clients in making the decisions that lead to solutions in a timely manner. Whereas the natural process of problem solving could take literally several years for an individual to work through, the process counselors utilize can be completed conceivably during the course of one interview. Counseling streamlines the problem-solving process by helping the client consider all the options. As you will see, this process involves three stages:

1. Identifying the current situation - where is the client now?
2. Setting goals - where does the client want to go?
3. Working to get there - how will the client reach stated goals?

Stage I: Where the client is now. It is important that counselors begin by gathering facts, incomes and expenses, and current levels of debt. Remember, personal finances are just that -- personal! The information that counselors seek is rarely disclosed even between friends. It is critical to establish client/counselor trust. Ask closed-ended questions to get factual information and confirmations. Use non-reflective listening techniques to encourage client communication.

Stage II: Where the client wants to go. Solving problems is more than just fixing something that isn't working. It involves setting viable objectives and putting into place whatever is necessary to achieve those objectives. In other words, instead of being reactive -- reacting to problems or sources of conflict -- the client/counselor team is proactive.

Stage III: Getting There. Once the current scenario is understood and goals have been specified, it is time to act. Whereas Stage II identifies what the client wants, Stage III identifies how the client will get there. It consists of brainstorming for options, evaluating each option, and acting on the best alternative. It means coming up with a plan that works.

The three stages of problem solving as utilized by counselors will provide the framework for the units that follow.

SUMMARY

1. A client-centered approach to problem solving acknowledges that it is the client who must be motivated toward positive change.

2. The Problem-Management/Opportunity-Development Model compliments financial counseling specifically by focusing on the two inter-related actions of managing problems (decreasing expenses) and developing opportunities (increasing income).

3. People are naturally motivated to resolve financial dilemmas.

4. The problem-solving process counselors utilize consist of three stages: identifying where the client is now, determining where the client wants to go and facilitating actions to meet client-directed goals.

REVIEW QUESTIONS

1. Describe what is meant by client-centered counseling.

2. List the steps in the natural problem-solving process.

3. Outline the problem-solving stages used by counselors to facilitate problem solving.

Unit 10: Where the Client is Now

OBJECTIVES:

- To differentiate between objective & subjective measures of financial well-being.
- To determine ways to assess the client's financial situation.
- To define budget analysis.
- To explore types of spending personalities and money relationships.

A clear sense of the client's current financial situation will set the stage for all future financial planning and goal setting. Assessing the client's financial condition involves not only dollars and cents calculations but also the client's attitudes and beliefs about money.

Where is the client now? To find out, counselors use objective measures such as the net worth statement, debt-to-income ratio, and budget analysis. Subjective assessments are no less important in determining a client's overall financial situation. These assessments explore cognitive and emotional issues linked to money -- how we make it, how we spend it, and how we feel about it.

As a counselor, you will undoubtedly encounter a variety of individuals or couples who will present a wide range of presenting concerns. These are the problems or issues that clients initially bring to the counseling process. In some cases, clients will be experiencing various levels of financial stress or dissatisfaction. In other cases, clients will be in a crisis situation stemming from excessive debt or sudden lack of income.

Your role as counselor is to listen to their concerns and issues in a non-judgmental way. Financial setbacks affect all but the lucky few in today's economic landscape of corporate downsizing, soaring medical costs, and easy access to credit. Finding solutions never begins by assigning blame but rather by taking a non-judgmental look at the client's current financial scenario and helping that client move forward.

OBJECTIVE MEASURES of the FINANCIAL CONDITION

CALCULATING NET WORTH

How much are you worth? That's the question to be answered when figuring net worth. Net worth is the difference between the total amount of your assets and the total amount of your liabilities. It is the single best estimate of your level of wealth at a particular time. Periodic assessments of net worth are important because:

The net worth statement provides a starting point from which to formulate financial goals. It is the YOU ARE HERE mark on the map from which to plot your financial course. Net worth is a way to measure financial progress. By calculating your net worth every six months or so, you can objectively gauge the success of your financial plan.

Calculating net worth begins by listing all assets. Assets are things you own that have market value. They can be physical possessions such as a house, car, boat, jewelry or furniture. They can also be in the form of paper -- cash, bank account balances, stocks and bonds, and investments.

Figuring the total value of your assets requires two steps:

1. Identify and list all items of value that you own.
2. Determine the market value for each item.

What Do You Own?

Step two is the more difficult since it is not always easy to appraise the value of an item particularly if it has sentimental value or is a family heirloom. Begin with liquid assets. A liquid asset is cash on hand, money in the bank or any other asset that can be converted into cash with a minimum amount of inconvenience and with no loss in market value.

The market value of homes should be figured by observing the selling prices of homes that are similar in terms of size, type and location. It's a good idea to then deduct seven percent for a realtor's commission. Values for automobiles can be determined by referring to the "blue book" of used car values. In other cases a professional appraiser may be needed to determine the worth of antique furniture or items resulting from hobbies or collections.

It is important to take a conservative approach in assigning value to assets. Fair market values for many used items may be twenty to forty percent less than what they are listed for as new.

What Do You Owe?

Liabilities will likely be easier to determine since lenders and billing departments make it a point to let you know exactly how much you owe. A liability is a debt obligation that must be paid some time in the future. Some balance sheets arrange liabilities in current (to be paid within one year) and non-current (debt obligations beyond one year) categories.

Housing will represent the greatest liability for most homeowners. It is the unpaid portion of a mortgage. Automobile installment loans are also a big ticket liability that can be determined by referring to a bank's payment schedule. Also, to be listed in the liabilities column are unpaid utility bills, credit-card balances and unsecured debts.

Different types of documents can be used to figure net worth. A balance sheet uses the mathematical equation:

Assets = Liabilities + Net Worth

The balance is between assets on the one hand and the sum of liabilities and net worth on the other.

Another document or financial statement in use today is the equity sheet which uses the more straightforward equation:

Assets -- Liabilities = Net Worth

WEB RESOURCES!

There are several free access net worth calculators online. There are also ebudget worksheets and cost-of-credit calculators available to the public. See *Appendix C: Consumer Resource Links* under "Consumer Tools."

TRACKING INCOME AND EXPENSES

To budget or not to budget -- that is the question. Budget by any other name is still a budget but you may wish to call it a spending plan. Budget is a word with a bad reputation. A derivative of the French word *bouge* meaning "small purse", it conjures up images of penny-pinching deprivation. Whatever you call it – a budget or a spending plan -- it is a valuable tool for reaching financial goals. It helps you to manage the cash that flows in and out of your life.

Customize Your Expense Categories

Some categories like MORTGAGE, UTILITIES, and CAR PAYMENTS will be easy to fill in because you will have a paper trail. Other areas like FOOD, CLOTHING, and PERSONAL will take some thought. It can be helpful to divide these categories into smaller units. For example, FOOD can be broken down to GROCERIES and EATING OUT. PERSONAL can be divided into PERSONAL CARE and ENTERTAINMENT.

Keep a Spending Record

It may be necessary to keep a daily expense record for the month so purchases can be accurately tracked. Guidelines for keeping an expense record are:

- Do not skip any days.
- Record every expense no matter how insignificant it might seem.
- Record the expense as soon as you make the transaction.
- Write down costs to the penny.

ANALYZING THE BUDGET

Once you have the clients monthly income and expenses, it is time to analyze just what the information tells you. Budget analysis is the process used to determine how well resources are being allocated in the household. It allows you the counselor to identify the expense categories that are in control and others that may need to be reduced or modified for the short-term.

Using a Spending Percentage Guideline

Although spending is (and should be) based on the specific needs, goals and values of the client, there are some general guidelines that can help clients achieve a healthier debt-to-income ratio. Here's one example:

SPENDING PERCENTAGE GUIDELINE

Expense Category	% of Overall Spending
Housing	25-35%
Utilities	5-10%
Transportation	10-15%
Healthcare	5-10%
Food	5-15%
Investments/Savings	5-10%
Debt Payments	5-10%
Charitable Giving	5-15%
Entertainment/Recreation	5-9%
Misc/Personal	2-7%

Here's a graphic version of a spending percentage guideline:

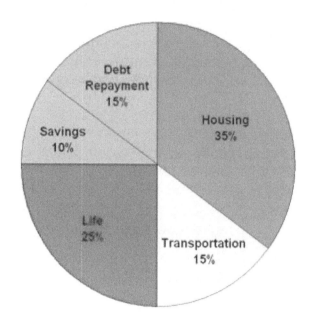

Divide the client's monthly income by each expense category percentage to get actual amounts. Then, you will know which categories of spending to adjust. Remember, guidelines should be tweaked to meet the needs of each individual's household.

DEBT-TO-INCOME RATIO

Another objective measure of a client's current financial condition is the debt-to-income ratio. It will tell you how much debt the client carries in relation to his or her income. Some calculations include mortgage or rent payments and some do not. Some experts recommend including all your current debt to get a more complete picture of the current debt load. It is also recommended to double the amounts of your minimum payments on revolving accounts since paying only the minimum each month is financially unhealthy.

To calculate debt-to-income ratio, add up all monthly payments and divide by the monthly net income. If you include mortgage or rent, a healthy debt-to-income ratio is 36% or less. If you do not include mortgage or rent, the ratio should be kept under 20%.

Different guidelines are used for different purposes. For example, the Federal Housing Authority (FHA) calculates two ratios -- a front ratio (mortgage divided by the gross monthly income) and a back ratio (total fixed payments divided by the gross monthly income).

EXPENSE BREAKDOWN

Fixed Expenses are expenses that do not vary from month to month such as mortgage and car payments.

Variable Expenses are those that change from month to month such as utilities, groceries, and clothing.

Discretionary Expenses are those the client has complete control over such as spending for gifts, recreation and entertainment.

SUBJECTIVE ASSESSMENTS of the FINANCIAL CONDITION

We are what we consume. If we look deeply into the items that we consume everyday, we will come to know our nature very well.

– Thich Nhat Hanh

Let's look at some subjective assessments of the financial condition. The client may wish to explore the possible reasons for the current scenario through any number of self-assessments. .. and like calculators, questionnaires that score for credit behavior and level financial literacy can be found online.

Getting control of spending is not easy especially when you consider that clients may possess a subconscious tendency to make spending mistakes. Is your spending personality costing you hundreds or even thousands of dollars a year? Take the Spending Personality Assessment developed by Grady Nash to find out more.

SPENDING PERSONALITY ASSESSMENT

Read each of the following statements and check each one that applies to you. Which category has the most checks?

The Fanatical Shopper

1. You shop for weeks for the best price. _____
2. Others consider your bargain hunting to be excessive. _____
3. You neglect quality in an effort to save money. _____

The Impulsive Buyer

1. You make unplanned, impulsive purchases often. _____
2. You have little willpower when considering a purchase. _____
3. You buy items you dont need because they are on sale. _____

The Passive Buyer

1. You put off making necessary purchases. _____
2. You are easily persuaded by salespeople. _____
3. You assign blame when the purchase is unsatisfactory. _____
4. You rarely ask questions or feel insecure when talking to salespeople. _____

The Ulterior Motive Spender

1. You shop to escape the pressures of life. _____
2. You spend money to get back at your spouse or significant other. _____
3. Buying certain items makes you feel superior. _____
4. You buy gifts out of guilt or to gain approval from others. _____

The Esteem Spender

1. You prefer to shop in prestigious stores. _____
2. You avoid discount stores. _____
3. You buy items because others have them. _____
4. You buy items to impress others. _____

The Special Interest Spender

1. You have a collection or hobby others might consider excessive. _____
  (If you did not check this item, skip this part.)
2. Others consider your spending on it to be excessive. _____
3. The collection, hobby, or activity is potentially harmful to your health or finances. _____
4. The collection, hobby, or activity is the cause of family conflicts. _____

The Hot Potato Spender
1. You worry about important purchases. _____
2. You put off important purchases for weeks and then make a sudden decision to get it over with. _____
3. When faced with complex financial decisions, you tend to get overwhelmed and make quick choices rather than thinking through all the variables. _____

OVERCOMING BAD SPENDING HABITS
Read the descriptions for each of the seven spending personalities. Think of three ways to overcome each type of problem spending.

1. The Fanatical Shopper. It's one thing to be frugal, but if someone's obsession with getting the lowest prices is taking up a lot of time and energy, he/she is not seeing the big picture. Some fanatical shoppers hunt for months to save ten or twenty dollars but think of all the time and travel expenses involved. The effort just doesn't make sense.

List 3 ways to overcome fanatical shopping.

Example: Place a value on your time and energy.

1.

_____
_____
_____

2.

_____
_____
_____

3.

_____
_____
_____

2. The Impulsive Buyer. This is the most common type of spender. That's why retailers put all those knickknacks near the check out! Impulsive buyers lack control and do not plan before they shop.

List 3 ways to overcome impulsive spending.

Example: Leave money at home when shopping.

1.
_____
_____
_____

2.
_____
_____
_____

3.
_____
_____
_____

3. The Passive Buyer. Passive buyers are pushovers. They are easily persuaded to buy items they may not really want or need. They generally do not like to shop and put very little time and energy into making purchases even when they are for big-ticket items.

List 3 ways to overcome passive buying.

Example: Ask questions when talking to salespeople.
1.
_____
_____
_____

2.
_____
_____
_____

3.
_____
_____
_____

4. The Ulterior Motive Spender. This type of spender uses shopping as a means of escape or to deal with stress. Often there are hidden emotions at play. For example, the ulterior motive spender may shop as a form of revenge against someone. They may also spend money as a way to win someone's approval.

List 3 ways to overcome ulterior motive spending.

Example: Explore other ways to manage daily stress.

1.

_____

_____

2.

_____

_____

3.

_____

_____

5. The Esteem Spender. This spender tries to keep up with the Joneses by shopping in the prestige stores and buying in order to impress others.

List 3 ways to overcome esteem spending.

Example: Identify what you value as opposed to what other people think is important.

1.

_____

_____

2.

_____

_____

3.

_____

_____

6. The Special Interest Spender. This type of spender has a hobby, collection, or activity that is eating up a good deal of income. In some cases, the special interest spender is addicted to gambling, alcohol or drugs. Reasons behind this type of spending could be boredom or a need to be unique.

List 3 ways to overcome special interest spending.

Example: Find new less expensive hobbies.

1.

_____
_____
_____

2.

_____
_____
_____

3.

_____
_____
_____

7. The Hot Potato Spender. These spenders procrastinate and worry about making new and unfamiliar purchases. Then, at the last minute, they buy as a way to quickly put the ordeal to an end. Trouble is, what they bought is probably far from what they really needed.

List 3 ways to overcome Hot Potato Spending.

Example: Research products before you buy them.

1.

_____
_____
_____

2.

_____
_____
_____

3.

_____
_____
_____

MONEY TALK

Destructive financial behaviors are driven by our subconscious expectations, attitudes, and beliefs about money. People do not deliberately set out to overspend or get into debt. They are motivated by emotions and assumptions just under the surface that fuel everyday interactions and transactions.

These feelings and ideas about money vary considerably from person to person. Let's listen in on some of the subconscious talk that plays in peoples' minds as they go about their daily activities:

I Deserve It! Some people have strong feelings of entitlement. They believe they deserve nothing but the best. Whether or not they can afford the best is a little detail they often overlook.

I Don't Expect Much. Others are just the opposite. Feelings of worthlessness keep these individuals from expecting any more than the basic necessities of life. Small expectations often lead to low paying jobs and shabby living conditions. When these individuals get money, they spend it recklessly because they dont feel they really deserve it. "Money in my pocket?", they ask, "It must be a mistake!"

I'm Waiting For A Miracle. You might just win the lottery. Or maybe your rich uncle will die and leave you a fortune. Maybe you'll make a killing in the stock market. Then, you will pay off all your debts in one mighty swoop. You just have to wait.

I'm Showing Them I Really Care. Some individuals see money as a way to show and express love and affection. How will they know how much they mean to me unless I put a price tag on it? But, when that special someone says, "You shouldn't have!", people in this category probably need to take that sentiment to heart.

I'm Not Like Everybody Else. These individuals rationalize their dysfunctional financial behavior by seeing themselves as a special case. Since they are so different and unique, they simply cannot be expected to follow the same rules as everyone else.

It Really Doesn't Matter. When one considers the immensity of the universe, worrying about debt is pretty insignificant.

I Need A Fix Now! When the going gets tough, these people shop! A new wardrobe is such a wonderful mood enhancer!

I'm Not Good With Money. These individuals feel they are hopeless when it comes to personal finances because they don't understand international economics or Calculus. Actually, balancing a checkbook rarely involves anything more daunting than simple addition and subtraction.

I Will Impress You. These individuals dress, eat out, travel, and spend, spend, spend to impress others. They are strongly motivated to display their level of success for all to see.

I Believe Money Corrupts People. This group of people shuns money as the root of all evil. Actually, it's the love of money that is said to be the root of all evil. But, it never hurts to be thorough, right?

Stop and listen to the chatter in your mind. What "money talk" do you hear? What message or messages about money are continually playing in your head? You can use the list above or come up with you own.

_____
_____
_____
_____
_____
_____

THE 3 As OF MONEY RELATIONSHIPS

Which money relationship category do you fall into?

1. **Money and Achievement.** In this category, money is strongly related to feelings of achievement. People who have this relationship with money work hard and want something tangible to show for it. A new sports car is the perfect pat on the back for a job well done. A pay raise means it's time for a bigger house.

2. **Money and Approval.** This group sets out to please others. They want everybody to like them. They want to be accepted into the group. Here's your "keeping up with the Joneses" set. They also tend to overspend on social occasions and gifts.

3. **Money and Agitation.** Spending is often fueled by our day-to-day emotions. People in this category purchase items to alleviate stress, feel better about themselves, or even to get back at someone. For these individuals, money is the drug of choice.

Consider your own relationship with money. Which of the "3 As"
describes your dominant money relationship?

_____

Give specific examples of how your money relationship fuels your spending.

_____
_____
_____
_____
_____
_____

 Understanding your own spending habits and money relationships is a crucial
step toward gaining insight into the forces that often push people over the
financial edge.

SUMMARY

1. There are objective and subjective ways for assessing a client's current
    financial condition.

2. Assessing the client's financial condition may involve determining net worth,
   analyzing the budget or calculating the debt-to-income ratio.

3. Exploring a client's relationship with money helps counselors gain a more
   complete picture of the current financial condition.

4. Budget analysis is a process used to determine how well resources are being
   allocated in the household.

5. A spending percentage guideline lets counselors compare client spending with
   national averages.

6. A spending or expense record may be necessary in order to get a more
   accurate picture of where the money is going.

7. Everyone exhibits various spending personalities when shopping.

8. Money relationships can be seen as falling into three major categories: money
   and achievement, money and approval and money and agitation - the "3 As."

87

1. Explain how a client's net worth is calculated.

2. Discuss how spending percentage guidelines can be utilized during budget analysis.

3. Explain how debt-to-income ratio is calculated.

4. Identify 3 types of spending categories.

5. Describe the Three As of Money Relationships.

Unit 11: Where the Client Wants to Go

OBJECTIVES
- To survey the seven phases of life-cycle planning.
- To determine the three components of a good outcome goal.
- To explore your own values as it relates to consumption.
- To explore Maslow's Hierarchy of Needs as it relates to consumption.

What is the definition of financial success? For some, it may mean paying off the mortgage or saving enough for their children to attend the college of their choice. For others, financial success may mean keeping a steady source of income and staying afloat between paychecks.

As a counselor, it is important to remember that clients may view financial success from vastly different perspectives. Therefore, it is best to define financial success in broader terms:

Financial success is obtaining maximum benefits from existing financial resources. In order to gain the maximum benefits from existing resources, planning is necessary. Let's take a look at seven areas of financial planning that occur throughout the life-cycle.

7 PHASES OF LIFE-CYCLE PLANNING
People pass through various phases in their lives and their financial goals shift and evolve as time goes on. Life-cycle planning can be broken down into seven areas: career planning, savings planning, debt planning, insurance planning, investment planning, retirement planning and estate planning.

1. Career Planning
Career planning typically starts when the individual is young and peaks in the college years, but it can continue throughout life. People may choose to change careers in mid-life or to re-enter the workforce after their children reach a certain age, after divorce or after additional education.

2. Savings Planning
No matter what the income, consumers must decide how much money to use for current expenditures and how much will be saved for the future. The funds set aside for saving is what will be used for investments, and investments are an important way to achieve lifelong financial goals. Savings planning is best accomplished using financial statements like net worth and spending plans.

89

3. Retirement Planning

In the past, people relied on pensions and Social Security after retirement. Today, there are few guarantees and individuals need to calculate the amount of income they will need and choose from a wide array of available options - IRAs, 401(k), or other types of investing.

4. Debt Planning

Debt is a part of life. Mortgages, car loans and lines of credit make it possible for us to attain life's necessities when we don't have tremendous amounts of cash at our disposal. It is important to keep our debt in check and not let it get out of hand. Shopping and qualifying for the best low interest loans and credit cards with consumer-friendly terms is key in debt planning.

5. Insurance Planning

Insurance planning also plays an important role in the life-cycle. For instance, when people are young, their ability to work and earn income is their most valuable asset, so they must be prepared should they lose that ability. Disability insurance is a way to guard against this. Later in life, things like life insurance and health insurance are paramount to the financial plan. Additionally, as consumers gain more and more assets, they need the proper insurance to protect what they own.

6. Investment Planning

Saving a percentage of one's income every year is only part of the retirement equation. The money saved will do little good stuffed in a mattress or piggy bank. Consumer's must decide how to invest it. The choices can be overwhelming, but the sooner money is invested, the greater the dividend will be.

7. Estate Planning

Financial planning is seemingly endless. Even after life is over, financial obligations can linger and plague family and loved ones. Preparing a will and a tax strategy is best handled by a licensed attorney.

REASONS FOR SAVING

Financial planning is necessary first and foremost in order to spread out resources throughout the life span. We may have our current consumption needs met but what about our future consumption needs? Saving is putting money aside for those future needs. Saving is also important if you wish to leave anything to your heirs. Last but certainly not least, saving lets you increase your investment assets; more money is making even more money.

FINANCIAL GOALS: THE "BIG 3"
The top three financial goals (generally speaking) are:

Paying for an education. With the cost of a college education rising yearly, it is impossible for most people to pursue higher education without some type of financial assistance. Student loans are properly considered investments toward higher earning potential.

Buying a home. For many, home ownership is the hallmark of financial success. It requires saving for a down payment and qualifying for a mortgage you can live with. It offers a sense of stability and security that renting cannot. However, owning a home is not for everyone. Renting allows for mobility while careers are being developed. Plus there is no property tax to pay.

Saving for retirement. Retirement income is of great concern today. Few people can rely on a pension or Social Security. More than ever, people need to fund their retirements through savings and investments. Options include 401(k)s, Individual Retirement Accounts (IRAs), and mutual funds. It is important to know and plan for the amount of income you will need after your working years.

PLANNING IN 4 STEPS
1. State goals in specific terms.
2. Create a plan on how to achieve each goal.
3. Evaluate progress toward the goal.
4. Decide whether to keep working toward the goal or to focus on a new one.

KEYS TO ATTAINING GOALS
The desire to resolve financial dilemmas becomes a goal through counseling. A specific plan is decided upon, a measurable outcome is monitored and solutions to obstacles are explored.

Setting goals is merely a means, not an end. Simply setting goals is not nearly as difficult as attaining those goals. A series of experiments and studies conducted by Gary Locke and Edward Latham have lead researchers to believe that there are fundamental aspects of goal setting that often enable people to achieve their desired outcome. These include setting short and long-term goals, making the goal-setting process participative, and using feedback.

Short-term goals. Researchers find that people are better able to reach long-term goals when they set short-term goals that are along the same path. These goals should be thought of as sections of the path towards the overall goal.

Long-term goals. Short-term goals should be set with the long-term goal in mind. Without a desired long-term goal in mind, the short-term goals have no final destination. The overall long-term goals should be the main concern, while the short-term goals are the means of getting there.

Participative Goal Setting. People are more often able to achieve goals when they have taken part in setting those goals. Commitment to goals is also higher when participative goal setting is applied. The client should take an active role in setting goals. It is more advantageous to facilitate goal setting rather than to suggest goals to the client, thus giving them a more active role.

Feedback. Without feedback, people will not know if they are on their way toward achieving their goals. Consistent feedback has been shown to positively influence goal attainment. It may be beneficial for clients to be aware of sources of feedback and seek those out.

All of these are important elements of goal setting. While they are not fail safe determinates of goal achievement, research suggests that they are often highly beneficial. Integrating these elements into the client's plan may increase the likelihood that they will be more committed to, as well as more likely to achieve, their desired goals.

TURNING WANTS INTO GOALS

Effective counselors work with clients to turn wants and desires into realistic outcome goals. An outcome goal contains three elements:

1. **It is specific.** Clients usually begin by communicating general or vague desires for change. For example, a client may say, "I need to cut my monthly expenses." Using a budget analysis sheet, the counselor will help the client decide which expenses can be either reduced or eliminated to achieve a specific reduction.

2. **It is measurable.** Without some way to objectively measure the results of an action, it is impossible to monitor its success. If the client wants to cut monthly expenditures, he/she needs to identify by what percent expenses will be reduced. The client will also need to determine an acceptable time frame to achieve the desired outcome. For example, "In three months, I want to establish and maintain a 15% reduction in my monthly expenses."

3. **It is viable.** Goals must be realistic. If objectives are made which are not likely to be met, frustration will ensue. For example, it is unrealistic to try to reduce all expenditures within one month. Instead, it is important to break client goals down into viable tasks that can produce successive accomplishments.

NEEDS VS. WANTS

According to psychologist Abraham Maslow, we all have various levels of needs. His Hierarchy of Needs is a good starting point for identifying some of the motivations behind client consumption. Some needs are universal and quite legitimate like needs for shelter, food and clothing. Other needs such as gold watches, cashmere sweaters and lattes may require a measure of scrutiny.

Maslow's Hierarchy of Needs can be visualized as a pyramid made up of five successive tiers each representing human needs ranging from the most basic to the higher-level needs for esteem and self-actualization.

self-actualization
morality, creativity, spontaneity, acceptance, experience purpose, meaning and inner potential

self-esteem
confidence, achievement, respect of others, the need to be a unique individual

love and belonging
friendship, family, intimacy, sense of connection

safety and security
health, employment, property, family and social stability

physiological needs
breathing, food, water, shelter, clothing, sleep

Physiological Needs. These are the basic survival needs such as food, air, water and warmth. These are life's essentials! However, how these essentials are procured may vary widely from one individual to the next. For example, drinking water can either be delivered by a service or simply poured from the tap. Food can either come from gourmet dining or frugal grocery shopping.

Safety Needs. The need for security becomes active once the basic needs for life maintenance have been met. The need for safety/security can influence such spending decisions as exclusive vs. modest housing or luxury vs. economy vehicles. Many products today are designed to give an illusion of security.

Needs for Love, Affection, and Belonging. Once a feeling of security is established, a need for love and a sense of belonging takes precedence. Many people buy items in order to fit into a perceived status quo or in order to attract love or affection from others. A large portion of a client's debt can accumulate from this form of emotional spending. The "need" to own a certain vehicle or live in a certain type of housing may stem from the underlying need for acceptance within a desired group. Attracting love and affection in others can result in erroneous purchases that include expensive clothing, jewelry or beauty treatments. Advertisers have been exploiting this human need for decades.

Needs for Esteem. Once an individual has met the first three levels of needs, the need for esteem becomes dominant. This includes gaining self-esteem and esteem from others. To satisfy this need, a consumer may buy in order to look or feel good about himself/herself or to project a certain image of success or authority. Such purchases may include designer clothing, a prestigious watch or other conspicuous items.

Needs for Self-Actualization. At the top of the Needs Hierarchy is the need to realize one's true potential. Needless to say, this is the hardest need to satisfy because it is often unclear exactly what it means to actualize your true potential. However, if this need is not met, the symptoms are quite identifiable. If an individual has met all the prior needs but lacks satisfaction in this one, the condition manifests itself in a certain restlessness, tension and edginess. The individual may spend in order to compensate for this particular feeling of emptiness. Purchases that arise from this need would then include merchandise or experiences that add diversion to life such as frivolous toys, trips or any purchase made to escape.

Self-actualization: To reach your full potential.
Esteem: To be appreciated and heard.
Social group: To belong and be accepted.
Security: To be safe from physical harm.
Physiological: To have food, clothing and shelter.

EXERCISE: DOES YOUR SPENDING REFLECT YOUR VALUES?

When making your financial plans, it is important to reflect upon what is truly important to you.

Step 1: Take a moment to think about what is most important to you. List the top five things you most value in life. For example, time with my family, a beautiful home, traveling, etc.

1.

_____

_____

_____

2.

_____

_____

_____

3.

_____

_____

_____

4.

_____

_____

_____

5.

_____

_____

_____

Step 2: For each value you have listed, think of three ways that the money you have today can help you realize that particular value. For example, if you value romance, you might list a vacation, fresh flowers or spending on a baby-sitter.

1.

_____

_____

_____

2.

_____
_____
_____

3.

_____
_____
_____

4.

_____
_____
_____

5. _____

_____
_____

Step 3: Consider whether or not your current spending reflects your values. For example, if music is important to you, do you go to see live performances or purchase recordings? Does your spending reflect your values?

_____
_____
_____
_____
_____
_____
_____
_____
_____
_____
_____

MAKING DECISIONS

The helping process involves many decision points. Effective counselors facilitate client decision making by understanding the dynamics and pitfalls that arise when confronted with choices.

Clients who voluntarily seek out counseling have already gone through one decision-making process by the time the initial interview begins. The other major decision points that clients and counselors encounter together are:

- deciding what goals to work on and
- how to achieve those goals.

3 STEPS TO RATIONAL DECISION MAKING

1. Information gathering. Gathering information is the basis for deciding what the problem is, what needs work, what could be better.

2. Processing the information. Once the information is gathered, the client must analyze it and draw conclusions from it.

3. Choice and execution. This is the point of commitment when the client decides to take action. That's the way it happens theoretically.

Client Variables

However, in real life, it is rarely that straightforward and objective. For example, clients may give or receive inaccurate information during Step 1. People, as you know, hear what they want to hear and this bias creates blind spots.

Likewise, Step 2 is subject to the client's feelings, beliefs, and attitudes. As we know, the same information can be interpreted differently by different people.

Step 3 is perhaps the most unpredictable step in the process. For example, many clients will skip the analysis (Step 2) and jump right into a choice (Step 3). Think impulse buying! Sometimes clients go through the analysis of the information halfheartedly having already made up their minds.

Other client variables that may compromise rational decision making:

- confusing quick decision making with being competent
- making a choice just to end the ordeal
- putting off choices by rationalizing or shifting responsibility and
- deciding one thing and doing another

Counselors help clients make better decisions by ensuring that information received is accurate and an objective assessment of the current scenario is discussed and agreed upon. From there, it's a matter of client commitment to act on the plan.

Once the client and counselor have gathered all information related to the client's financial situation and identified where it is the client wants to go, it is time to act. Counselors work with clients to develop a bias toward action. They emphasize the importance and value of doing as opposed to doing nothing. Next, we will explore some of the dynamics behind taking action as well as some concrete strategies for helping clients realize their goals.

SUMMARY

1. Financial goals shift and evolve throughout the lifespan.

2. The 7 phases of life-cycle planning are career planning, savings planning, retirement planning, debt planning, insurance planning, investment planning and estate planning.

3. Client goals must be specific, measurable and viable.

4. It is important to set short-term goals as a way to work toward long-term goals.

5. It is also important for goals to be created by the client.

6. Maslow's Hierarchy of Needs can be applied to understanding patterns of consumption as well as differentiating between needs and wants.

7. Effective counselors help their clients to understand the decision-making process and challenge them to base their decisions on their values.

REVIEW QUESTIONS

1. Give your own definition of financial success.

2. List the seven different phases of life-cycle planning.

3. How can Maslow's Hierarchy of Needs be used to gain insight into a client's spending habits?

4. What are the three steps to decision making?

5. What are the key aspects of goal setting as described by Locke and Latham?

Unit 12: How the Client Will Get There

OBJECTIVES

- To explore the dynamics behind taking action and achieving goals.
- To determine the benefits of creating a spending plan.
- To examine specific strategies for cutting costs.
- To learn ways to overcome self-defeating behaviors.
- To gain awareness about the Solution-Focused Counseling.

INITIATING ACTION

Clients and counselors may understand the current scenario, identify desired outcomes, and come up with a viable plan for addressing an issue or goal but unless action is taken, the goal will remain out of reach.

Taking action may be hindered by states of inertia or other barriers to positive change. Some of these obstacles to personal progress result from self-defeating behaviors that serve to sabotage success. It is important for counselors to consider the dynamics behind a client's lack of motivation or failure to act even when specific goals are defined.

Individuals who need to get control of their financial situation may need to develop a new and empowering perspective that will engender positive change. What is preventing clients from actually solving problems and acting on viable solutions could be the result of underlying belief systems about how much control and power they have over the world around them.

Let's look at two psychological models which address this issue of the power we have over the world around us: Bandura's Self-Efficacy and Rotter's Locus of Control.

BANDURA'S SELF-EFFICACY

Albert Bandura theorized that an individual's willingness to take action depends on the presence of two necessary conditions:

1. Outcome expectations. In order to act, the individual must believe that the action will result in a desired outcome. For example, the individual understands that maintaining a budget is crucial for getting control of spending.

2. Self-efficacy expectations. This is the can-do attitude. For action to take place, the individual must believe that he/she can successfully engage in the necessary behavior to achieve the desired outcome. For example, the

individual is reasonably sure he/she can do what it takes to resolve outstanding debt. This means making consistent payments as well as creating all necessary conditions to ensure sufficient funds by cutting expenses, increasing income, etc.

If either of these two conditions is missing, taking action will be avoided. On the one hand, the client may wholeheartedly believe a particular plan of action is the best option given the current circumstances. However, the client may question his or her ability to actually do what it takes to complete the necessary actions. The client will then resist taking action and find reasons -- real or imagined -- to continue to do nothing.

On the other hand, the client may possess the can-do attitude but resist taking action because the action plan is not fully understood as the best course to take. Again, action will be avoided in favor of doing nothing.

INCREASING SELF-EFFICACY

Help clients acquire necessary skills. Self-efficacy is based on ability. You believe you can do something because you have the skills and the resources to achieve it. Therefore, increasing self-efficacy means increasing the skills required to accomplish a desired outcome. A client may resist applying for a better paying job because he/she lacks interviewing skills. Interviewing skills can be acquired through practice. This then positively impacts the client's self-efficacy with regards to the hiring process.

Monitor progress. Clients need to see the positive outcomes of the actions they take. Acknowledgment of small successes can help bolster the confidence to tackle bigger problems.

Inspire by example. Seeing is believing and believing is what self-efficacy is all about. Tell clients about others who overcame obstacles and resolved their problems.

Encourage and challenge. "You can do it!" often leads to "I can do it!" Self-defeating beliefs need to be challenged and replaced by the idea that desired outcomes are not only possible but also realistic.

Help clients overcome anxiety. Fear of failure is a sure recipe for non-action. Help clients by listening to and acknowledging their fears. Then help them to dispel them with good, solid information.

ROTTER'S LOCUS OF CONTROL

According to J.B. Rotter, each of us operates with either an internal or external locus of control. Those with an internal locus of control believe that the circumstances and events surrounding them depend on their own ability or behavior. Conversely, those with an external locus of control see events and circumstances as outside their direct control. Things happen by chance.

Possessing an internal locus of control empowers the individual whereas an external locus of control subordinates the individual to outside forces which act irrespective of whatever the individual might do. Locus of control determines to a large extent how clients view the positive and negative circumstances in their lives. It informs their belief in what they can and cannot do and what they are responsible for. Therefore, it directly impacts the willingness to act.

Individuals with an external locus of control may view creditors as preying on and victimizing consumers who end up in debt because they were fooled and confused by lending agreements they could not understand. In their view, these consumers are well-intentioned pawns in a game of intricate deception.

However, those with an internal locus of control are more likely to view themselves as ultimately responsible for their own financial problems. An internal locus of control is advantageous for two reasons:

1. Internal locus of control fosters responsibility. Consequences and outcomes are seen as direct results of the individual's actions. The individual is less likely to blame outside forces for negative outcomes. Also, the individual is more likely to take credit for positive outcomes. This, in turn, garners self-respect and motivation to accomplish more.

2. Internal locus of control engenders self-efficacy. The individual possesses the power to affect change. Obstacles can be overcome and necessary resources can be accessed and utilized to solve problems.

Curious about your own locus of control? Learn more about this important human dynamic by completing the following self-assessment.

For each pair of statements, choose the one you most agree with.

1. a) Children get into trouble because their parents punish them too much.
   b) The trouble with most children nowadays is that their parents are too easy with them.

2. a) Many of the unhappy things in people's lives are partly due to bad luck.
   b) People's misfortunes result from the mistakes they make.

3. a) One of the major reasons why we have wars is because people don't take enough interest in politics.
   b) There will always be wars, no matter how hard people try to prevent them.

4. a) In the long run, people get the respect they deserve in this world.
   b) Unfortunately, an individual's worth often passes unrecognized no matter how hard he tries.

5. a) The idea that teachers are unfair to students is nonsense.
   b) Most students don't realize the extent to which their grades are influenced by accidental happenings.

6. a) Without the right breaks, one cannot be an effective leader.
   b) Capable people who fail to become leaders have not taken advantage of their opportunities.

7. a) No matter how hard you try, some people just don't like you.
   b) People who cant get others to like them, don't understand how to get along with others.

8. a) Heredity plays a major role in determining one's personality.
   b) It is one's experiences in life which determine what they're like.

9. a) I have often found that what is going to happen, will happen.
   b) Trusting to fate has never turned out as well for me as making a decision to take a definite course of action.

10. a) In the case of the well prepared student, there is rarely, if ever, such a thing as an unfair test.
    b) Many times exam questions tend to be so unrelated to course work that

studying is really useless.

11. a) Becoming a success is a matter of hard work, luck has little or nothing to do with it.
    b) Getting a good job depends mainly on being in the right place at the right time.

12. a) The average citizen can have an influence in government decisions.
    b) This world is run by the few people in power and there is not much the little guy can do about it.

13. a) When I make plans, I am almost certain that I can make them work.
    b) It is not always wise to plan too far ahead because many things turn out to be a matter of good or bad fortune anyway.

14. a) There are certain people who are just no good.
    b) There is some good in everybody.

15. a) In my case, getting what I want has little or nothing to do with luck.
    b) Many times, we might just as well decide what to do by flipping a coin place first.

16. a) As far as world affairs are concerned, most of us are the victims of forces we can neither understand nor control.
    b) By taking an active part in political and social affairs, the people can control world events.

17. a) Most people don't realize the extent to which their lives are controlled by accidents.
    b) There really is no such thing as luck.

18. a) One should always be willing to admit mistakes.
    b) It is usually best to cover up one's mistakes.

19. a) It is hard to know whether or not a person really likes you.
    b) How many friends you have depends upon how nice a person you are.

20. a) In the long run, the bad things that happen to us are balanced by the good ones.
    b) Most misfortunes are the result of lack of ability, ignorance, laziness or all three.

21. a) With enough effort, we can wipe out political corruption.
    b) It is difficult for people to have much control over the things politicians do

in office.

22. a) Sometimes I can't understand how teachers arrive at the grades they give.
    b) There's a direct connection between how hard I study and the grades I get.

23. a) A good leader expects people to decide for themselves what they should do.
    b) A good leader makes it clear to everybody what their jobs are.

24. a) Many times I feel that I have little influence over the things that happen to me.
    b) It is impossible for me to believe that chance or luck plays an important role in my life.

25. a) People are lonely because they don't try to be friendly.
    b) There's not much use in trying too hard to please people. If they like you, they like you.

26. a) There is too much emphasis on athletics in high school.
    b) Team sports are an excellent way to build character.

27. a) What happens to me is my own doing.
    b) Sometimes I feel that I don't have enough control over the direction my life is taking.

28. a) Most of the time I can't understand why politicians behave the way they do.
    b) In the long run, the people are responsible for bad government, on a national, as well as on a local level.

Score one point for each of the following:

2.a, 3.b, 4.b, 5.b, 6.a, 7.a, 9.a, 10.b, 11.b, 12.b, 13.b, 15.b, 16.a, 17.a, 19.a, 20.a, 21.b, 22.a, 24.a, 25.b, 27.b, 28.a.

A high score = External Locus of Control
A low score = Internal Locus of Control

Albert Ellis believed that thoughts come before emotions when it comes to making decisions. Therefore, if the thinking is corrected, the emotion can be controlled. Clients finding themselves under financial strain are likely to listen to that inner voice that chants, "I MUST have this and I MUST buy that." The reality is that these "musts" cannot always be accommodated by the client's income.

Don't fall for irrational musts. Think about the word *must*. Is saying "I must have a lambskin jacket for the winter season" a rational statement? Obviously it isn't. Absolutely no harm will come to someone from not having a lambskin jacket. Leave the "musts" for referring to things like hot meals and shelter. Consumer luxuries are never a must. Encourage clients to change this season's *musts* to this season's *must nots*.

Use rational coping and self-statements. A good cognitive exercise is to trade the irrational "must" for a rational statement that moves the client toward financial well-being:

"If I went out on the town one less night a week, I could put that money toward credit-card debt without radically changing my lifestyle."

"It will take time and discipline to stick to a spending plan, but it will be worth it to get my finances under control."

Take the bad with the good. People who overspend often focus on the supposed benefits of purchasing items while ignoring the pitfalls. If overspending is a problem, concentrate and write down the disadvantages of the behavior. Similarly, concentrate and write down all the reasons to stick to the spending plan.

Never underestimate the power of distraction. To combat feelings of disappointment and frustration, the simple directive to get your mind off things works wonders. Keep the mind occupied with hobbies, exercise, spending time with friends, watching movies, doing chores, or just about anything else besides money and expenses.

BECOMING SOLUTION-FOCUSED

Imagine that you are in a restaurant and you notice that the man seated at a nearby table suddenly clutches his throat while his face proceeds to turn a bright shade of purple. You could go over to the man and ask him if he is all right, but now he is getting up and violently thrashing his arms around.

You might ask him what he ordered from the menu but, at the present moment, he can't speak. Maybe he has a medical condition. Possibly the panicked woman at his table can tell you if he has had a history of heart problems.

You might even confer with the other diners in the restaurant; perhaps they've seen this sort of thing before. Or you could save the man's life by performing the Heimlich Maneuver.

The Solution-Focused Approach to counseling espouses the positive notion that change is a natural, everyday process, that people are not destined to be stuck in a rut, and that solutions to problems can result from simple, sometimes small adjustments made by the individual.

The key is to help the client access what he/she already knows. The man in the illustration above who is choking on food knows the answer to his problem; the obstruction must be removed so he can breathe again. But he needs help. This is where the Solution-Focused Approach comes in.

This approach is particularly valuable in financial-based counseling for the following reasons:

1. **Financial-based counselors are not therapists.** The word therapy comes from the Greek word meaning "to cure." This implies that the client is a patient that needs to be treated rather than a capable individual who requires assistance with current financial issues. The Solution-Focused Approach departs from the idea of therapeutic care. Instead, the counselor helps the client discover and activate his or her own strengths and resources.

2. **Solution-Focused Counseling is goal-oriented.** Clients are encouraged to identify their short and long-term goals and to identify the obstacles that are keeping them from reaching those goals. Then, it's a matter of removing the obstacles. This can be a highly motivational exercise.

3. **The Solution-Focused Approach highlights client strengths rather than weaknesses.** Any real, long-term solution to a client's problem must come from the client. Thus, the counseling session becomes positive and self-affirming for the client.

106

4. Solution-Focused Counseling focuses on the future. Little time is spent on the past, the mistakes and the patterns of self-deception. The present moment -- the counseling session is used as a springboard to discover and actualize a positive future.

REFRAMING

Reframing involves a change in perception that activates possibilities. It takes a situation out of its old context and places it into a new context that offers a positive outcome. For example, a client may focus on the negative aspects of excessive credit-card debt. By reframing the situation, the client can view the problem as an opportunity to organize finances and change destructive spending habits.

A laid-off worker focuses on the dismal economy and the lack of jobs. In contrast, the focus could be on gaining new skills and/or career exploration. A student who has accumulated a mountain of credit card debt can, through reframing, use his or her personal experience with debt to initiate a campus-based education program concerning the proper use of credit.

Let's look at two techniques based on the concept of reframing which are utilized in Solution-Focused Counseling.

The Miracle Question

This is a counseling technique that helps clients visualize a future in which their problems no longer exist. It begins by asking the client the following question:

"Let's imagine that tomorrow you wake up and are free from the burden of excessive debt. It is a miracle but since you were asleep when it happened, you are not immediately aware that anything has changed. What will you begin to notice about yourself and your surroundings that will clue you in that a miracle has occurred? How will you know the miracle has taken place? What will be different?"

By identifying the outward effects of the miracle, the client can begin to visualize the specific conditions that created it. For example, the miracle of being free of outstanding debt may include a home where there is little or no stress, where creditors are no longer calling, and where family members are not in conflict over limited financial resources. Now, what specifically has the client done to create this scenario? Does the client have a different job? Has the client moved? What kind of car does the client drive? Most importantly, how does the client act within the miracle scenario?

The Exception Question

Another technique, The Exception Question, helps clients recognize those times when things were better. The counselor asks the client to recall a time when debt was not a problem. What was different about his or her situation or behavior that created a manageable debt scenario?

Both The Miracle Question and The Exception Question have 3 benefits:

1. They help clients explore what it is they want different in their lives.
2. They help clients identify the strengths and resources to make these desired differences a reality.
3. They situate a desired future squarely in the present moment.

CREATING A SPENDING PLAN

Many clients will tend to equate budgeting with denial, sacrifice, and the postponement of gratification. They may find the act of recording expenditures and incomes a mundane chore. In fact, clients with substantial credit debt may have avoided budgeting for fear of being overwhelmed with the truth.

It is important for counselors to help their clients gain a new perspective about budgeting. One strategy they can use right away is to avoid the word *budget* with all its connotations of belt tightening and instead use the term *spending plan*. *Creating a spending plan* sounds better than *making a budget*. It implies freedom while the other implies restriction.

Another thing counselors can stress is that a personal budget or spending plan, far from being a mundane chore, is key to realizing financial goals. It is nothing less than an indispensable tool for mapping out a course toward increased financial freedom.

Creating a spending plan has 4 primary benefits:

1. **Helps to identify overspending.** Once all the numbers are on paper (or on the computer screen), the client and counselor can see exactly where the money is going. Problem areas can be detected. For example, what percentage of income is going to housing costs? What is the client's debt-to-income ratio?

2. **Promotes honest interpersonal communication and accountability.** Clients in debt don't live in a vacuum. Their debt affects everyone around them. As you may know, money and how it is spent is a leading cause for arguing

and discontent between partners and family members. A solid spending plan is an objective starting place for making the adjustments necessary to reach financial goals.

3. Increases motivation. When clients identify what they really want from the money they make, a tangible goal has been created. Yes, resolving financial problems can sometimes require short term sacrifices. People generally do not do without the products and services they have come to value simply because self-denial is virtuous. It is because they know there is a light at the end of the tunnel. The spending plan is like a map leading toward future rewards.

4. Tracks your success. Without a plan, there is no measuring stick to use to tell whether or not you are reaching your goals. With a spending plan in place, you can easily monitor the level of your success.

When a spending plan is utilized correctly and client motivation continues, it will function as an on-going action plan. Make sure the client keeps the plan up-to-date for each new month. Also, it is important to keep the plan flexible. Spending plans that are too strict are destined to failure.

At the beginning of each month, the client will allocate spending for each of the categories under the appropriate column. At the end of that month, the actual amount spent will be recorded. These two amounts are then compared to see if the client's goals for that month have been achieved.

There are many types of spending plans including computer-based programs with built-in calculators. Keep in mind that some of the best spending plans are formulated on plain legal pads or, in some cases, even on the backs of envelopes!

CUTTING CUTS
When you stop to think about it, there are many ways to economize -- that is, to reduce expenses. There's coupon and sale shopping, careful meal planning with utilization of leftovers for lunches and snacks, substituting generic products for name brand ones, watching household electricity consumption -- the list is endless.

When clients experience a loss or reduction of income, they must re-examine their current expenditures to determine which ones are essential and which ones are non-essential. In many cases, a short-term adjustment in spending may be all that is necessary. In other cases, sacrifices over the long term may be in order. The important thing is to understand how to economize and to see that cutting costs can be a source of personal satisfaction and accomplishment.

Let's begin by defining what it means to economize. Economizing is allocating spending so that it has the maximum benefit for everyone in the household. During times when money is scare, economizing also helps to minimize hardship. It does not necessarily mean spending less. It simply means making use of available resources for the greatest benefit.

In fact, there are circumstances in which economizing warrants spending more. For example, loss of employment may necessitate that the client invest in his or herself through job training, education, re-locating, or purchasing new clothes for interviewing. Spending more may also be necessary when a client decides to utilize a particular skill and turn it into a way to make money. For example, someone who can bake or sew would need to invest in the materials from which to make the products they would sell.

4 WAYS TO ECONOMIZE

1. Substituting products or services for less costly alternatives. This does not necessarily mean giving up quality. For example, substituting dry cleaning services for do-it-yourself dry cleaning does not mean you will be wearing dirty clothes.

2. Conserving resources to get the most out of them, avoiding waste, and using what you have efficiently. Part of conserving is maintaining the things you own and keeping them in good working order. This includes your possessions, your skills, and your health.

3. Cooperating with others to reduce expenses. Common examples include carpooling and sharing baby-sitting, food and housing costs.

4. Utilizing community resources. Communities everywhere offer a wealth of free services and recreation like parks, museums, and libraries. A picnic lunch at a public park often provides a more spectacular view than most restaurants. This category of economizing also includes all the various assistance programs designed to help those who need it.

EXERCISE: BRAINSTORMING WAYS TO CUT COSTS

For each of the following spending categories, list ideas for economizing.
Give specific examples for each of the four ways to economize.

1. CUT FOOD COSTS BY:
Substituting. Example: Buying generic brands when suitable.

_____
_____
_____
_____
_____
_____
_____

Conserving. Example: Wrap and store food properly.

_____
_____
_____
_____
_____
_____
_____

Cooperating. Example: Plan a community garden.

_____
_____
_____
_____
_____
_____
_____

Utilizing community resources. Example: Apply for food assistance.

_____
_____
_____
_____
_____
_____

2. CUT TRANSPORTATION COSTS BY:

Substitute. Example: Drive a car that is more fuel efficient.

_____
_____
_____
_____
_____
_____

Conserve. Example: Do preventative automobile maintenance.

_____
_____
_____
_____
_____
_____

Cooperate. Example: Carpool with co-workers.

_____
_____
_____
_____
_____
_____

Utilize community resources. Example: Use public transportation.

_____
_____
_____
_____
_____
_____

3. CUT HOUSING COSTS BY:

Substitute. Example: Shop for the better mortgage agreement.

_____
_____
_____
_____
_____
_____

Conserve. Example: Conserve heating with insulation, weather stripping.

_____
_____
_____
_____
_____
_____

Cooperate. Example: Trade home repair skills with friends and neighbors.

_____
_____
_____
_____
_____
_____

Utilize community resources. Example: Use local assistance with energy costs.

_____
_____
_____
_____
_____
_____

4. CUT CLOTHING COSTS BY:

Substitute. Example: Shop for baby clothing and toys at thrift stores and consignment shops.

_____
_____
_____
_____
_____
_____

Conserve. Example: Keep clothes clean; remove stains promptly.

_____
_____
_____
_____
_____
_____

Cooperate. Example: Swap baby clothes and accessories.

_____
_____
_____
_____
_____
_____

Utilize Community Resources. Example: Shop at rummage sales.

_____
_____
_____
_____
_____
_____

Things to consider...
Substituting one thing for another does not necessarily mean foregoing quality. Articles of clothing sold at outlets, for example, are of comparable quality to those sold in department stores. In the case of food, it's important to consider the nutritional value of items.

It is interesting to note that a survey conducted in the 1960s determined that people living in poverty had healthier diets than wealthy people. (This is no longer the case due the explosion of fast food.) The food items that often cost the most tend to be processed food which has little or no nutritional value, whereas the poor man's staple of rice and beans is undeniably a healthier, more efficient source of nutrition.

Substituting is also the category where comparative shopping comes in. You substitute what you may have bought in the past with something less costly as you shop with new and more cost-conscious considerations.

Conserving has a lot to do with lifestyle. Good planning and management of resources helps a consumer avoid unnecessary waste and reap the full benefits from each resource. In this day and age, most people are aware of the importance of recycling. It is important to apply conservation principles to everyday life.

Cooperating with others can be challenging, but it can also be fun. Neighborhood garage sales and informal potluck dinners not only help save money but increase community ties and provide low-cost entertainment.

In the next section, we will explore some of the financial knowledge necessary to put goals into action. How a client achieves financial well-being depends in large part on his or her understanding of credit and debt. The next modules focus on these two areas of personal finances.

SUMMARY

1. One of the goals of counseling is to help clients develop a bias toward action.

2. According to Bandura's Theory of Self-efficacy, in order for an individual to take action, he or she must:

    a. believe that the action will result in a desired outcome *and*
    b. believe that he or she possesses the ability to do what it takes to see the action through to completion.

3. According to Rotter's Locus of Control, individuals possess either an internal or an external locus of control.

4. Solution-Focused Counseling highlights a client's strengths as opposed to weaknesses.

5. There are four primary benefits when a spending plan is established and utilized:

   a. It helps to identify overspending.
   b. It promotes honest interpersonal communication and accountability.
   c. It increases motivation.
   d. It tracks your success.

6. Economizing means allocating spending so that it has the maximum benefit for everyone in the household.

7. Four ways to economize are substituting, conserving, cooperating and utilizing community resources.

REVIEW QUESTIONS

1. Discuss Bandura's idea about self-efficacy. What two conditions does he say affect an individual's willingness to take action?

2. Discuss the differences between an individual with an internal locus of control and individual with an external locus of control.

3. List the four primary benefits for establishing and maintaining a spending plan.

4. What are the four ways to economize described in this unit?

Module IV: Demystifying Credit

Credit can be a good thing. The ability to receive funds, goods, and services in the present and pay for them over time presents us with vast opportunities that otherwise would be extremely difficult to realize. Buying a home, a car, paying for higher education, starting a business would be out of reach for most people if it weren't for the availability of consumer-friendly loans and lines of credit.

Credit also offers a convenient way to do business. You don't need to carry around large amounts of cash. Credit cards allow you to reserve a hotel room in a far off city, and once there, to rent a car and pay for emergency services if need be. The credit card offers a sense of security when traveling.

However, credit has a dark side. For the uninitiated, the credit card can be a gateway into a debilitating debt situation of late fees and collection notices. Stress and frustration trigger family conflicts while credit card balances grow and bank accounts shrink. Current trends indicate that consumers are using a higher percentage of their disposable incomes toward credit card debt at the expense of savings. In fact, credit card debt is the fastest growing form of consumer debt.

CAMBRIDGE SURVEY
If credit is such a powerful financial tool, then why are so many Americans experiencing it negatively? Part of the answer might be found in a survey conducted by Cambridge Credit Counseling Corporation. They asked prospective credit counseling clients:

What was the main reason or recent event that made you realize you need help with your unsecured debt?

Frustration with high bank rates and fees was the number one reason cited for seeking credit counseling. This reason was given by nearly 30% of respondents while lack of financial education was cited by about 10%.

What does this tell us? Given the fact that people generally do not like to put all the blame for their debt squarely on their shoulders, frustration with high bank rates and fees can be seen as a way for consumers to point their fingers at lenders as, at least, part of the problem. After all, many lending agreements today are often far from consumer-friendly.

However, a lot of the frustration that consumers are experiencing is a direct result of lack of financial education. If consumers knew about the credit system and how to manage their credit to their advantage, those high interest rates and fees would not be there in the first place.

CREDIT LITERACY

Educating your clients about credit is an extremely important part of counseling the financially stressed. The goal of counseling is not to get people to stop using credit even though they may need to stop credit card use for the short term. Ultimately, the goal is to help clients get credit and use credit the smart, informed way so they can avoid excessive debt in the future.

Establishing good credit, maintaining good credit habits, and knowing the best ways to resolve credit-card debt are all topics counselors and clients alike need to learn more about.

By completing this module, you will:

- gain awareness about how the credit system works.
- determine the different types of credit available to the consumer.
- know the difference between types of credit cards.
- understand how credit-card issuers calculate finance charges.
- know the many fees associated with credit cards.
- gain awareness about current credit card trends.
- be introduced to the Truth in Lending Act.
- learn ways to avoid credit-card debt.
- understand the components of creditworthiness.
- be introduced to the Equal Credit Opportunity Act.
- understand consumer rights as they apply to billing errors.
- learn ways to avoid identity theft.
- ascertain how to receive a credit report.
- be introduced to the Fair Credit Reporting Act.
- be able to identify the 4 categories of information in a credit report.
- understand consumer rights as they apply to credit reporting errors.
- gain awareness about credit scoring

Unit 13: Credit Basics

- To understand the system of borrowing and lending.
- To explore the different types of consumer credit.
- To determine how finance charges are calculated.
- To gain awareness about credit-card fees.
- To learn ways to prevent credit-card debt.

HOW CREDIT WORKS

Using credit wisely begins by understanding the credit system. Credit is really all about credibility. Lenders extend credit to individuals they judge to be trustworthy. Any loan, whether it is a student loan, a mortgage or a revolving line of credit, is granted based on the expectation that it will be paid back to the lender. In return for the use of funds, consumers give lenders their promise that they will repay. Since trust is more valuable than a promise at transaction time, consumers pay the lender interest.

Just how much interest depends on the consumer's track record. Has there been previous loans? Were payments made on time? What about income? How much debt does the consumer already have? Is the consumer stable? Does the consumer own a home?

Lenders try to find out as much as they can so they can determine a particular consumer's risk factor. After all, there is a certain gambling element involved in extending credit and knowing the odds beforehand is a great advantage.

Over time, a system developed that serves to reduce the lender's risk that you will default on the loan. The basic conditions of a loan agreement are filled with incentives for on-time payments and penalties for late or missed payments. The most important incentive for making regular payments on time is the establishment of good credit. Lenders report consumer credit transactions and repayments to the three credit reporting agencies.

When a consumer establishes and maintains a good credit record, he/she becomes less of a risk in the eyes of the lender. Then, there are more options for getting new credit at better terms.

However, when borrowers do not fully understand the system and fail to play the credit game by the system's rules, severe financial consequences can result. First and foremost is a damaged credit rating. Also, unresolved credit card debt doesn't just go away. In fact, it is likely to grow beyond the consumer's ability to

119

manage it. This leads to bankruptcy. If and when the consumer tries to re-establish credit, he/she has to start all over with the lowest credit limits and the highest interest rates.

Credit Cards By The Numbers

Average credit card APR: 15.5%
Average APR for cash advances: 24%
Average late fee: between $25 to $35
Average number of cards per individual: 8
Percentage of card holders who carry balances from month to month: 46.7%

4 KEY PLAYERS

Consumers need the leverage of credit to buy things that cost more than they are willing or able to purchase using their available cash. For example, the vast majority of the population needs the leverage of a mortgage to buy a home. People also use credit for the sake of convenience to make everyday purchases.

Merchants welcome the use of credit because they know that consumers with credit tend to buy more. Credit card issuers charge retailers a nominal service charge for each transaction. Retail stores that offer merchant cards extend credit directly to the consumer.

Lenders act as a bridge between the consumer and the products and services offered by merchants. They grant loans based on the projected profit they will make through the interest they charge. Lenders then borrow more funds from other lenders so they can continue to make more loans. Banks can borrow money directly from The Federal Reserve Bank.

The "Fed" makes loans to banks so they can keep on lending. More consumer loans help to make a healthier economy. Banks themselves play the trust game. Will they repay on time? The only player who does not have to go through a credit check is the Federal Reserve Bank. When it needs more money, it can simply print more, raise taxes, or borrow it from you, the consumer, by selling bonds.

4 TYPES OF CREDIT

Secured credit is any loan backed by collateral. Mortgages and auto loans are examples of secured credit. In the event that the consumer defaults on the loan, the lender can seize the property that was pledged as collateral.

Unsecured credit is not backed by collateral so the risk is much higher for the lender. If the consumer fails to repay, the lender must win a court judgment in order to recover any unpaid debt. It is granted solely on the consumer's creditworthiness which includes credit history and current financial picture. Credit cards are the most prevalent examples of unsecured credit.

Installment credit can be either secured or unsecured. Consumers are granted a loan or credit, which must be repaid in equal installments over a specific time period. Common installment loans are automobile, student, and personal loans.

Non-installment credit is any loan repaid in one payment by a specified date. Any bill you receive that says, Payment due in full upon receipt of this bill, this non-installment credit. Examples include monthly utility and medical services.

4 TYPES OF CREDIT CARDS
Credit cards yield high dividends for their issuers, accounting for as much as 75% of the profits generated annually by banks. Many companies charge an annual fee for issuing a credit card, and most companies charge late fees, over-the-limit fees, and other miscellaneous charges. Lenders also profit by charging merchants and service providers a fee each time a customer uses the company's credit card in the merchants establishment.

There are 4 major types of credit cards available to consumers:

1. Bank Cards are issued by banks, savings and loans, and credit unions. Examples include Visa, MasterCard, and Discover. Bank cards may or may not come with an annual fee. Interest rates and terms vary considerably depending on the consumer's credit rating and company policies.

2. Travel and Entertainment Cards, despite their name, are not limited to travel and entertainment at all. Any consumer items and services may be obtained with these cards. Clients may be charged an annual fee and be required to pay the full balance each month. Lenders who issue these cards are less tolerant of late payments and quick to revoke privileges.

3. Merchant Cards are offered by most major department stores. Oil companies and airlines also issue merchant cards. These types of credit cards seldom charge annual fees and often provide discounts, frequent flier miles, and other features.

4. Secured Credit Cards draw funds from money the consumer has deposited in a savings account. By borrowing his or her own money to make purchases, the consumer is able to exhibit good credit behavior by making regular payments to the account. This type of card is a good way to establish credit or repair a bad credit rating. Some cards come with a conversion feature so that after a period of regular payments, the consumer can upgrade to a regular credit card.

DEBIT CARDS

Debit Cards look like credit cards but they are not. Banks originally offered these types of cards called ATM cards expressly for withdrawing cash from an automated teller machine.

Today, consumers habitually use debit cards to make deposits, account inquiries, and money transfers. They also use their debit cards to make everyday purchases. Essentially, they are electronic replacements for checks. When paying with a debit card, the amount of a store purchase is automatically (and immediately) deducted from a consumer's checking account.

CREDIT LIMITS

Credit limits can vary considerably from a few hundred dollars to thousands. Some banks are quite lenient with credit. The more they lend, the more interest they can charge. Others are more conservative.

Banks consider several factors when deciding how much credit the consumer will have access to. Most important is the consumer's credit rating. Other factors include company policy, competition from other lenders, the availability of funds, and the economy. Clients need to be wary of receiving credit limits that go beyond their ability to pay.

The Far-Reaching Effects of Credit

How you manage credit is one of the most scrutinized aspects of your life. It not only affects your ability to get new credit but also affects your mortgage rate, your automobile insurance rate, and whether or not you are hired by an employer who does a background check. For example, you need to show a good credit history for jobs requiring that you handle money.

You may need a credit card to...
- guarantee a hotel room
- rent a car
- pay for emergency service away from home
- pay a doctor or dentist who requires immediate payment
- use as identification to cash a check

FINANCE CHARGES
Finance charges are based on the lender's annual percentage rate (APR) which is the rate of interest charged on an annual basis. They can vary considerably from 8 to 21% or higher.

The cost of credit is not only determined by the interest rate but also by how the interest is calculated. Because of this, consumers need to consider the lender's balance computation method.

BALANCE COMPUTATION METHODS

Average Daily Balance. This is by far the most common computation method. It credits your account from the day payment is received by the issuer. To figure the balance due, the issuer totals the beginning balance for each day in the billing period and subtracts any credits made to your account that day. While new purchases may or may not be added to the balance, depending on your plan, cash advances typically are included. The resulting daily balances are added for the billing cycle. The total is then divided by the number of days in the billing period to get the average daily balance.

Adjusted Balance. This is the most advantageous method for card holders. Your balance is determined by subtracting payments or credits received during the current billing period from the balance at the end of the previous billing period. Also, purchases made during the billing period are not included.

Previous Balance. This is one of the least advantageous methods because finance charges are based on the amount owed at the end of the last billing cycle. It does not take in consideration any payments or new purchases you may have made.

Two-Cycle Average Daily Balance. For consumers who carry balances from month-to-month, this is another method to be avoided. In this case, the average daily balance is derived from both the previous and the current billing cycles.

HIDDEN FEES

Many fees besides interest contribute to the cost of credit. They are often hidden in the fine print. Sometimes referred to as nuisance fees, they include:

Transaction Fees. Unfortunately for credit card issuers, many cardholders keep credit-card payments current. They pay off their balance within the card's grace period thereby avoiding finance charges. To compensate and increase revenue, many issuers impose transaction fees. Typically, transaction fees are 2 or 3% of the amount of a purchase. Transaction fees can add up quickly when cards are used frequently.

Late Fees. Late fees can be as high as $39 -- more than triple the $11.96 average in May 1994 and it is now much easier for credit-card companies to charge late fees. Many creditors have decreased the amount of time between when the bill is mailed and when payment is due. It is also now common for late payments to trigger a substantial increase in the interest you pay.

Over-The-Limit Fees. Charges made beyond the credit limit do not always result in a credit card being rejected by the merchant. It could result in an added fee. Over-the-limit fees nearly tripled from $12.56 in 1994 to an average of between $29 to $35 until the CARD Act of 2009 put an end to these fees being an automatic feature of credit-card terms.

Pay-Off Fees. Sometimes a bank will actually penalize a cardholder for making all payments on time. In this case, finance charges cannot be added to the bill so a flat rate is included instead.

Annual Fees. Some credit-card issuers charge annual membership or participation fees. They often range from $25 to $50, sometimes up to $100; gold or platinum cards often charge between $75 and several hundred dollars.

Charges for Cash Advances. Many cardholders are unaware that the interest rate charged for cash advances can be substantially higher than the rate charged for purchases. Some of these rates are as high as 30% or more. Cash advances typically do not provide grace periods for avoiding that hefty finance charge.

GRACE PERIODS

Some people confuse the idea of a grace period with the amount of time you have to pay your credit-card bill without incurring a late fee. Actually, a grace period is the time a consumer has before a credit-card issuer starts charging interest on new purchases. Stay within the grace period and it's like getting an interest-free loan.

However, the terms of credit are never quite that simple. All grace periods are not created equal. Let's take a look:

Typical Grace Period. This most common type of grace period uses the average daily balance including new purchases for applying interest. In this case, you pay interest on all new purchases unless you have paid your previous month's balance in full.

Full Grace Period. Few cards have this most desirable feature. This type of grace period comes with cards that use the average daily balance excluding new purchases. Here, interest is not applied to new purchases whether or not your previous balance has been paid off.

No Grace Period. In this least desirable scenario, the average daily balance including new purchases is applied but whether or not you have paid off your previous balance doesn't matter. You still pay interest.

Which grace period is right for you? If you pay on time every time, either the typical or the full grace period will work for you. If you pay off your monthly balance only sometimes, then you will want the full grace period. No grace period is to be avoided.

You can determine a card's grace period by finding the balance computation method listed on the back of the statement. For no grace period cards, look for a statement indicating that you will pay a finance charge from the date of the transaction.

CREDIT CARD TRENDS

Universal default. This has been one of the most controversial trends in recent years. Based on the practice of risk-based pricing, a lender can change the terms of a credit agreement from the normal to the default terms. That often involves a substantial increase in the interest rate. How does it work? If your credit card has a universal default clause in it's agreement, you can be late on one card one time and it will affect your interest rate on all your cards. Penalty rates are applied universally to all your accounts. In some cases, universal default can affect your auto insurance rates. The good news for consumers is that most forms of universal default have been prohibited by the CARD Act of 2009.

Minimized payments. Typical minimum payments at 2% of the balance often create a condition called negative amortization. This occurs when the monthly credit-card payment consistently falls short of covering all finance charges and fees assessed during the billing cycle and the outstanding balance continues to grow. Simply put, minimum payments don't add up!

Shrinking grace periods. The average grace period in 1990 was 30 days. By 2006, it was 21 days, making it harder to enjoy interest-free credit-card purchases. With the CARD Act of 2009 (effective February 2010), standard credit cards cannot have a grace period less than 21 days.

THE TRUTH IN LENDING ACT
This act requires that all credit-cared issuers disclose:

- The Annual Percentage Rate (APR)
- The monthly finance charge (APR divided by 12)
- Whether the rate is fixed or variable. If it is variable, the lender must disclose how it is calculated
- The interest rate applied to cash advances
- The duration of the grace period -- the time in which a cardholder can pay off the balance without incurring interest
- By what method finance charges are calculated
- Additional fees such as late payment fees, over-the-limit fees, or cash advance fees
- Early interest posting dates. Purchases made on these cards are posted from the time of the transaction which translates into higher finance charges.

PREVENTING CREDIT CARD DEBT

It is clear that owning and using a credit card is a powerful and often expensive privilege for today's consumer. It is easy to understand how someone can unwittingly accumulate debt in a relatively short amount of time.

The ability to charge on impulse coupled with the fine print of credit agreements is a combination that can quickly create out-of-control debt. Here are some ways to avoid the pitfalls of credit-card use:

1. **Limit the number of credit cards you maintain.** Usually, there is no good reason to have more than one or two credit cards. In the case of a client with extensive debt problems, all credit accounts should be closed except the one with the lowest finance rate and balance.

2. **Do not maintain cards with the following feature:**
   High interest rates. If the only card a client plans to keep active has a high interest rate but the payments are up-to-date, he/she may request an interest rate reduction.

3. **Avoid credit cards with complicated billing policies.** If you cannot understand the language of the disclosure portion of a credit offer or the provisions listed on the credit contract, do not sign up.

4. **Minimum payments don't add up.** Many consumers get locked into the idea that if they can make their minimum monthly payments, their credit debt will remain manageable. This simply is not true. If the consumer is making new purchases every month and only making the minimum payments, the debt will never go down. In fact, it will continue to grow. This, in turn, increases the finance charges which accrue based on the increasing balance. (See negative amortization above.)

5. **Limit the credit limit.** Banks and credit card issuers may increase your credit limit even when you have not requested it. Do not believe that this increase is a reward or that it somehow indicates your increased ability to pay for purchases. Basically, a high credit limit translates into higher monthly balances which, in turn, means higher interest payments.

SUMMARY

1. The ability to obtain and maintain good credit is a key component of financial well-being.

2. There are four types of credit extended to consumers: secured, unsecured, installment and non-installment.

3. Credit cards can cause severe debt problems quickly because they allow for impulse purchases and they often carry hidden fees.

4. Lenders carry different annual percentage rates and calculate finance charges through different balance computation methods.

5. Credit limits are based primarily on a consumer's credit rating.

6. Consumers need to be wary of credit-card offers; they must read the fine print and understand it fully.

7. The Truth in Lending Act requires that credit-card issuers disclose their balance computation method and their APR.

REVIEW QUESTIONS

1. List some of the reasons why credit is important in today's society.

2. Explain the difference between secured and unsecured credit.

3. List three ways lenders calculate finance charges.

4. List three nuisance fees that lenders may add into monthly statements.

5. Explain what the Truth in Lending Act requires lenders to do.

6. What are some ways to prevent credit-card debt?

Unit 14: Choosing Credit Wisely

OBJECTIVES

- To determine the components of creditworthiness.
- To examine what to look for in credit-card offers.
- To understand the importance of the Equal Credit Opportunity Act.
- To determine the true cost of credit.

Choosing the best credit card involves fully understanding loan agreements and assessing repayment options. Consumers are inundated with credit-card offers that feature pre-approved introductory rates and attractive looking perks.

It is best to shop for credit just as you would any other product. This means being pro-active by learning about the product, the terms and conditions that go with the product and how it compares with the competition.

Getting the best deal is the first step to successfully managing credit. A consumer-friendly credit card can offer convenience and the ability to payback the principal without incurring any interest. Conversely, there are cards on the market today that make managing credit bills an extremely frustrating experience. Therefore, choosing credit should involve careful assessment by the consumer.

ASAP: QUALIFYING FOR CREDIT

When applying for credit, a person is officially asking for a loan. The credit-card application is designed to gather the information that will determine the consumer's level of creditworthiness. One way to look at the components that make up creditworthiness is to think ASAP.

A S A P -- Ability, Stability, Assets and Performance.

A stands for the Ability to pay back the amount of the loan granted. Lenders evaluate level of income as well as monthly expenses to determine how comfortably a consumer can handle payments. They do this by calculating the consumer's debt-to-income ratio.

Stability is also considered as a factor of creditworthiness. Stability is a reflection of character. The idea is that if a person has worked and lived at the same place for at least two years, he/she is likely to make regular payments on credit bills because he/she shows regularity in maintaining the same job and the same address.

The second A stands for Assets. Lenders more readily extend credit to consumers who have things -- houses, cars, boats, antiques, jewelry -- things that can be liquidated, if necessary, to pay back outstanding debts. Lenders know, with all the hard penalties they can incur to prompt payments, consumers with assets can get cash under pressure.

P is for Performance. Many people do not realize it, but as soon as they are granted credit in any of its forms, they walk onto a stage. The audience is made up of the credit reporting agencies who act as critics. They gather up all your academy award nominations as well as your box office flops and disseminate them to prospective creditors who then scrutinize how you have performed over time with credit. Just like in gymnastics, consumers are given a three-digit numerical code, which acts as a predictor of future payback performances.

SHOPPING FOR A CREDIT CARD

Features to consider when choosing a credit card are finance charges, annual fees, grace periods, penalty fees, and balance computation methods.

Credit card features to look for:

- Low interest rate
- No annual fee
- Long grace period
- Low penalty fees
- Adjusted balance computation method

Credit card features to avoid:

- High annual fees that can increase over time
- Penalty fees for not using your card regularly
- Low interest rates that quickly increase
- Increased finance charges due to late payments
- Increased finance charges due to exceeding your credit limit

The big print giveth and the fine print taketh away.

-- Tom Waits

THE TRUE COST OF CREDIT

Minimum payments maximize finance charges. The minimum payment on a credit card is calculated as a percentage of the current balance. The minimum payment will decrease as the balance is paid. However, through the magic of compound interest, the balance will remain for a long time.

For example, let's say there is a balance of $500 on a card with an interest rate of 18%. If the minimum payment is figured at 5% of the balance ($25), it would take 50 months to pay off the balance in which time $168.15 in interest will have been paid!

However, if a consumer maintains payments at $50 a month regardless of the balance, the balance can be paid off in 11 months and the cost of interest would only amount to $45.81. That's a savings of $122.34. Also consider that by paying off the balance in less than a year as opposed to over four years, a consumer greatly reduces the risk of adding new charges to the account, thus incurring yet more interest. When calculating the true cost of credit, you begin to see how debt can have a life of its own!

THE EQUAL CREDIT OPPORTUNITY ACT

This act oversees how credit is granted to consumers. That includes the entire credit evaluation and application process. Under its guidelines, lenders must inform you within 30 days whether your application has been accepted, rejected, or found incomplete.

If your application has been rejected, you will receive a rejection letter containing two required pieces of information:

- The specific reason or reasons you were turned down
- The name of the credit bureau used to obtain your credit report

Some of the common specific reasons for rejection that meet the ECOA requirements are:

- Insufficient income
- Failure to pay previous obligations as agreed
- Insufficient number of revolving accounts
- Excessive inquiries
- Too many credit obligations
- No checking or savings account
- Too brief a period of employment

Reasons that do not appear to meet the ECOA requirements are:

- credit history
- information in credit report or
- your qualifications do not meet our standards.

Notice that these reasons are vague and unspecific.

It is important to do some homework before applying for credit. Consumers should have a good idea as to whether their application will be accepted or denied before submitting it. Too many rejections adversely affect a credit score as we will see later in this module.

SUMMARY

1. Choosing credit wisely means fully understanding the terms and conditions stated in credit-card offers and disclosures.

2. It is important to realistically assess how you plan to use and pay for your credit privileges.

3. One way to remember the components of creditworthiness is to think ASAP -- Ability, Stability, Assets, and Performance.

4. Desirable credit-card features include low interest rate, low penalty fees, and a long grace period.

5. Undesirable credit-card features include interest rates that can increase due to variable rates or to penalize the cardholder, high late and over-the-limit fees, and short or no grace periods.

6. Under the Equal Credit Opportunity Act, creditors must inform the consumer whether an application for credit has been approved, rejected, or found incomplete within 30 days. If credit is denied, creditors must provide the consumer with the specific reason or reasons for the rejection.

7. Minimum payments serve to maximize the finance charges that can be added to the remaining balance.

1. What are the four components that make up a consumer's creditworthiness?

2. List some of the desirable features in credit-card offers.

3. What features should be avoided in credit-card offers?

4. Explain the purpose of the Equal Credit Opportunity Act.

5. Explain why paying the minimum balance each month ultimately increases the cost of credit.

Unit 15: Using Credit Wisely

OBJECTIVES

- To understand how to use credit advantageously.
- To understand the importance of monitoring billing statements and communicating with creditors.
- To determine how to resolve billing errors.

THE REAL POWER OF CREDIT

Credit provides convenience, flexibility, and buying power to consumers who know how to use their cards advantageously.

Contrary to what it may feel like when it's sizzling in one's hand, a credit card is not an extension of income. When clients develop a solid spending plan, they will know what they can comfortably afford and what they cannot.

A good rule of thumb is the same that many lenders use to judge creditworthiness: Do not let monthly housing costs exceed 36% of your gross monthly income. For example, if the monthly income is $2000 and the house payment is $600, a person is already at 30%. Therefore, encourage clients not to let the power of credit allow them to make purchases they could not otherwise afford.

Credit cards cannot take the place of savings. Whether a consumer wants a new home entertainment system or a trip to Aruba, it makes a lot more sense to set a short-term financial goal and save the necessary funds beforehand. Otherwise, that home theater or trip will end up costing a lot more, and the consumer will end up paying for them long after the value of the product has decreased or the experience has ended.

For many consumers, maxing out their credit cards on spending sprees, entertaining, and traveling is what's fun and exciting about credit cards. Inevitably, the excitement is short-lived. Before long, the billing statements appear in the mail with balances that, at first, bewilder and then, frustrate the uninitiated.

The real power of credit comes with the understanding that credit is an opportunity to, over time, increase the ability to receive new and better credit. Getting the best mortgage rates, car loans, and insurance rates all depends on how someone has used credit in the past. When credit is used wisely, a person is paving the road to higher levels of financial freedom while enjoying the credit now for the convenience and flexibility it affords.

134

WISE CREDIT WAYS

Here are some important guidelines consumers need to follow if they are going to reap the full benefits of credit:

Obtaining credit. Shop for the best deals. There are some excellent sources online to begin searching for the best card for you. Watch out for variable interest rates or introductory rates that can turn monstrous overnight.

Making purchases. It is usually not a good idea to use credit to pay for everyday expenses like groceries. Also, try not to use credit to pay for unexpected expenses such as car or home repairs. Your spending plan should provide funds for these types of emergencies.

Cash Advances. Most cards allow for cash advances. Don't do it!

Monitor your account. Many people fail miserably at the credit game simply because they are not paying attention to what is going on with their accounts. Read over the billing statement carefully the same day it arrives in the mail. If there are unfamiliar charges or fees, call the customer service number. Watch for any unexpected changes in rates, terms, or conditions.

Paying bills. It is best to pay the balance in full each month to avoid any finance charges. However, if this is not realistic, try to pay more than the minimum payment. A good idea is to decide on a fixed amount to pay each month until the balance is either paid off or, at least, manageable.

Check the credit report once a year. Get a copy of your report from each of the three credit reporting agencies -- TransUnion, Equifax, and Experian. Dispute any errors.

COMMUNICATING WITH CREDITORS

A cardholder's communication with the lender primarily consists of the following:

The creditor sends a monthly billing statement and the cardholder pays all or a portion of the balance.

However, there are times when further communication is necessary. For example, a person may need to call the credit-card issuer because he/she notices an error on a billing statement. A cardholder may also need to call the lender to get explanations for any changes that occur in the terms and conditions of the loan.

Communicating with creditors is not always easy, but it is important to make the effort. If there is a problem, creditors want to be informed about it. By keeping the lines of communication open, a cardholder is seen as being actively involved with the account. If communication is avoided, lenders will think the cardholder ignores problems when they arise.

RESOLVING BILLING ERRORS

It is the cardholder's responsibility to monitor any changes in the lending agreement and to check for billing errors. Although itis not always easy to communicate with lenders, disputes are usually resolved without a problem.

Cardholders have the right to dispute billing errors under The Fair Credit Billing Act. They can then withhold payment on the specific account in question and request that the card issuer investigate and resolve the dispute.

Common billing errors include:

- Unfamiliar charges
- Clerical errors
- Fraud

Disputing by Phone

Many billing errors can be resolved by calling the customer service number on the back of your credit card. Half of all disputes are due to consumers not recognizing a charge. One reason this is so prevalent is because the merchant identifiers listed on the billing statement often use the corporate name rather than the familiar store front name.

Many clerical errors can also be cleared up by telephone. Cases of fraud are usually resolved quickly because the card issuer wants to maintain customer confidence.

Disputing by Letter

Other billing errors require a dispute letter. In this case, the credit-card issuer must receive the letter within 60 days from the date on the statement in question. Usually, there is an address for disputes listed on the monthly statement. Include copies of all documents supporting the dispute.

The issuer then has 30 days to acknowledge receipt of the dispute letter and 90 days to resolve the matter.

According to Consumer Reports, the number of people who dispute credit-card charges is in the millions. It costs at least $25 to process each dispute.

Billing errors that may require a dispute letter are:

Unauthorized charges. These include automatic charges you authorized when, for example, you signed up for a cable service but have since canceled.

Cramming. This is when a credit-card issuer tacks on additional charges such as insurance or other services without your knowledge. Sometimes you accept the additional charges by not signing a fine-print refusal or bill stuffer.

Goods not delivered. Request proof that the item was delivered. This means a signature of receipt -- not a computer-generated delivery confirmation.

THE BILLING DISPUTE LETTER

Here is a sample letter for disputing a billing error. Use the following checklist as a guide for what to include in the letter:

- Address it to the specific department that handles billing errors.
- Identify the cardholder and the account number.
- Give the date the statement was received.
- Describe the problem.
- Request evidence of the charge.

Be sure to make copies of all correspondence to creditors. When disputing an amount from a transaction, be sure to include a copy of the receipt. It is also a good idea to keep records of all letters sent with the name of the creditor, the date it was sent, and the reason for the dispute.

Sample Letter for Disputing a Billing Error

Date
Your name
Your ID number
Your address
Your telephone number
Your Social Security Number
Your date of birth

Name of creditor
Billing Inquiries
Address
City, State, Zip Code

Dear Sir or Madam:

I am writing to dispute a billing error in the amount of $_____ on my account. The amount is inaccurate because [describe the problem]. I am requesting that the error be corrected, that any finance charge and any other charges related to the disputed amount be credited to my account and that I receive a new and accurate statement.

Enclosed are copies of documents [describe any enclosed information such as sales slips or payment records] supporting my position. Please investigate this matter and correct the billing error as soon as possible.

Sincerely,
Your name
Enclosures: [list what you are enclosing]

AVOID LATE PAYMENTS

A payment is past due even if it is one day late. Therefore, it is a good idea to make payments at least one week prior to the due date. Late payments not only incur penalty fees but they also give lenders the opportunity to increase finance charges. If that wasn't enough, late payments lower credit scores.

HOW TO CANCEL A CREDIT CARD

If you don't want a particular credit card anymore, don't just toss it in the trash. Here is the right way to cancel an account:

1. Notify the card issuer by telephone.
2. Follow up by notifying the card issuer in writing.
3. Get a copy of your credit report and make sure that it accurately records the cancellation -- that is, that the cancellation was at the cardholder's request.
4. Repeat steps 1 - 3 if necessary.

The cancellation steps in detail:

Call the telephone number on the back of the credit card to be canceled. Confirm the status of the account and make sure the balance is 0. It is recommended that you pay off the balance first.

Notify customer service of the desire to cancel. Hold firm! They will try to keep your business by promising lower rates or special deals. Always get the name of the customer service representative as well as the name of the person to whom you should address correspondence.

Write a short letter to a specific person and state the following:

- I am closing the account.
- I want my credit report to show that it has been canceled by me.

Give your name, address, and account number. Send by certified mail or return receipt requested.

Allow 30 days for the account to be closed. Then, request a copy of your credit report from all three credit bureaus. Make sure it reads "Closed at customer's request." Make sure it does not read "Closed by creditor" as that would negatively affect the credit report.

If the report says that the account was closed by the creditor, the cardholder must start all over again. Call customer service and explain the mistake. Send a follow-up letter with a copy of the original letter. Check the credit report again after 30 days.

Reasons for canceling include the following:

1. To lower potential debt. Unused credit available may lower a credit score.
2. To eliminate the temptation of plastic and easy access to funds.
3. To close out a card that was a bad deal.

IDENTITY THEFT

The Federal Trade Commission acknowledges identity theft as a growing dilemma. Experts estimate that there are hundreds of thousands of victims each year. Every 79 seconds, a thief steals someone's identity, opens accounts in a victim's name and goes on a buying spree.

Credit-card fraud accounts for 50% of identity theft. Victims reported that a credit card was opened in their name or that unauthorized charges were placed on their existing credit card.

80% of the victims do not know the perpetrators while the remaining 20% could identify the fraudsters. Here's a further breakdown on who is committing these crimes:

35% of identity theft victims notice the theft within one month. However, some victims are unaware for up to five years! The average time it takes for victims to notice that someone has snatched their identities is 14 months. That's plenty of time to devastate a consumer's finances and credit rating.

- Protect your bills and credit cards by keeping track of your mail and the physical whereabouts of all your credit cards.
- Frequently review credit-card and bank statements for unauthorized charges.
- Guard your credit-card number. Do not give your number over the phone unless it is a company you have done business with before.
- Do not use your credit card to make Internet purchases unless the website has a secure server.
- Be wary of e-mails asking for personal information to update files.

SUMMARY

1. Credit cards should not be viewed as an extension of income or as a substitute for savings.

2. An important part of using credit wisely is to read and fully understand the monthly billing statement.

3. Communicating with creditors is essential in order to resolve billing errors and to ask about any changes that appear in the terms and conditions of the credit-card account.

4. Purchases made with credit cards should not include everyday expenses such as groceries. Cash advances should be avoided.

5. Responsible consumers monitor their credit report at least once every year.

6. Consumers should avoid making only the minimum payments each month. If paying off the account in full each month is unrealistic, it is best to arrive at a fixed amount to pay each time the billing statement arrives.

7. Consumers have the right to dispute billing errors under the Fair Credit Billing Act.

8. There is a systematic way to cancel unwanted credit cards so that the cancellation is reported correctly by the credit bureaus.

9. Identity theft has become increasingly problematic for consumers. Always be wary of telephone or online offers that ask for personal information.

10. Avoiding identity theft means keeping track of you mail, your credit-card and bank statements, and the whereabouts of your credit cards at all times.

1. Describe some of the ways to use credit wisely.

2. List two of the most common types of billing errors.

3. Describe the steps necessary for canceling a credit card.

4. What does the Fair Credit Billing Act give consumers the right to do?

Unit 16: Credit Reports

OBJECTIVES
- To understand the importance of your credit report.
- To determine how to request your credit report.
- To examine the information included in a credit report.
- To identify the steps involved in fixing credit report errors.

GETTING YOUR CREDIT REPORT
Various changes in a consumer's circumstances could signal the need for a current credit report. Career changes, promotions, or relocation should prompt a review of any information that an employer might view as derogatory. Some job applications request permission to do a credit check.

Purchasing a new home or vehicle are times when a consumer will want to be sure there are no unpaid accounts or inaccurate information. Clients filing for separation or divorce would need to verify accountability on joint accounts and insure proper assignment of liability to outstanding loans and financial responsibilities.

THE FAIR CREDIT REPORTING ACT
Under The Fair Credit Reporting Act, anyone obtaining or reading a consumer's credit report for reasons other than those listed here may face heavy fines or imprisonment:

- Written permission for employment or other authorized reasons
- Application for government license
- Application for business license
- Credit or insurance transaction
- Court subpoena from a federal grand jury
- Requirement for setting child support

The Fair Credit Reporting Act also requires that negative reporting be erased 7 years from the date initiated. This includes a Chapter 13 Bankruptcy. A Chapter 7 Bankruptcy can remain on a credit report for up to 10 years.

Within 60 days of denied credit, employment, insurance, or housing, a consumer may request a free copy of their report. Reports are issued free to consumers on welfare or if there is a reason to suspect fraud.

It is highly advantageous for consumers to monitor their credit reports at least once a year.

1. If a consumer has been denied credit, employment, or insurance within the last 60 days, mail written proof of being turned down to the three credit-reporting agencies. It is important to get all three reports since the information contained on each will vary.

2. Beginning in October 2005, all states are required to provide consumers one free copy of their credit report per year. You can request your credit report online by visiting each of the three credit bureau websites at:

   www.experian.com   www.equifax.com   www.transunion.com

3. You can also get one merged report online for a fee by going to www.myFICO.com. It includes consumer rights under The Fair Credit Reporting Act. Contact information for "The Big Three" are listed below:

   Experian, P.O. Box 390, Allen, TX 75013-2104, 1 (888) 397-3742

   Equifax, P.O. Box 740241, Atlanta, GA 30374-0241, 1 (800) 685-5000

   TransUnion, P.O. Box 2000, Chester, PA 19022, 1 (800) 916-8800

FREE CREDIT REPORTS
The result of the Federal Trade Commission's final ruling under The Fair and Accurate Credit Transactions Act allows U.S. citizens to obtain 1 free copy of their credit report every 12 months from each of the 3 credit reporting agencies.

Go to: www.annualcreditreport.com.

Include the information below if you are requesting a report by mail:

Your name
Date of birth
A photocopy of your social security card
A photocopy of your driver's license
Current address

Former address if you lived there within the last 5 years
A copy of letter denying credit, employment, or insurance (if you are requesting a
  free copy)

Name
Date
Address
Home and Work Phone
Social Security Number

I [your full name], request a complimentary copy of my complete credit report.
This is in accordance with state regulations and the Fair Credit Reporting Act of
1970, which states the credit agency must provide me with a complimentary copy
of my credit report once a year upon request at no charge. Please send a
complete complimentary copy of my credit report to the address provided above.

To help ensure that the correct report is generated, the following additional
information is provided: Date of Birth, Previous Names (Aliases, previous
marriages, name changes, or name shortening), Previous Address and
Employers (if you have been at your current address or employment for less than
five years), Spouse's First Name (if you are married)

Sincerely,
Your Signature
Enclose a copy of your Driver's License (certain states) or a current utility bill.

Name
Date
Address
Home and Work Phone
Social Security Number

I [your full name], request a copy of my complete credit report. Included is the fee
of $_____ plus tax, which is the cost you have set for generating this credit
report.

To help ensure that the correct report is generated, the following additional
information is provided: Date of Birth, Previous Names (Aliases, previous
marriages, name changes, or name shortening), Previous Address and

Employers (if you have been at your current address or employment for less than five years), Spouse's First Name (if you are married)

Sincerely,
Your Signature

Enclose a copy of your Driver's License or utility bill and the application fee.

READING A CREDIT REPORT

When consumers get their credit reports, they may be surprised about what information is included and what is left out. It is important to realize that a credit report is not a comprehensive picture of the consumer. There are two reasons for this:

1. The three credit reporting agencies do not get their information from the same subscribers. Different creditors subscribe to different bureaus.

2. Many creditors do not report consumer activity on a regular basis. In fact, some do not report information on consumer accounts unless the accounts are in default.

Some accounts are listed and some are not

To many consumers, credit reports may not seem fair. For example, mortgage companies and auto dealers sometimes do not report consistent on time payments. However, information will show up if the accounts are past due, in collections, or in legal proceedings.

Below is a list of accounts regularly reported:

- Bankcards
- Merchant cards from large chains
- Travel and entertainment cards
- Federal student loans

The following list shows accounts not normally reflected in a credit report ... unless they are in default:

- Utility bills
- Medical bills
- Mortgage or rent
- Automobile loans
- Merchant cards from small or local retailers

As you can see, a consumer may be on time over a long period with mortgage and car payments and it will never be reflected by the credit bureaus. However, be one day late with a payment and it will show up on the report.

4 CATEGORIES OF INFORMATION

Deciphering a credit report is not as hard as cracking a secret enemy code, but it can seem like it. It is important to remember that, although the three credit reporting agencies use different formats, they all contain the following four categories of information:

1. Personal identification information
2. Account history information
3. Public record information
4. Inquiries

The order in which they are presented differ among the credit reporting agencies. A breakdown of the three formats appears below.

TransUnion
- General Information
- Summary Line
- Public Records Information
- Account Information
- List of Inquiries
- Consumer Statement
- Optional information

Equifax
- Personal Identification Information
- Public Records
- Collection Agency
- Credit Account
- Additional Information
- Companies that requested credit file

Experian
- How to read this report
- Your credit history
- Your credit history was reviewed by
- Please help us help you
- Identification information

INQUIRIES

Anytime a request is made to see a consumer's credit report, it is reported as an inquiry on that consumer's credit report. If a person applies for a lot of credit cards in a short time, it will produce a lot of inquiries on the report. When a consumer is denied credit because of too many inquiries, there is no legal recourse under existing legislation.

Consumers should not give their name and address to a merchant until they are ready to apply for credit there. Some merchants illegally run credit checks to get an idea as to what they can try to sell the consumer and how.

Too many inquiries on a credit report indicate that a person is "credit hungry." Most inquiries are disregarded if they occurred six or more months ago. All credit inquiries should be removed from a report after two years.

2 Types of Inquiries

There are two types of inquires -- hard and soft. Hard inquiries occur when the consumer applies for credit. Soft inquiries are those that come from companies that want to send out promotional information to a pre-qualified group or current creditors who are monitoring your accounts. Soft inquiries also occur when a consumer requests a copy of their credit report.

Inquiries are what generate credit reports

There is a mistaken idea that credit reports are keep in enormous files and are constantly being updated as you go about your financial life. The reality is that credit reports do not exist until they are requested. Initiating an inquiry is what creates a credit report.

FICO scoring models (see Credit Scoring) ignore a vast majority of inquiries. For example, these models have buffer periods that ignore inquiries within 30 days of getting a mortgage or car loan. They also count two or more hard inquiries in the same 14-day period as just one.

RESOLVING CREDIT REPORT ERRORS

It is up to nobody but the individual to make sure the information in his/her credit report is correct. Credit bureaus report what creditors tell them. They do not check for accuracy. Many experts acknowledge that up to 80% of all credit reports have some kind of misinformation.

- Information is mixed up with another report belonging to someone else with a similar or identical name.
- The name of a former spouse appears on the report.
- The name is misspelled, the address is wrong, or the Social Security number is incorrect.
- Duplicate accounts show up.
- Account information is inaccurate or incomplete. This includes incorrect account balances, showing closed accounts as opened, or paid-off accounts still showing as delinquent.
- Outdated information is included. Negative account information must be removed after seven years. A Chapter 7 Bankruptcy must be removed after ten years.
- Unauthorized inquiries are listed.
- There is a failure to show that a tax lien has been released.

2 things to keep in mind when fixing credit report errors:

1. There is a standard procedure for getting rid of mistakes on a report under the terms of the Fair Credit Reporting Act.

2. Erasing report errors by telephone or letter exchanges can take time. New online procedures can offer faster results.

Here's what to do:

1. Complete the special investigation request form that will come with the report. Follow all the form's instructions.

2. Attach a letter to the completed form along with any documentation that helps prove the error. This includes copies of canceled checks, receipts, account statements, as well as copies of previous correspondence between the consumer and the creditor involved.

3. Maintain a copy of the completed investigation request form, letter, and all accompanying documentation. The date on the letter will signal when a response should come from the credit bureau. According to guidelines of the Fair Credit Reporting Act, the credit bureau must respond within 30 days of receiving an investigation request form.

4. Send the request by certified mail with a request for a return receipt. When you get the receipt, file it with the other documents. Below is a sample letter for

correcting errors on a credit report. Be sure to attach a copy of the credit report to the letter. Have the specific errors highlighted.

Sample Letter for Disputing Errors on a Credit Report

Name of Agency
Attn: Customer Relations
RE: Your Name
Your ID#
Your Address
Your Telephone Number
Your Social Security Number
Your Date of Birth

Please begin an investigation of the following items listed on my credit report that do not belong in my credit file.

Company's Name	Account #	Reason For Dispute
_____	_____	_____
_____	_____	_____
_____	_____	_____

Please update my credit report and send me a copy at the conclusion of your investigation. Send the results to the organizations that have reviewed my credit report in the past six months and/or to employers that have reviewed it during the past two years. Thank you for your help and prompt attention to this matter.

Your Signature

Credit Report Mistakes are Common

According to a report issued in 2004 by The Public Interest Research Group, 1 in 4 reports contain errors serious enough to disqualify consumers from making major purchases. Over 75% of the reports from the study contained some kind of error. More than half of these errors involved personal information like misspelled names or outdated information.

Individuals with common last names or suffixes (Smith, Jones, Brown, or Sr., Jr., II, III) often become confused with other people. Also, identity theft is on the rise. Individuals have been misrepresented or have had accounts opened in their name without their knowledge.

Should a client discover any disputable items, a claim may be filed with the credit reporting agency which supplied the report. The client will need to fill out the special investigation request form that is included with the credit report. According to the Fair Credit Reporting Act, the credit bureau is required to resolve the problem in a reasonable amount of time -- generally 30 days. During that period of time, a Statement of Dispute will be added to the credit history. It is advisable for clients to request their report once a year to safeguard against errors that may damage their credit rating.

What the Credit Bureaus Must Do

After completing their investigation, each credit bureau has 5 business days to send you written notice of its findings. It must delete or modify the contested information immediately if:

1. the information being disputed has been determined to be inaccurate, or
2. the information cannot be verified.

However, if the credit bureau later receives proof that the disputed information is accurate, it can reinsert the information into the report. Along with the credit bureau's written notice of its findings, the consumer should also receive a revised copy of the credit report to verify that the requested changes have been made.

After receiving the corrected report, wait a couple of months and then request another copy of the report. This is to make sure that the error does not reappear due to a glitch in the system.

If a consumer disagrees with the credit bureau's findings, he/she may insert a statement free of charge. The statement must be included every time the report is sent out. Send the letter by certified mail and keep the receipt and a copy of the report. As long as the charge is in dispute, the dispute will appear on the credit report.

Your Rights Under The Fair Credit Reporting Act

The credit bureau is required to resolve the problem in a reasonable amount of time -- generally 30 days.

If a consumer feels that the credit bureau has not responded promptly and fairly to his/her situation, contact the State Attorney General or The Federal Trade Commission in Washington at (202) 326-2222.

SUMMARY

1. Consumers should obtain their credit reports at least once a year in order to check for possible errors and to ascertain their credit scores.

2. A ruling under the Fair and Accurate Credit Transactions Act allows consumers to obtain one free copy of their credit report from each credit bureau every 12 months.

3. The Fair Credit Reporting Act requires that negative items on a credit report including Chapter 13 Bankruptcy be erased seven years from the date initiated. Chapter 7 Bankruptcy must be erased after ten years.

4. Credit reports from all three credit-reporting agencies contain four categories of information: personal identification information, account history information. public record information, and inquires.

5. Consumers can fix errors on their credit report by following a standard procedure involving phone calls and certified correspondence or they can now access and fix their reports online by visiting the credit reporting agency websites.

6. The vast majority of credit reports contain some kind of an error. According to The Public Interest Research Group, 1 in 4 contain errors serious enough to disqualify consumers from making major purchases.

REVIEW QUESTIONS

1. Explain what the Fair Credit Reporting Act requires of credit-reporting agencies.

2. What should be included in a letter requesting a credit report?

3. What are the three credit-reporting agencies?

4. What are the four types of information that go into a credit report?

Unit 17: Credit Scores

OBJECTIVES
- To understand the importance of FICO scores.
- To determine the five major items a FICO score considers.
- To explore ways consumers can raise their FICO scores.

FICO SCORES

A credit score is a number lenders use to help them decide: If I give this person a loan or credit card, how likely is it that I will get paid back on time? A score is a snapshot of a person's credit risk picture at a particular point in time.

There are many types of credit scores but the most commonly used are credit bureau scores. Credit bureau scores are based solely on information gathered from consumer credit reports that are maintained at one of the credit-reporting agencies. The most widely used credit bureau score is based on a statistical model developed by Fair, Isaac. It is commonly known as a FICO score.

Understanding credit scoring can help people manage their credit. A FICO score looks at the same information in a credit report that a lender will also use. By knowing how credit risk is evaluated, a consumer can take actions that will lower credit risk, and thus, raise the score over time.

Your Credit Report -- The Basis of Your Score

Credit-reporting agencies process information on millions of borrowers. Lenders making credit decisions buy credit reports on their prospects, applicants, and customers from the credit-reporting agencies.

Your report details credit history as it has been reported to the credit-reporting agency by lenders who have extended consumer credit. A credit report lists what types of credit are used, the length of time accounts have been opened, and whether or not bills have been paid on time. It tells lenders how much credit has been used and whether the consumer is seeking new sources of credit. It gives lenders a broader view of credit history than do other data sources, such as a bank's own customer data.

A credit report does not really exist until the consumer or a lender asks for it. It is then compiled by the credit-reporting agency based on the information stored in that agency's files. This information is supplied by lenders, by court records and by the consumer.

Tens of thousands of credit grantors -- retailers, credit-card issuers, banks, finance companies, credit unions, etc. -- send updates to each of the credit-reporting agencies, usually once a month. These updates include information about how their customers use and pay their accounts.

A credit report reveals many aspects of borrowing activity. All pieces of information are considered in relationship to other pieces of information. The ability to quickly consider all this information is what makes credit scoring so useful.

HOW SCORING WORKS

Along with the credit report, lenders can also buy a credit score based on the information in the report. That score is calculated by a mathematical equation that evaluates many types of information from the credit report at that agency. Exactly what formula is used to calculate a score is shrouded in mystery and protected by the Federal Trade Commission. By comparing this information to the patterns in hundreds of thousands of past credit reports, the score identifies a consumer's level of credit risk.

In order for a FICO score to be calculated from a credit report, the report must contain at least one account that has been opened for six months or more. In addition, the report must contain at least one account that has been updated in the past six months. This ensures that there is enough information and enough recent information in the report on which to base a score.

More About FICO Scores

Credit bureau scores are often called FICO scores because most credit bureau scores used in the United States and Canada are produced from software developed by Fair, Isaac and Company (FICO). FICO scores are provided to lenders by the three major credit-reporting agencies: Equifax, Experian and Trans Union.

FICO scores have different names at each of the three credit-reporting agencies. All of these scores, however, are developed using the same methods by Fair Isaac, and Company and have been rigorously tested to ensure they provide the most accurate picture of credit risk possible using credit-reporting data. Fico score names for each credit bureau are listed below:

Credit Reporting Agency	FICO Score Name
Experian	Experian/Fair, Isaac Risk Model
TransUnion & TransUnion Canada	EMPIRCA
Equifax & Equifax Canada	BEACON

At present, FICO scores provide the best guide to future risk based solely on credit report data. The higher the score, the lower the risk. No score, however, can predict whether a specific individual will be a good or bad borrower

Also, while many lenders use FICO scores to help them make lending decisions, each lender has its own strategy, including the level of risk it finds acceptable for a given credit product. There is no single cutoff score used by all lenders.

More Than One Score

In general, when people talk about your score, they are talking about your current FICO score. However, there is no one score used by lenders to make decisions about you. Here's why:

Credit bureau scores are not the only scores used. Many lenders use their own scores which may include the FICO score as well as other information about the consumer.

FICO scores are not the only credit bureau scores. There are other credit bureau scores although FICO scores are by far the most commonly used. Other credit bureau scores may evaluate a credit report differently than FICO scores. In some cases, a higher score may mean more risk, not less risk as with FICO scores.

An individual's score may be different at each of the three main credit-reporting agencies. The FICO score from each credit reporting agency considers only the data in the credit report at that agency. If a person's current scores from the credit-reporting agencies are different, it is probably because the information those agencies have on that person differs.

An individual's FICO score changes over time. As the data changes at the credit-reporting agency, so will any new score based on that credit report. A FICO score from a month ago is probably not the same score a lender would get from the credit-reporting agency today.

WHAT A FICO SCORE CONSIDERS

There are 5 main categories of information that are used to calculate a FICO score. The categories have different levels of importance.

1. Payment History: What is the track record?
   Approximately 35% of a score is based on this category.

The first thing most lenders want to know is whether a consumer has paid past credit accounts on time. This is also one of the most important factors in a credit score.

However, late payments are not an automatic score-killer. An overall good credit picture can outweigh one or two instances of late credit-card payments. By the same token, the absence of late payments in a credit report does not necessarily translate into a perfect score. Approximately 60 - 65% of credit reports show no late payments at all. Payment history is just one piece of information used in calculating the score.

Payment history takes into account:

- Payment information on many types of accounts. These will include credit cards (Visa, MasterCard, American Express and Discover), retail accounts (department store credit cards), and installment loans (loans where you make regular payments, such as car loans, finance company accounts and mortgage loans).

- Public record and collection items -- reports of events such as bankruptcies, foreclosures, lawsuits, wage attachments, liens and judgments. These are considered quite serious, although older items and items with small amounts will count less than more recent items or those with larger amounts.

- Details on late or missed payments (delinquencies) and public record and collection items -- specifically, how late they were, how much was owed, how recently they occurred and how many there are. A 60-day late payment is not as risky as a 90-day late payment, but recency and frequency count too. A 60-day late payment made just a month ago will count more than a 90-day late payment from five years ago. Note that closing an account on which there was a previously missed payment or satisfying a judgment or collection item does not make the late payment or item disappear from the credit report.

- How many accounts show no late payments. A good track record on most of your accounts will increase a credit score.

2. Amounts owed: How much is too much?
Approximately 30% of the score is based on this category.

Having credit accounts and owing money on them does not mean a person is a high-risk borrower with a low score. However, owing a great deal of money on many accounts can indicate that a person is overextended and is more likely to make some payments late or to not pay at all. Part of the science of scoring is determining how much is too much for a given credit profile.

155

Amounts owed takes into account:

- The amount owed on all accounts. Note that even if credit cards are paid in full every month, a credit report may show a balance on those cards. The total balance on the last credit card statement is generally the amount that will show on the credit report.

- Whether there is a balance on certain types of accounts. In some cases, having a very small balance without missing a payment shows a consumer has managed credit responsibly and may be slightly better than no balance at all. On the other had, closing unused credit accounts that show zero balances and that are in good standing will not generally raise a score.

- How many accounts have balances. A large number can indicate higher risk of over-extension.

- How much of the total credit line is being used on credit cards. Someone closer to maxing out on many credit cards may have trouble making payments in the future.

- How much of installment loan accounts is still owed compared with the original loan amounts. Paying down installment loans is a good sign that a consumer is able and willing to manage and repay debt.

3. Length of Credit History: How established is an individual's credit history? Approximately 15% of the score is based on this category.

In general, a longer credit history will increase a score. However, even people who have not been using credit long may get high scores, depending on how the rest of the credit report looks.

Length of credit history takes into account:

- How long the credit accounts have been established. The score considers both the age of the oldest account and an average age of all accounts.

- How long specific credit accounts have been established. Different accounts are evaluated in different ways.

- How long it has been since certain accounts were used. FICO scores consider not only how long an account has been opened but also whether or not it is active.

4. New Credit: Is an individual taking on more debt?
Approximately 10% of the score is based on this category.

People tend to have more credit today and to shop for new credit more frequently than ever. Fair, Isaac and Company scores reflect this fact. However, research shows that opening several credit accounts in a short period of time represents a greater credit risk -- especially for consumers who do not have a long credit history.

New credit takes into account:

- Recent requests for new credit. Inquiries remain on a credit report for two years, although FICO scores only consider inquiries from the last 12 months. Note that if a credit report is ordered from a credit reporting agency or www.myfico.com, the score does not count this, as it is not an indication that a person is seeking new credit. Also, the score does not count requests a lender has made for a credit score in order to make someone a pre-approved credit offer, or to review an account, even though these inquiries may be seen on a credit report.

5. Types of Credit in Use: Is it a healthy mix?
Approximately 10% of the score is based on this category.

The score will consider the mix of credit cards, retail accounts, installment loans, and finance company accounts. It is not necessary to have one of each, and it is not a good idea to open credit accounts just to have them in the mix. The credit mix usually will not be a key factor in determining a score, but it will be more important if a credit report does not have a log of other information on which to base a score.

Types of credit in use takes into account:

- What kinds of credit accounts there are and how many of each. The score also looks at the total number of accounts. For different credit profiles, how many is too many will vary.

What Determines Your Credit Score?

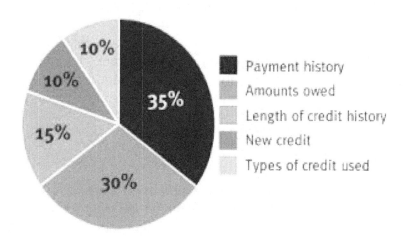

The Credit/Mortgage Connection

Mortgage lenders and brokers use FICO scores to determine mortgage rates. The FICO score will also determine how a client applies and qualifies for a mortgage. A FICO score is a three-digit number between 300 and 850 that tries to gauge a consumer's creditworthiness.

If a score is higher than 700, a client will not only qualify for the best loan terms, but lenders may also grant the loan without asking questions about income and assets. These loans are referred to as no-docs and are fast and easy to get.

If a score is 660 or better, a client will get the best rates available from virtually all lenders. However, full documentation of income, assets, and current debt must be provided.

If a score is between 620 and 660, a client may get a preferred-rate loan but will have fewer lenders to choose from. Lenders will look more closely at any transgressions on the credit report to determine whether they can push the client into the dreaded subprime market.

If a score is less than 620, lenders will consider that client a subprime borrower. Subprime borrowers pay at least 1% more in interest on a home loan and may have to accept features like pre-payment penalties. "What's one percentage point?", you might ask. Just one percentage point difference costs $23,410 for each $100,000 borrowed over thirty years!

TOP TEN REASONS FOR A LOW SCORE

Here are the top 10 most frequently given reasons for low scores. Note that the specific wording given by a lender may be different from these:

1. Serious delinquency
2. Serious delinquency and public record or collection filed
3. Derogatory public record or collection file
4. Time since delinquency is too recent or unknown
5. Level of delinquency on accounts
6. Number of accounts with delinquency
7. Amount owed on accounts
8. Proportion of balances to credit limits on revolving accounts is too high
9. Length of time accounts have been established
10. Too many accounts with balances

RAISING YOUR FICO SCORE

It is important to note that raising a FICO score is a bit like getting in shape -- it takes time and there is no quick fix. In fact, quick-fix efforts can backfire. The best advice is to manage credit responsibly over time.

One general tip is to make sure the information in the credit report is correct. Check the credit report for accuracy at least 90 days before planning any major purchases such as applying for a mortgage. If errors are detected, have them corrected by the lender as well as any credit-reporting agency involved.

Specific tips for raising a score include:

- Pay bills on time. Delinquent payments and collections can have a major negative impact on a score.

- If there have been missed payments, get current and stay current. The longer a consumer pays bills on time, the better the score.

- Be aware that paying off a collection account will not remove it from the credit report. It will stay on the report for seven years.

- If an individual is having trouble making ends meet, encourage him/her to contact current creditors to negotiate an easier payment schedule. This will not improve the score immediately, but if credit begins to be managed with bills paid on time, the score will get better over time.

- Keep balances low on credit cards and other revolving credit. High outstanding debt can affect a score.

- Pay off debt rather than move it around. The most effective way to improve a score in this area is by paying down revolving credit.

- Do not open a number of new credit cards just to increase available credit. This approach could backfire and actually lower the score.

- If the credit history is not long, do not open a lot of new accounts too rapidly. New accounts will lower the average account age, which will have a larger effect on the score when there isn't a lot of other credit information. Also, rapid account buildup can be seen as risky business.

- FICO scores distinguish between a search for a single loan and a search for many new credit lines, in part by the length of time over which inquiries occur. Therefore, do rate shopping within a focused period of time.

- Note that it is OK to request and check one's own credit report and one's own FICO score. This will not affect a score as long as the credit report is ordered directly from the credit-reporting agency or through an organization authorized to provide credit reports to consumers.

- Apply for and open new credit accounts only as needed. Do not open accounts just to have a better credit mix -- it probably will not raise a score.

- Have credit cards but manage them responsibly. In general, having credit cards and installment loans (and making payments on time) will raise a score.

- Note that closing an account that contains a balance does not make it go away. A closed account will still show up on a credit report and may still be considered by the score.

Interpreting the Score

When a consumer or a lender receives a Fair, Isaac and Company credit bureau risk score, up to four score reason codes are also delivered. These explain the top reasons why the score was not higher. If the lender rejects a request for credit, and the FICO score was part of the reason, these score reasons can suggest why your score was not higher.

These score reasons are more useful than the score itself in helping a consumer determine whether a credit report might contain errors and how the consumer might improve the score over time. However, if the score is already in the mid - 700s or higher, some of the reasons may not be very helpful, as they may be marginal factors related to the last three categories described previously (length of credit history, new credit, and types of credit in use).

What Does NOT Go into a FICO Score?

- Race, color, religion, national origin, sex or marital status. U.S. law prohibits scoring from considering these facts, as well as information concerning public assistance or the exercise of any consumer right under the Consumer Credit Protection Act.

- Age is not a consideration. Other types of scores may consider your age but FICO scores cannot under the Equal Credit Opportunity Act.

- Salary, occupation, title, employer, date employed or employment history. Lenders may consider this information, however, as may other types of scores.

- Place of residence.

- Any interest rate being charged on a particular credit card or other account.

- Any items reported as child/family support obligations or rental agreements.

- Certain types of inquiries. The score does not count requests the consumer has made for his/her credit report. It also does not count promotional inquiries -- requests made by lenders in order to offer pre-approved credit or administrative inquiries -- requests made by lenders to review an account. Requests that are marked as coming from employers are not counted either.

- Any information not found in the credit report.

- Any information that is not proven to be predictive of future credit performance.

FALLACIES AND FACTS

Fallacy: A poor score will haunt a person forever.

Fact: Just the opposite is true. A score is a snapshot of a person's risk at a particular point in time. It changes as new information is added to bank and credit bureau files. Scores change gradually as a person changes the way he/ she handles credit. For example, past credit problems impact a score less as time passes. Lenders request a current score when a consumer applies for credit, so they have the most recent information available.

Fallacy: Credit scoring is unfair to minorities.

Fact: The Equal Credit Opportunity Act prohibits lenders from considering race, nationality, gender or marital status. Independent research has monitored and continues to monitor the effectiveness of the ECOA .

Fallacy: Credit scoring infringes on privacy.

Fact: FICO scores evaluate a credit report alone which lenders already use to make credit decisions. A score is simply a numeric summary of that information. In fact, lenders using scoring can often ask for less information about a consumer. They may have fewer questions on the application form for example.

Fallacy: A score will drop after applying for new credit.

Fact: Probably not much. If several credit cards are applied for within a short period of time, multiple requests for credit report information (called inquiries) will appear on the report. Looking for new credit can equate with higher risk, but most credit scores are not affected by multiple inquiries from auto or mortgage lenders within a short period of time. The FICO score treats these as a single inquiry which will have less impact on the credit score.

Fallacy: The score determines whether or not a consumer gets credit.

Fact: Lenders use a number of facts to make credit decisions, including the FICO score. Lenders look at information such as the amount of debt a person can reasonably handle given his/her income, employment history, and credit history. Based on their perception of this information as well as their specific underwriting policies, lenders may extend credit although the score is low, or decline a request for credit although a score is high.

162

SUMMARY

1. The most widely used credit bureau scores use a statistical model developed by Fair, Isaac and Company and are known as FICO scores.

2. Lenders purchase consumer credit reports of loan applicants in order to assess a prospective consumer's past credit performance.

3. At present, FICO scoring is the best way to determine future risk based solely on credit report data.

4. There are five main categories of information that are used to calculate a FICO score:

- payment history
- amounts owed
- length of credit history
- new credit
- types of credit in use

5. In addition to a credit bureau risk score, consumers and lenders also receive up to four score reason codes. These explain the top reasons for the score and help consumers to locate errors and determine how to improve their score.

6. Tips for raising your score include: pay bills on time, keep credit-card balances low and negotiate with creditors if you are having difficulty staying current with payments.

7. U.S. law prohibits scoring based on race, color, religion, national origin or marital status.

1. What does FICO stand for?

2. What items does a FICO score consider?

3. List some ways consumers can raise their FICO score.

4. What are some types of information that are NOT factored into a FICO score?

Module V: Understanding & Dealing with Debt

PREVIEW

Clients who are unsure or apprehensive about the current options available to the consumer will benefit from the objective, non-judgmental guidance that the counselor can offer. The role of the counselor is to help the client evaluate each alternative and to facilitate decision making by providing timely information. Each client will require a different strategy for resolving financial dilemmas which, in some cases, were years in the making.

Module 5 takes a close look at debt -- its many causes as well as its many cures. In between, it examines the process of debt collection and the legal consequences of unpaid debt. Fear of the unknown is replaced by solid information.

By completing this module, you will:

- learn about the many sources of debt.
- gain insight about the psychology behind spending.
- gain awareness about predatory lending.
- learn about gambling addictions.
- understand that indebtedness is a condition that affects people differently.
- determine who is authorized to collect unpaid debt.
- become familiar with the rules governing the collection of debt
- know the consequences of unpaid debt including foreclosure, repossession and lawsuits.
- learn about ways for resolving debt.
- understand the processes involved in bankruptcy.
- become familiar with the new bankruptcy legislation of 2005.
- determine the components that make up pre-bankruptcy counseling.

Unit 18: Getting Into Debt

OBJECTIVES

OBJECTIVES
- To gain awareness about causes behind delinquent debt.
- To explore the psychological motivations behind spending.
- To gain awareness about the effects of indebtedness on clients.

According to the U.S. Census Bureau, credit-card debt has reached 1.4 trillion dollars. This debt drives nearly one and a half million consumers to file bankruptcy each year while a large percentage of the population struggles with monthly bills and expenses. Many are without adequate savings on which to fall back on should financial setbacks occur.

It is important for financial counselors to gain insight into why their clients are in debt in the first place. By helping clients identify the sources of their debt, counselors can help them pinpoint financial stumbling blocks and adjust their spending habits to a sound financial plan.

Understanding the dynamics behind spending and over-extending credit also serves to increase a sense of empathy for clients. As you will see, a very small percentage of debtors are "credit criminals." The vast majority of consumers experiencing the stress of delinquent debt are well-intentioned individuals who have either suffered major financial setbacks or who have unwittingly gotten over their heads with bills.

SOURCES OF DEBT
Let's look at some of the most prevalent reasons for indebtedness:

1. **Easy access to credit.** Credit card companies target nearly every sector of society with savvy credit offers that give the illusion of getting something for nothing. As a result, everyone seems to be carrying plastic -- some with outrageous finance charges.

2. **Easy access to money.** ATMs and debit cards are everywhere you go and everywhere you spend money. If you have a PIN number, you can effortlessly withdraw whatever you need (and more) from your bank account. With easy cash and a debit card, you always spend more.

3. **Consumer culture.** Americans are increasingly becoming media-driven. Instead of comparing themselves to their neighbors, millions are tuning in to movies and television shows as their reference points of success and style.

And those in the media are quite a bit harder to keep up with!

4. Changing technology. Our changing technology accounts for a significant increase in big ticket purchases that appear to be absolutely necessary in our fast-paced society. Many computer savvy people admit that in order to keep up with the advances in computer technology, consumers must purchase a whole new system every 18 months. New hi-tech features in cars, household appliances and wireless communication increase what consumers pay.

5. Lack of financial literacy. Many individuals in debt fail to evaluate credit offers properly, do not understand interest rates and finance charges adequately and are not pro-active in the management of their personal finances.

6. Financial setbacks. These include loss of income (job loss), medical emergency, death in the family or some unexpected cost. These setbacks are the facts of life that savings are supposed to help out with. However, many Americans no longer have the ability to save. Why? See above reasons.

7. Spending too much. According to VISA, who asked 50,000 consumers filing bankruptcy the cause of their indebtedness, as much as one-third cited overspending! Why do consumers spend more than they have? What are the psychological factors behind overspending?

THE PSYCHOLOGY OF SPENDING

Several books have been written which attempt to understand the motivations that ultimately drive people into debt and to identify various categories of spenders. By understanding the psychology behind debt, counselors, as well as the clients they serve, can predict negative outcomes and identify specific obstacles to financial well-being.

Anselm Bassano (2001), writing for *Legal and Trade Collectors Ltd.*, explains the benefit of understanding the causes of debt in terms of dollars and cents:

"Listening to each debtor and attempting to understand the state of mind can be an effective tool in securing payment. Indeed, when counselors pinpoint client motivation to spend, they are better able to help adjust that motivation to pay off debt and achieve control over their financial futures."

In her book, *The Overspent American*, Juliet Schor identifies several "neurotic" spending styles. Competitive spenders aggressively try to establish and maintain status by keeping up with their particular reference group. As mentioned in the primary reasons of indebtedness, the reference group of choice no longer lives in your neighborhood. They live in the media where style and success are defined. The problem is, for most Americans, the level of opulence portrayed in the media is simply unattainable.

Other spending styles are described in the books, *Emotional Business* by David Krueger and *Consuming Passions* by Ellen Mohr-Catalano and Nina Sonenberg. They include:

Compulsive spending is the attempt to alleviate a sense of emptiness by binge shopping and frivolous spending.

Co-dependent spending tries to create dependency in others by showering them with perceived necessities.

Narcissistic spending is an attempt to overcome feelings of inner inferiority by spending to look good. This could include designer clothing, hair and skin treatments, and products that signify status like expensive watches and jewelry.

Revenge spending usually occurs in relationships where one person exacts punishment on another by spending their money. They literally get them in the pocket.

The problem with categorizing people as neurotic spenders is that this serves to pathologize consumers as somehow mentally unstable or ill. It is not the goal of the counselor to categorize spenders. Rather, it is important to explore the various psychological motivations behind overspending in order to recognize them as patterns of behavior all people exhibit from time to time.

Some reasons behind overspending are based on erroneous beliefs. For example, many over-spenders rationalize their spending by thinking that their income will increase. This is the assumption that advertisers prey upon when they announce no payments until next year or better yet, next millennium. By then, many believe, they will have accumulated savings, received an inheritance, or won the lottery.

Other beliefs are products of our childhood and the messages we received about money as we were growing up. Some of us were told that money is the root of all evil. We heard fairy tales about misers who horded their riches only to meet a tragic end, pirates who sank to the bottom of the sea weighed down by treasure, and evil queens adorned in gold. These stories and images help to shape our relationship with money. Do we fear it? Do we embrace it? Do we need to spend it in order to realize its power? Or do we understand that its real power is in creating financial freedom?

The sources of excessive debt include the current lending climate and trends in borrowing and extending credit. Predatory lenders do just what the name implies. They exploit borrowers, especially vulnerable groups such as the elderly, minorities and people with poor credit histories by charging high interest rates and excessive fees. Many of these types of lenders use deceptive sales practices to trick people into getting loans they cannot afford to repay. The results can lead to foreclosure, eviction and homelessness.

Predatory lending has become a growing problem nationwide. For this reason, federal and state governments have responded with increased regulatory enforcement and educational outreach efforts. One example is a campaign by Freddie Mac called "Don't Borrow Trouble." Federal Reserve Banks have also become actively involved with this issue.

There is no one precise definition of predatory lending. Rather, it consists of a number of practices that unfairly exploit consumers. Predatory lending includes both technically legal but high-cost loans and outright fraud through deceptive sales practices.

A common element of all predatory loans is exploiting a consumer's ability (or inability) to repay. Borrowers are often lent amounts far in excess of what their incomes can support. In the case of mortgage loans, lenders are assured of a profit either through loan repayments or foreclosure. Another characteristic is interest rates and fees that are well in excess of what is required to compensate for risk and to earn a reasonable profit.

Predatory lenders often justify their high interest rates and fees by citing the additional risk posed by borrowers. In reality, most predatory loans are low risk because they are secured by the borrower's home, automobile, or other property. Therefore, there is no need for the substantial risk premium.

Traditional loans from banks and credit unions often charge loan rates according to risk (e.g. higher rates for unsecured loans). With predatory loans, there is little or no relationship between cost of credit and the risk assumed by the lender. All borrowers pay high rates and fees.

CHARACTERISTICS OF PREDATORY LOANS

Frequent Refinancing. Making multiple loans to the same customer is a great way for predatory lenders to maximize their profits. They typically encourage borrowers to refinance an existing loan into a bigger, longer-term loan -- often at a higher interest rate. This practice is called "loan flipping."

Ability to Repay is Disregarded. Consumers are encouraged to borrow more than they can afford. Predatory lenders do not care if the borrowers cannot keep up with the monthly payments. Borrowers can always refinance. Or predatory lenders can simply start the foreclosure process.

Payment History is NOT Reported. Predatory lenders generally do not report the borrower's payment history to the credit bureaus. So even if the borrower is able to keep the loan current, it is not reflected in the credit report or the borrower's credit score.

Balloon Mortgages. A balloon mortgage is a loan in which the borrower makes small monthly payments for five to seven years after which the loan becomes due and must be paid off in one large final payment. This practice pretty much guarantees that the borrower will refinance.

Exorbitant Fees. Fees are usually much higher than those charged by reputable banks and credit unions.

LOANS TO WATCH OUT FOR

Payday Loans -- also known as cash advance loans or post-dated check loans -- issue short-term, single payment loans aimed at low-and middle-income workers who live paycheck to paycheck.

Car Title Loans usually require no credit check and few questions are asked. However, the borrower must use his or her car as collateral.

Tax Refund Anticipation Loans, also known as rapid refunds, appeal to people who are short on cash and expect an income tax refund. Typically, a high interest rate is charged for a relatively short amount of time.

GAMBLING AND ADDICTIONS
You don't have to go to Las Vegas. Gambling is everywhere today. Once confined to backrooms and pool halls, gambling has become mainstream. Over 80% of Americans have gambled at least once. Gambling is legal in 48 states.

Besides casino gambling, there are now state lotteries, cruise ship and riverboat gambling, scratch card games, slot machines, keno, sports wagering, horse and dog race gambling and poker games targeting teenagers. Gambling now seems to cater to the entire family. Some of our Congressmen even want to tie in voter registration with playing the lottery!

Gambling really produces no winners. Can anyone declare that they are a successful gambler or that they make their living by gambling? Gambling makes the casino owners rich, not the gamblers. Gambling is more likely going to ruin relationships and destroy family resources. In fact, the very concept of money is hijacked through gambling. No longer is money viewed as a tool for realizing financial goals. Instead it becomes the means by which the gambler stays in the action.

According to a study conducted by the National Institute of Mental Health, 4.2 million Americans are addicted to gambling. Sixty percent of them have annual incomes of less than $25,000.

If you or someone you know has a gambling problem:

You can learn more by visiting the website of the National Council on Problem Gambling at www.ncpgambling.org or by calling them at (800) 522-4700.

The National Council on Problem Gambling states:

Although no substance is ingested, the problem gambler gets the same effect from gambling that someone else might get from taking a tranquilizer or having a drink. The gambling affects the person's mood and the gambler keeps repeating the behavior attempting to achieve the same effect. But, just as tolerance develops to drugs and alcohol, the gambler finds that more and more of the gambling experience is needed to achieve the same emotional effect as before and creates an increased craving for the activity and the gambler finds they have less and less resistance as the craving grows in intensity and frequency.

Problem gamblers like substance abusers may require intervention and treatment in order to control compulsive and destructive behaviors. Although financial difficulties most frequently drive gamblers to seek counseling, the problem goes beyond personal finances.

Unless the gambler recognizes the source of the problem and has successfully abstained from all gambling activities for at least 30 days, focusing on finances is premature. Active problem gamblers need to confront their behaviors first! This most frequently involves therapy which is beyond the scope and expertise of the financial counselor.

Signs of problem gambling include:

- Increased frequency of gambling activity and money spent.
- Neglecting family and job due to gambling.
- Preoccupation with gambling.
- Deriving intense pleasure and excitement from gambling.
- Gambling continues regardless of negative effects.
- Gambling is used as a way to escape anxiety and stress. After a loss, or series of losses, taking greater risks.
- Borrowing money to continue gambling.
- Moods are tied to winning or loosing.
- Hiding gambling activities and evidence.

SELF-ASSESSMENT: ARE YOU A PROBLEM GAMBLER?
The following 20 questions may help determine if someone has a compulsive gambling addiction.

1. Do you lose time from work due to gambling?
2. Is gambling having a negative effect on your home life?
3. Is gambling affecting your reputation?
4. Have you ever felt remorse after gambling?
5. Do you ever gamble to get money to pay debts or solve financial difficulties?
6. Does gambling negatively affect your productivity or ambition?
7. After losing, do you feel an urge to get back in the action?
8. After winning, do you feel an urge to try and win more?
9. Do you ever gamble until your last dollar is gone?
10. Have you ever borrowed to pay for your gambling?
11. Have you ever sold anything to finance gambling?
12. Do you keep a gambling fund separate from other money?
13. Does gambling make you careless with respects to the welfare of you or your family?
14. Do you ever gamble longer than you had planned?
15. Do you ever gamble to escape worry or trouble?
16. Have you ever committed or contemplated an illegal act to finance gambling?
17. Does gambling interfere with your sleeping?
18. Is gambling fueled by arguments, disappointments or frustrations?
19. Do you have an urge to gamble as a way to celebrate?
20. Have you ever considered suicide as a result of gambling?

If you answered "yes" to seven or more of these questions, you may have a gambling addiction.

THE CONDITION OF INDEBTEDNESS

Being in debt has its own effects which often serve to exacerbate the situation. Patterns appear and reappear as debtors repeat past mistakes. Perhaps one of the best research-based appraisals of the various types of delinquent debtors is from Kevin Keleghan. As Chief Credit Officer for Sears Credit, he conducted 200 structured interviews with customers who had delinquent accounts.

What he came up with are six types of debtors:

1. The Imprudent. These are consumers who have no money put away for a rainy day. Generally, they live one day at a time without any financial goals. Setbacks such as interruption of income, medical emergency, health problems, or marital breakup can knock down their lifestyle, assets, and credit as if they were bowling pins.

2. The Naive. Many consumers today do not know the consequences of unpaid debt. Some think that if they just ignore their debt, it will eventually go away. What usually goes away, however, is any chance for financial freedom.

3. Fortune's Victim. Yes, some people in debt have done everything right. They planned, they saved, they practiced responsible spending and lending. And yet, they suffer financial collapse due to some catastrophic life event. It's not fair, but indebtedness can and often does happen to conscientious, money-savvy people.

4. The Reckless Spender. These are people who, for whatever emotional reason, spend more than they have. They may impulse buy, cave in to salespeople, spend money on friends due to a need to be liked or have deep feelings of entitlement -- the "I deserve it" syndrome.

5. The Unethical. These are the fraudsters who borrow on credit with absolutely no intention of paying back their loans.

6. The Impoverished. Some high-risk consumers are issued credit cards by accident. Once they have it, they use it to make necessary purchases like food and clothing now with the added cost of finance charges.

Keleghan suggests that for each of these types of debtors, different methods are needed in helping settle their accounts. His study is based on the premise that a debtor's history can be used as a predictor of what will ultimately motivate the debtor to pay down delinquent debt.

For example, a client who appears to be fortune's victim may already possess a strong commitment toward the resolution of debt whereas the unethical debtor will have none. The imprudent and naïve debtors could use some help with being pro-active with their financial goals and learning more about lender policies. The reckless spender may need some quality time working out a disciplined budget and finding new ways to relieve stress.

The condition of being in debt feels different for different types of people. Many young people in debt express dismay and fear. They sincerely dont know how the amounts on their billing statements got so high. Often, they are the most susceptible to harassing calls from collectors because they lack knowledge of their consumer rights.

Older debtors, on the other hand, may take their debt more personally or as a sign of weakness. They may express embarrassment or humiliation. Outstanding debt can cause stress and distress in every aspect of an individual's life -- self-esteem, relationships, parenting, job performance and health.

The Fine Art of Tea

A visitor to Japan described his experience while visiting a famous tea house where the service of a cup of tea has been established as a fine art. While looking over the menu, he became puzzled why the price of a certain cup of tea was the equivalent of one U.S. dollar while another cup of tea on the menu costs $100. He asked the elderly proprietor for an explanation for the difference in price. The old man said, "The difference is that the cup that costs one dollar costs one dollar and the cup that costs $100 costs $100." With that, he bowed slightly and walked away.

This is an example of buying a product or service vs. buying a spending experience. Many people go clothes shopping to make themselves feel better. They bring the clothes home, hang them up in the wardrobe and never wear them. They are consumers of the experience only. The product itself is not important. Does the $100 tea taste better? Not really. But the $100 tea gives he who selected it a special feeling that the dollar tea can't. It's a pure spender's high.

DEALING WITH DEBT: THE GOOD, THE BAD AND THE WORST

Anselm Bassano identified four types of debtors in terms of how they handle their debt:

1. Panickers fail to prioritize their debts properly and regularly borrow more to pay off existing debts.

2. Mourners initially maintain a state of denial about their debts. Finally, when the situation sinks in, they get angry and blame creditors for their problems.

3. Rationalists do it the right way. They rank order their debts according to importance and negotiate payment plans based on available resources.

4. Fraudsters set out to abuse the system with no intention of ever paying back what was extended to them.

As a counselor, you will come in contact with all these types and more. Listen to them, assess their circumstance and appraise their emotions concerning their debt. Some clients may chuckle over their debt while others suffer from severe stress and anxiety. Clearly, different approaches are necessary in working to motivate and empower individuals who come from all walks of life and exhibit a wide variety of attitudes about money and debt.

SUMMARY

1. It is important for counselors to gain an understanding of the sources of debt for two reasons:

    a. it helps to increase counselor empathy toward clients in debt.
    b. it helps clients and counselors identify past financial stumbling blocks.

2. Prevalent reasons for indebtedness include easy access to credit and a lack of financial literacy among consumers.

3. Many consumers overspend due to unhealthy spending styles which include compulsive spending, co-dependent spending and revenge spending.

4. Consumer spending patterns may result from erroneous beliefs, attitudes and expectations about money.

5. Predatory lending is a growing trend in today's consumer culture; it is yet another source of problematic debt.

6. Indebtedness is a condition that affects different people in different ways.

1. Identify three of the most prevalent reasons for consumer debt.

2. Name at least two types of over-spenders.

3. Define predatory lending.

4. Describe how the condition of indebtedness can affect different clients.

Unit 19: Debt Collection

- To determine the different types of collectors.
- To learn about the Fair Debt Collection Practices Act.
- To learn what methods collection agencies may not use in collecting debts.

A consumer's account becomes delinquent when no payments are received by the end of the billing period. Usually, a letter will be sent by the creditor reminding the consumer that payment is due either immediately or by a specific date after which time late charges or other fees will be added to the outstanding balance. The majority of delinquent accounts are paid at this point by consumers who probably forgot to pay or who misplaced the billing statement. The relationship between consumer and creditor remains congenial and mutually productive.

When no payments are received after the second billing cycle and no positive negotiation has been worked out, the original creditor will mail out formal warnings to pay. These are, for the most part, not threatening but firm in tone. The creditor walks a thin line here because a consumer's business is to be valued and hopefully developed over time as a source of profit. At the same time, payment must be collected.

Generally, the lender does everything in its power to collect debt without resorting to tactics that may ultimately end a positive consumer/creditor relationship. Phone calls will be made asking for payment. Irate or evasive customers will be noted. Still, the creditor will probably handle the situation in a polite manner.

Debt delinquency becomes more serious after about three unpaid billing cycles. Something is wrong. Lenders know that the longer a debt goes unpaid, the less likely collection will be successful.

THREE TYPES OF COLLECTORS

1. Credit Grantors. Most original creditors have a collections department in which delinquent payments are segmented into buckets. A bucket identifies the billing cycle the account falls under. For example, bucket one indicates 30 days late while bucket two means 60 days late, etc. If the client is late within the first few cycles, he/she may be able to rescue the account from going to a collection agency. Creditors will re-age the account or mark current after several consistent payments.

177

However, once accounts have been charged-off (written off as a loss), the balance due may be outsourced to a collection agency or to an office owned by the creditor under another name. Sometimes a client will receive an alarming letter from an unknown collector. However, this may simply be the result of an overwhelming number of accounts being handled by the in-house collection department. The creditor simply hired out a low cost operation off-site.

2. Collection Agencies. Anytime an account falls between bucket 3 and bucket 6, a creditor may contract an outside agency to assume responsibility for collecting the unpaid debt. Collection agencies are given authorization by the credit grantor to collect money owed on a commission basis. Generally, they keep 50% - 60% of all the funds collected -- not a percentage of the actual debt.

Collection agencies also charge creditors a fee each time they contact the debtor. This, in part, accounts for the frequency of calls and letters a debtor may receive. Collection agencies may be hired out by the credit grantor or they may purchase the debt at discount. If the agency owns the debt, they have the right to sue for the amount of that debt. In the former case, the credit grantor reserves the right to implement legal action.

3. Attorneys. When a collection agency uses every possible legal tactic and is still unsuccessful in collecting a debt, the account may be referred to an attorney. This is usually done only when the amount of the debt is substantial since attorney fees can be quite high. Consumers who ignore letters from credit grantors or phone calls from collection agencies generally take notice of a formal letter from a lawyer. Attorneys often have special means for tracking debtors and confiscating missed payments. These practices often entail obtaining information from voter registration records, credit bureaus, utility and post offices, family or acquaintances, and former employers or landlords.

The attorney may take legal action against a debtor by filing a lawsuit. A summons is then served to the debtor. Most states have laws to deal with individuals who try and avoid being served a summons. If the process server is unable to find the debtor after three legitimate attempts, the summons may then be served to a substitute. This may be a relative, neighbor, friend, or co-worker. A duplicate summons is then mailed to the debtor relating that the summons has been served.

WHAT CAN THEY DO?

Compared with mortgage companies and other lenders of secured credit, unsecured credit grantors and hired collection agencies cannot do nearly as much harm. Basically, there are three things they can do:

1. Revoke credit privileges. Unless the credit extender has a monopoly on a product or service the debtor desires, this, in and of itself, should not cause alarm.

2. Damage credit rating. Some collectors may threaten damage to the debtor's credit in order to prompt immediate payment. In reality, if a debtor is behind on payments, it has already been reported to the credit bureau.

3. Sue to collect the debt. Many credit grantors are reluctant to sue for the collection of debt because litigation is expensive and time consuming. Most often, creditors threaten lawsuits in an effort to scare a debtor into paying delinquent bills.

DEALING WITH COLLECTORS

1. Prevent harassment before it begins. It is never advantageous to completely ignore an unpaid bill. The creditor should be contacted and the situation should be explained politely and truthfully. Never agree to a payment negotiation that is unrealistic. Once a creditor knows you are sincere in wanting to pay, the account will most likely not be turned over to a collection agency.

2. Request termination of contact. Once an account is handled by a collection agency, a letter requesting that all contact cease will eliminate harassing phone calls and letters. A reason for non-payment or description of previous harassment may be included. The collector may then send a final notice stating any further action to be taken. Always maintain a copy for personal records. If the collection agency continues contact, the collection agency could be in violation of The Fair Debt Collection Practices Act.

3. Dispute all billing errors. According to The Fair Credit Billing Act, consumers have 60 days after the receipt of a bill to dispute it in letter form. They must send a dispute letter to the address of the customer service department usually located on the back of the billing statement. Consumers include their name, account number, and why they believe the bill is in error. Copies of receipts of other purchases made within the period in question may be helpful in clarifying the billing error. As with all correspondence, the consumer should keep a copy for a personal file.

Within 30 days, the creditor must respond with some explanation of the charge. The consumer cannot be reported to the credit bureau as delinquent until the dispute is settled. (The creditor can, however, continue to add finance charges on the amount.) The dispute must be resolved by the creditor within two billing cycles and no later than 90 days. (See Unit 15: Using Credit Wisely for sample dispute letter.)

4. Dispute the debt. Within 5 days of the initial contact, a collection agency must send a written statement informing the consumer of the nature of the debt and the right to dispute the debt. Because the collection agency may attempt to hide this statement of rights within their letter, a consumer must thoroughly read all correspondence. If a client decides the debt is not justified, he/she needs to respond immediately by registered or certified letter.

Has the consumer ever been billed for merchandise returned or never received? Has a credit-card issuer ever charged the consumer twice for the same item or failed to credit a payment? While frustrating, these errors can be corrected. It takes a little patience and knowledge of the dispute settlement procedures outlined in the Fair Credit Billing Act.

5. Correspond in writing and keep records. Communicate all requests, responses and complaints by letter and keep copies of all correspondence. Use registered or certified mail for documentation.

6. Do no succumb to scare tactics. Never let threats mar judgment where financial decisions are at stake. Knowledge of consumer rights mitigates fear.

WHAT DEBT COLLECTORS CAN AND CANNOT DO

The Fair Debt Collection Practices Act (FDCPA) was passed in 1977 as a means to protect consumers and debtors from harassment or unfair treatment by debt collectors. In 1986, an amendment was made to include attorneys who collect debts as a regular part of their practice. Debt collectors must abide by FDCPA rules when attempting to collect delinquent debts.

Although this law has afforded debtors some protection, private collectors may still resort to underhanded scare tactics. If the collector is from the original retailer or lending institution, the FDCPA holds no restriction to debt collection practices. In this case, complaints of excessive telephone calls within a short time period or threatening correspondence are often hard to restrict.

Collection Agencies May Not:

1. Give misleading or false information about the debt to others.
2. Call after 9:00 p.m. or before 8:00 a.m. within client's time zone.
3. Interrupt the work routine of a clients employment.
4. Make excessive calls to clients at home or work as a method of harassment.
5. Send any letter that may appear to be an official government document.
6. Threaten a client or family member in a physical manner.
7. Imply that physical damage may occur to client's property.
8. Deposit a post-dated check before the date on the check.
9. Misrepresent themselves as a government agency or a law practice.
10. Continue to harass a client after being notified in writing to cease.

Collection Agencies Must Abide by the Following:

1. The initial collection call must be made between 8:00 a.m. and 9:00 p.m. at the debtor's home. The agent cannot harass, threaten physically or annoy the debtor. However, the agent can be forceful and explain in a normal tone the consequences to the debtor if he/she does not meet his/her obligation.

2. If the agent contacts the debtor, he must identify his employer and relate the reason for the call. The debtor is entitled to know the identity and reason for the call.

3. The agent can attempt to motivate the debtor by offering incentives for partial or full payment of the debt.

4. The agent can ask for personal information but the consumer does not have give it.

5. The agent has the right, using a normal speaking voice, to let the debtor know the legal options that are available to the agent and that the agent may use any legal action available. The agent also can tell the debtor the consequences if a judgment is won in favor of the collector.

6. An agent can file a proof of claim and request a meeting with the debtor. As a debtor, remember if the agent is making a secured claim, the debtor has the right to redeem certain secured merchandise by paying the creditor only the fair market value as determined by the court.

7. The agent can ask the debtor to renegotiate a new note. The debtor does not have to comply but an agent has the right to ask.

8. If the debtor is deceased, the agent may file a creditor's claim against the deceased debtor's estate, if any estate exists.

9. The agent, when attempting to contact the debtor at home and is informed that the debtor is not at home, may ask permission to telephone the debtor at work or wherever he may be at the time. If permission is given by the person answering the telephone, the agent may proceed and call the debtor at that number.

Remember, the collection agencies have rights, but they also have responsibilities. Make sure that they abide by their responsibilities and they do not abuse your client's rights.

Collection agencies will use every method available to them under the law. Agencies may try to confront the client in person. Another tactic employed by agencies is to call the client continuously at home or work. The agency will use this tactic to harass the client and disrupt his work routine. This could cause embarrassment in front of family members or co-workers.

As a counselor, give support and reassurance to the client. Don't let your client become intimidated. You must also, when establishing a plan, set up ways to prevent the collection agency from harassing the client. Familiarize yourself with the rights and responsibilities of debtors and take the measures necessary in assisting the client concerning confrontational collectors.

Determine the date of the first notice the client received from the collection agency and the last date the client made any payment on his/her debt. Most agencies will try to get the client to respond to its notices or calls within 60 days. This is the time frame when the probability of collecting the amount owed is highest. The longer the time period from the initial contact, the less chance there is of collecting the debt.

SUMMARY

1. The three types of representatives authorized to collect debt are credit grantors, collection agencies and attorneys.

2. The Fair Debt Collection Practices Act helps to protect consumers from the harassment of debt collectors.

3. Effective counselors are familiar with consumer rights and provide assurance to clients who are facing agency scare tactics.

4. Lenders of unsecured credit have the power to revoke credit privileges, negatively affect a consumer's credit report and initiate legal action.

5. The Fair Credit Billing Act helps provide consumer protection with regards to billing errors.

REVIEW QUESTIONS

1. Identity the three different types of collectors.

2. What is the purpose of the Fair Debt Collection Practices Act?

3. List three things collectors can do in the attempt to get consumer's to pay their debts.

4. List three things collectors are NOT allowed to do when attempting to collect unpaid debts.

Unit 20: The Consequences of Unpaid Debt

OBJECTIVES
- To gain awareness of the legal repercussions of unpaid debt.
- To understand why secured credit is a priority to pay back.
- To understand the processes of foreclosure, eviction and repossession.
- To explore what clients can do to avoid negative, sometimes devastating, outcomes.

Whenever a consumer has delinquent debts, it is important to decide which accounts are essential to pay and which are not as critical to resolve. This can be done only by understanding the consequences of each type of debt delinquency. Should a bank or creditor take legal action against a client, you must advise the client to seek legal representation. However, there are steps that can be taken to avoid worst-case scenarios.

SECURED OR UNSECURED?
Is the outstanding debt secured or unsecured? This should be the first question when prioritizing a payment schedule. We remember that secured credit is a loan backed by collateral. Collateral is property (real or otherwise) that can be seized in the event of a debt delinquency.

Common examples of secured credit are home mortgages and automobile loans. Should mortgage payments fall behind, the lender can seize your home (foreclosure). Should car payments lapse, the bank can literally drive your car away (repossession). Credit card companies that enlist collection agencies to harass for immediate payments should not deter you from settling secured debts first.

Lenders of unsecured credit do not have the legal powers that lenders of secured credit have. This is because lenders of unsecured credit must first seek and win a court judgment before money or property can be seized. Generally speaking, threats to sue for monies owed are often never carried out because litigation is a costly and time-consuming process. Therefore, decide which debts are secured and pay them first!

Victory Over Fear
Clients may express fear and uncertainty in light of frightening notices from collection agencies or court orders from lenders or attorneys. Fears can be diminished through knowledge. What can lenders really do? What can't they do? When and how should a client negotiate with creditors? What can be done to avoid the damaging repercussions of outstanding debt?

What follows are brief descriptions of what can happen when debts are not paid. They include foreclosure, eviction, repossession, utility shut-offs, and judgment liens that can result in bank account seizure, garnishment of wages, as well as other types of liens.

As a counselor, you will want to know how your client can avoid the worst from happening. There are also tactics listed for getting payment amounts decreased should the client be unable to keep essential debts current.

Contrary to popular myth, you will not go to jail for unpaid bills (with the exception of non-payment of child support). You can, however, be imprisoned for committing fraud. When negotiating with lenders or their attorneys, it is imperative that you are forthcoming and honest with all information you may furnish them.

FORECLOSURE

This is a homeowner's worst nightmare. Typically, if you have missed one or two mortgage payments, the lender will contact you by letter and telephone asking for the outstanding balance plus any late fees. These can be 5% - 6% of the monthly payment. After 60 to 90 days, if you do not pay or make contact with the lender, you will receive a formal notice in the mail. This is called the Notice of Default. It is the first step in the foreclosure process. At this point, you have 90 days to cure the debt by making up all your missed payments plus late charges. This will re-instate your loan and stop a foreclosure from proceeding.

If you still do not pay or contact the lender in the allotted amount of time, another formal notice will arrive in the mail -- the Notice of Acceleration. Literally, what you owe the lender is accelerated so that the full amount of the mortgage is due immediately to avoid a foreclosure sale.

In some states, a court order is required before the lender can move to actually foreclose on your property. This will come delivered in the form of a summons at which time you will have the opportunity to respond and raise a defense. If you do not respond, a judgment to foreclose will proceed and the Notice of Sale is sent to your house. It gives the time and date that the foreclosure will take place.

Foreclosure can take anywhere from 6 to 18 months to complete depending on how fast the lender moves, individual state laws and the circumstances and actions of the homeowner.

AVOIDING FORECLOSURE

Avoiding foreclosure means keeping your mortgage payments current and paying property taxes and insurance on time. If a client is behind on his/her mortgage or even if he/she has already received a Notice of Default, there are strategies and options available for either reducing monthly payments or deferring certain expenses.

Up until the date of foreclosure sale, consumers have certain rights as homeowners including the right to sell. The question is: Can the homeowner realistically keep up with the mortgage payments or is the financial setback only temporary? If it's temporary, a workout may be the answer. If paying the monthly mortgage bill is simply not feasible given income versus expenses, then the house should be sold before a foreclosure sale ends the current homeowner's right to do so.

Mortgage Workouts

If a client is having trouble paying the mortgage, he/she can negotiate for an easier payment schedule either temporarily or permanently with the lender. This is known as a mortgage workout. Recently, banks and mortgage companies have become more willing to negotiate workouts with consumers to avoid the cost and time associated with foreclosure. Remember, a foreclosure can be a long, complicated process requiring documentation, correspondence and, in some states, court hearings. A workout can avoid all that. A common workout is an arrangement to cure a default by adding a percentage of the outstanding debt, known as the arrears, to the regular monthly payments until the debt becomes current.

Another option is recasting the outstanding debt. If the homeowner is able to make the monthly mortgage payments, but cannot make up any past due installments, the arrears can be deferred or recast so that it is no longer a present obligation. It is recast as payment due at the end of the loan term.

Consumers may also ask for a temporary (or in some cases permanent) interest rate reduction. They can even request a temporary moratorium on mortgage payments depending on the situation. Late fees and other penalties are commonly waived as long as the consumer communicates a sincere wish to resolve the debt. Workouts are no longer limited to one year. Today, arrangements lasting up to 36 months are common.

Once the lender accelerates the loan and the full amount of the mortgage is due, options diminish. Few people have the money necessary to satisfy a Notice of Acceleration. Often, a second loan is procured to pay off the first one. This may delay foreclosure, but it makes little sense. Generally, the terms of the second loan will be even more difficult to satisfy than the first one.

EVICTION

Being evicted from an apartment is, at the very least, disruptive. It can also be dangerous given that it can mean becoming homeless should the renter have no alternative place to live. When the rent is due and not paid, the landlord has the right to force the renter out through the eviction process. Just how this is accomplished varies considerably depending on state and city laws. For example, in New York, California, and Massachusetts, an eviction can take as long as a couple of months whereas in states that provide less consumer protections, a landlord could evict in a matter of two weeks.

The first step in the eviction process is when the renter receives the Notice to Quit -- sometimes called the Notice to Vacate -- from the landlord. Basically, it tells the renter to pay up or vacate the premises within a very short amount of time. It is not a court order but a warning which gives renters the right to stay put if they pay the amount owed in back-rent (cure the debt).

After the time allotted on the Notice to Quit has expired and the renter has not paid the debt, the landlord can file an eviction action in court. In some states, a landlord can file an action in court without the benefit of a formal warning. A hearing is then scheduled and the renter will receive a summons to appear in court.

If the renter does not attend the hearing, the landlord gets a default judgment against him/her. The landlord then takes it to the sheriff whose job it is to enforce the eviction. Some states require a week's notice before the renters are forced out. Often the actual eviction takes longer depending on the sheriff's schedule. If the renter is not out by the date of eviction, his/her belongings can be removed and put on the street.

Ignoring the eviction process is disastrous. When people are forced to move against their will, they are, in effect, refugees. Their circumstances are turned upside down. Their expenses will actually increase as they scramble to find shelter, storage, parking for a vehicle, and food. Also, the landlord, like any extender of credit, has the right to sue for all unpaid back-rent.

If the renter signed a lease, he/she is also legally bound to pay for all future months until the end of the lease period.

AVOIDING EVICTION

This frightening scenario illustrates the absolute necessity for paying rent on time. If a client is having trouble coming up with the money due to a temporary financial setback, have him/her contact the landlord and explain the situation. The landlord may agree to a temporary rent reduction. Another option is to negotiate for the acceptance of weekly rent payments until the renter is caught up. If moving out is inevitable, have renters do so on their own terms. Ask for reduced rent payment in exchange for voluntarily moving by a certain date.

Of course, the landlord has no obligation to agree to anything. He/she may wish to avoid the eviction process, but that depends on the desirability of the rental property and his/her rapport with the renter.

Renter's Rights

Whether or not a renter has a defense, he/she should attend the eviction hearing to make sure that the amount of back-rent the landlord is suing for is correct. Also, that is a good time to present mitigating circumstances such as an illness or job loss to get an extension before the eviction takes effect.

Landlords cannot seize personal property without a court order or lock tenants out of their home. If these actions take place, renters have the right to countersue. Also, landlords cannot evict in retaliation for reporting substandard housing conditions. If a tenant becomes involved in any of these circumstances, they should get legal representation.

AUTOMOBILE REPOSSESSION

Theoretically, a default occurs as soon as one payment of any installment loan is missed. The lender then has the right to seize whatever property was guaranteed as collateral. In the case of automobile loans, the lender can put a lien on the car and sell it to recoup some of the money owed. Some states require the lender to send a Notice of Default giving the car owner the opportunity to cure the loan. However, in a state without this requirement, people may not even know they are in default!

Therefore, it is essential to keep track of secured loan payments. If it is uncertain whether a car is subject to repossession, check the lender's contract to see if the vehicle is listed under security. Also, check the certificate of title to see who is listed as owner. If the lender is listed as owner, then the consumer is leasing the car -- so it is subject to repossession anytime the loan is in default.

Henchmen with crowbars coming to take your automobile is a myth. The "repo man" cannot take a car by force. Any breach of the peace is illegal and a person has the right to sue should this occur. Still, the car can be taken at any time, opened with a duplicate key and even hot-wired.

Cars can be taken from open garages and, in some states, unlocked closed garages. When a person is in default of the automobile loan, he/she is probably under surveillance. The lender provides the "repo" man (or woman) with personal information about a person's whereabouts, workplace, address, school schedule, or anywhere he/she habitually drives to and leaves the car unattended. Cars are then most often driven away quietly.

Getting a repossessed automobile back is expensive and, in some cases, difficult. In a specified, short amount of time, it may be possible to re-instate the loan under its original conditions by paying the amount owed, plus late fees, plus the expense the lender paid to repossess and store the vehicle. This could amount to several hundred dollars more than what was owed at first default.

The lender has the right to reject attempts to re-instate the loan if the car has been repossessed in the past or there is fraudulent information on the credit application. Also, if there was an attempt to hide your vehicle from the possibility of repossession or if the re-possessor was assaulted, reinstatement likely will be denied.

The Deficiency Balance. Relinquishing an automobile and letting the lender sell it does not end the trouble. Typically, repossessed cars are sold at private sales where used automobile dealers bid and purchase vehicles at drastically reduced prices. A car valued at $14,000 might go for as little as $6,000. After the sale, it's up to the person who defaulted to make up the difference to the lender. This is known as the deficiency balance. For example, if $8,000 on the car loan is owed, but it sold for only $3,500, then the difference as well as the expenses incurred in the process of repossessing, storing and selling the former property is owed.

OPTIONS

If a car is repossessed or if a notice of default has been received, contact the lender and request that the loan be reinstated long enough for the owner to sell the car on his/her own. Provided that the vehicle has been maintained properly and shows no damage, an independent sale will raise more money to pay back the lender than a repossession sale would.

Lenders also have been known to waive the deficiency balance if there is obviously no way to pay and no assets to seize. However, the amount forgiven by a lender must be reported to the IRS as income.

It is also possible to negotiate a workout with the lender, especially if the value of the car is less than the amount owed on the loan. Typically, the lender would agree not to seize the vehicle as long as reduced monthly payments were maintained.

The chosen option in the face of repossession should depend on the importance of the vehicle to a consumer's everyday life, how much has been paid into it, and the risk of incurring a deficiency balance. Also, the client must realistically determine his/her ability to pay for and maintain the vehicle over the long haul.

UTILITY SHUT-OFFS

Unlike credit-card companies and department stores that must resort to collection agencies to recoup unpaid debts, utility companies can discontinue essential services when bills are not paid on time. These service companies provide the modern conveniences that are actually indispensable for living comfortably and productively in today's society.

Any interruption of service whether it be water, heat, electricity or telephone presents an extreme disruption. Service termination also brings unforeseen expenses into the picture. For example, if the electricity is turned off, cooking and storing food is not an option. This means eating out for every meal. If the water is cut off, the home is virtually uninhabitable. Without a telephone, the link to the outside world is severed. Making calls would require a drive around the block and a bag full of change. Receiving calls would no longer be possible without standing by a pay phone for a good part of the day. Update: Pay phones are becoming a thing of the past!

Publicly owned utility companies must, by law, send a notice stating that they will terminate service unless bills are paid. The customer is then given the opportunity to pay within a specified amount of time. Usually the threat of a shut-off is enough to convince the customer to pay all or a portion of the outstanding bill immediately. Privately owned companies may not be required to notify the customer and can simply cut service without warning.

Getting the utility service turned back on after termination is not always easy. It usually requires full payment of back-bills plus late charges, plus a re-installment fee and, in some cases, a deposit. A customer may try and get the additional fees waived by convincing the utility company of a temporary financial setback that is now resolved. Also, customers may negotiate to pay their past-due bills in installments over a certain period of time. When a deposit is required, it is generally equivalent to the average of two monthly bills. A deposit requirement may be avoided by providing the signature of a co-signer who then becomes responsible for payment of defaulted bills.

REDUCING UTILITY BILLS

If a client has had problems in the past keeping up with utility payments, chances are those same problems will continue in the future unless monthly service bills are reduced. Here are some options available to the consumer when current utility bills become burdensome or simply unaffordable.

Discount Plans. Clients may qualify for reduced rates on their utility bills through public assistance. Many utility companies have programs available for low-income customers. Information about these plans can be obtained by contacting the utility company or your state public utility commission.

Changing or Eliminating Unnecessary Services. Some utilities are nonessential and should be voluntarily canceled during financially hard times. Some of these discretionary services include cable television, internet service, extra telephone lines, and cellular telephone service. Additionally, there are ways to customize bills for service contingent on specific usage. For example, telephone companies offer a variety of payment plans that reduce rates at certain times of the day or on weekends. The same is true for companies that provide electricity.

Reducing Your Utility Usage. There are several ways to cut utility bills through energy efficient light bulbs, low flow faucets and winterization. Customers may be eligible for low-cost or even free conservation assistance. Again, check with the utility company or contact the federal Low Income Home Energy Assistance Program (LIHEAP).

Remember, effective problem solving depends on knowledge and the creative ability necessary to take steps to avoid negative contingencies. If you do have a client facing eviction or foreclosure or utility terminations, you will want to be able to provide reassurance and strategies to minimize financial setbacks.

CONSUMER RIGHTS

Protections against termination of utility services as well as eligibility for government assistance varies depending on who your provider is. However, the general rules by which companies must adhere are as follows:

- Utility companies must provide notification of impending shut-off.
- Customers have a right to a hearing.
- Customers have a right to arrange for deferred payments.
- Customers are protected from shut-offs during winter months.
- The seriously ill are protected from service termination.
- Landlords cannot terminate service to their renters.

LAWSUITS

When a consumer falls behind on payments to a lender of unsecured credit, the lender has the legal right to sue to get what is owed. Since property was not pledged as collateral, a court judgment is required in order for the lender to seize either property or assets to satisfy the amount of the debt. The consumer can choose to fight the lawsuit which, in some cases, is enough to get the creditor to drop the case. If the case is not contested, the lender wins a default judgment against the consumer.

This may or may not be cause for alarm since the lender may not follow through to actually seize the property. More often than not, threats to seize personal property are just that. The resale value on bedroom furniture or a piece of heirloom jewelry may be negligible, but the possibility of someone taking an item of sentimental value from someone may very well convince the consumer to arrange payment. Threats to seize heirloom jewelry or furniture are often effective tactics creditors use to collect debts.

Successful lawsuits filed by creditors can result in the following:

Judgment Liens. When a lien is placed on a piece of property, whether it be a home, vehicle, furniture, or electronic equipment, the title on that property is unclear. Until the title is cleared up (by settling the debt) the owner is prohibited from selling or re-financing the property involved in the lien. Once the judgment lien is won, the lender has the right to examine the assets. Then the lender must make a formal request to the court or sheriff to seize or sell the property. Certain possessions are exempt from seizure. These include household items of little resalable value. Your shirt cannot literally be taken off your back! Other items are protected from seizure depending on individual state laws including homes in some cases.

Wage Garnishment and Bank Account Seizures. Up to 25% of a person's take-home pay can be intercepted and seized. More can be taken if the debt involves unpaid child support. In most cases, a consumer has the right to a hearing before wages are garnished. If a court order is won, the order for garnishment is relayed either directly to the person's employer or to his/her bank. Laws vary widely from state to state regarding garnishments. In some states, it is quite common while in others, it is virtually impossible to carry out. Attending hearing proceedings is imperative and obtaining legal counsel is strongly advised.

THE IMPORTANCE OF NEGOTIATION

When a lawsuit is filed, or even if it is threatened as a collection tactic, the special relationship between creditor and consumer is in dire jeopardy. It is almost always in the best interest of lender and debtor alike to try and maintain a mutually satisfactory arrangement through a feasible workout of some kind.

The lender wants customers not litigants. If a debtor is unable to keep up with any agreed upon payment schedule, contact the lender and explain the situation. Avoiding calls from creditors and collection agencies will result in the debtor being seen as a "credit criminal" -- someone who has no intention of settling debts incurred through products or services already obtained. Avoiding contact may cause lenders to increase the severity of collection tactics and move forward with legal action.

It is better to be seen as a consumer who, like many, has over-estimated his/her ability to afford what has been purchased. Creditors want to see that customers acknowledge the debt and want to resolve it. From there, a compromise either can be drawn up in the form of a document or agreed to verbally over the telephone. That way, the lender maintains another customer and the consumer keeps the benefits of credit open.

SUMMARY

1. When prioritizing debts, secured credit should be resolved first.

2. Understanding the legal consequences of unpaid debt and how to mitigate them gives clients power over fear.

3. Foreclosure can be a long, complex process requiring 6 - 18 months to complete.

4. Common mortgage workouts include curing the debt and recasting past-due installments.

5. Eviction is a devastating and often swiftly executed procedure.

6. Effective counselors inform their clients about their consumer rights and the available options for resolving unpaid debts.

7. Negotiating is key to mitigating the severest outcomes of unpaid debt.

8. Retrieving a vehicle from repossession is difficult and expensive; relinquishing it to the lender will result in a deficiency balance.

9. Consumers have several options for reducing or altering their utility billings.

10. Lenders of unsecured credit have the right to sue for what is owed them. More often than not, they do not follow through with court actions due to the expense of time and money.

REVIEW QUESTIONS

1. Briefly outline the process of foreclosure.

2. Provide three examples of common mortgage workout agreements.

3. Explain what a deficiency balance is with regards to automobile repossession.

4. Explain why threats by creditors to seize personal property are usually never carried out.

5. List possible actions that may be taken by a creditor who has won a court judgment against a debtor.

Unit 21: Getting Out of Debt

OBJECTIVES

- To explore consumer options for dealing with debt.
- To examine the difference between Chapter 7 and Chapter 13 Bankruptcy.
- To identify what debts CANNOT be discharged in a Chapter 7 Bankruptcy.

Consumers who are struggling with unresolved debt have two basic options:

1. They can resolve the debt.
2. They can file bankruptcy.

Most consumers will wish to avoid bankruptcy if at all possible. Bankruptcy is available to the consumer as a last resort when the amount of unpaid debt is simply beyond the consumer's ability to pay back.

Therefore, it is important to carefully consider all the options available to resolve debt issues with the least detrimental effects to both the consumer's current spending plan and his or her credit rating. You will see that there are several options for avoiding bankruptcy but some are misleading and may even exacerbate a situation that is already desperately out of control.

RESOLVING THE DEBT

For the most part, clients will want to resolve their debt issues through some kind of workout. That means paying back their creditors all or at least an agreed upon portion of the debt. This plan of action presents several alternatives. Arrangements for repayment include a lump-sum discount or reduced payment amounts with an increased term of repayment. Reduction or elimination of interest may or may not be a feature with these arrangements.

The options available to the consumer facing unresolved debt will depend on his or her financial circumstance. Generally, the more dire the circumstance, the fewer the options. Let's take a look:

Consumer Workouts. Consumer workouts occur when those who are having trouble paying their bills contact their creditors directly and attempt to negotiate an agreed upon arrangement for payment. Usually creditors accommodate sincere consumers when they try to remedy their difficulty or inability to pay a bill. However, as soon as consumers fall behind in payments -- even by a month or two -- the creditor has the upper hand. Creditors can easily penalize those who do not pay on time by charging late fees and adding blemishes to a credit report. In other words, negotiating with creditors is not always easy to say the least. Resolving debt without professional assistance can be a viable option for those experiencing a temporary financial setback. However, negotiating with creditors requires motivation, commitment and a spending plan.

Debt Consolidation Loans. Debt consolidation loans give consumers the ability to pay off their high-interest accounts typically through lowered monthly payments. However, the term of the loan agreement is longer. This type of repayment plan requires that the consumer apply and qualify for the loan. That means the consumer must have the ability to make on time payments. It also means the consumer's credit rating has to be in relatively good shape.

The most common type of consolidation loans today are home equity loans. Homeowners who find themselves in debilitating debt have the option to pay off their accounts by using the equity they have earned as collateral to procure a loan. The downside, of course, is that consumers are trading their unsecured debt for secured debt. If they default on a home equity loan, the lender could initiate the foreclosure process. Consumers who opt for a home equity loan must have self control so they do not continue to use credit as they have in the past. A survey conducted by Consumer Bankers Association found that within one year, 70% of the people who got home equity loans were again running up credit debt.

Another type of debt consolidation is 0% transfers. These offers sound good but can be extremely costly for the consumer. Your unpaid balance from a high-interest loan is transferred to a new 0% interest account. This could be beneficial if the consumer is truly committed to making consistent payments. However, there are some startling disadvantages to this plan.

First, any new purchases are still charged interest. Furthermore, any payments the consumer makes go only to the transferred balance amount. So, you can't take care of the balances arising from new purchases until the transferred amount is paid off. 0% transfers typically come with severe penalties. For example, if the consumer makes one late payment, that 0% is history. Consumers who choose this method of dealing with debt must restrain themselves from making new credit purchases until the transferred account is paid in full.

Chapter 13 Bankruptcy is a court approved consolidation.

Credit Counseling. Credit counselors may enroll clients in debt management plans or DMPs that involve one monthly payment. That payment is handled by the agency and dispersed to the various creditors. They receive what is known as fair share from the creditors which is a percentage of the collected payment. To qualify for credit counseling, consumers must have a steady source of income in order to make regular monthly payments. They also must be committed to resolving their outstanding debt as a DMP may take up to four years to complete depending on the amount of debt.

Debt Settlement. Debt settlement, sometimes referred to as debt negotiation, offers consumers the option to resolve their debts with a lump-sum payment. The debtor must come up with the agreed upon amount in order to pay off the debt all at once. This could require a period of time in which to save the necessary funds. In some cases, a client in debt settlement pays into an account. As cash accumulates, the debt negotiator works out a reduced settlement amount with the creditors.

This alternative holds promise for consumers with sizable debt issues who wish to avoid a declaration of bankruptcy. Typically, clients in debt settlement must endure a period of increased debt collection activity while they cease making regular payments to their creditors. However, for many debtors, this is a viable alternative to a Chapter 7 Bankruptcy.

Budget Counseling. Many individuals who are experiencing financial stress would benefit from budget counseling. This type of counseling is offered by agencies to help consumers analyze their monthly expenses and develop a spending plan so they can pay their bills on time. In some cases, budget counseling is also offered to support clients who enroll in debt management and debt settlement plans.

Consumers in debt must wrestle with a number of issues if they are to resolve overdue bills. First and foremost is coming up with the money to cover the debts. Many individuals and families are simply over their financial heads with unpaid debt. Basically, they must cut their expenses, increase their income, or both.

Another big issue to consider is the consumer's credit rating. How will it be affected by a particular repayment option? This is especially important when consumers have maintained a good payment history and their credit rating is in good standing. However, some consumers will have been delinquent for an extended period of time causing their credit rating to have already been severely damaged.

In all cases, dealing with debt requires three things:

1. The client must fully understand his or her financial situation. That includes knowing all incomes and monthly expenses as well as his or her current credit score.

2. The client must develop a plan of action based on personal goals and a complete evaluation of all options appropriate for the client.

3. The client must be committed to paying off delinquent debt. Paying off debts needs to be seen as a way of taking control of life and getting free from financial stress. Resolving debt can literally take anywhere from several months to several years. Clients need a stick-to-it attitude to succeed.

Reasons NOT To Go It Alone

Many consumers are reluctant to seek help with their debt issues. They may feel that their personal financial problems are a private matter. They may also feel that reaching out for assistance is a sign of weakness. However, there are a couple of points to consider that may help clients realize that personal debt issues, especially severe debt, can best be resolved with professional help.

First, dealing with debt is not pleasant. It requires time on the telephone talking to creditors who may or may not wish to negotiate with you. It takes a certain level of tenacity that many people just do not possess. Also, going it alone can create a lot of aggravation and stress.

Debt management and debt settlement agencies are often in a much better position to negotiate with creditors. They have developed working relationships with lenders and credit-card issuers. Also, because of the large number of accounts that organizations handle, they have the opportunity to receive volume discounts. Finally, agencies know about the latest industry trends and special offers for resolving delinquent accounts.

Effective counselors help clients to consider *all* the alternatives.

A CLOSER LOOK AT CREDIT COUNSELING

According to the Pension Protection Act of 2006, credit counseling agencies must tailor their services to meet the individual needs of the client. The best agencies already adhere to this now mandatory standard.

Effective agencies strive to emphasize the counseling aspect of credit counseling -- especially during the initial interview. Gathering incomes and expenses from vulnerable clients takes time. It also takes time to determine the type of service most appropriate for the client. Effective counselors focus on the client's complete financial picture.

In some cases, a client's debt situation can be addressed through a debt management plan. A debt management plan or DMP is the implementation of an agreement between the agency and the client's creditors. It allows the client to make one single payment that is then distributed to the creditors participating in the plan. Typical plans can last from three to five years.

How a Debt Management Plan Works

A DMP begins when the creditors accept an individualized proposal for repaying delinquent loan amounts. An accepted proposal is known as a Debt Management Agreement. For participating in a repayment plan, clients will often receive concessions from the creditors.

TYPICAL CREDITOR CONCESSIONS

Interest rates are lowered or eliminated. After the client establishes regular payments, many creditors will reduce or eliminate interest fees. More of the client's money goes towards paying off the principle as opposed to finance charges.

Accounts are re-aged. Even before a client has paid off an account, the creditor will often re-age the account so that its status is current. Usually, this benefit occurs after the client has made three or four on-time payments to the DMP. In some cases, the account is re-aged when the proposal is accepted by the creditor.

Late and over-the-limit fees are eliminated. Depending on the creditor, late and over-the-limit fees are eliminated at the point when the proposal is received or when the account is re-aged (made current). Some creditors do not impose late fees as long as the client is in a DMP. Others, however, will continue to charge late fees in the event that payments are not on time.

In some cases, these benefits to the client are automatic. In other cases, the client receives the concession after the payment plan has been established through regular, on-time payments.

SUPPORT AND MAINTENANCE OF THE PLAN

Throughout the DMP, clients can expect assistance from the agency. Large agencies usually have a customer service department to handle any problems or issues that might come up. Throughout the process, the counselor or customer service agent acts as a liaison between creditor and client to resolve problems. Issues that may arise include:

Billing errors. A late fee or other type of fee may appear on a billing statement that is not listed in the agreement.

Payment not received by creditor. Payments involve money orders, cashiers checks, or automatic account withdrawals. It is a priority that these payments are received on time.

Changes in the DMP. During the course of the plan, various changes may occur. Creditors may be added or, when an account is paid off, removed from the plan. Also, the client may initiate various changes as to when and how they will make their monthly payments.

APPROPRIATENESS OF A DMP

Whether the program is appropriate for a particular client depends on:

The amount of debt. The debt load must be within the parameters set according to the policies of individual agencies. If the amount of debt is lower than the threshold amount, other options may present themselves during the counseling session. Over a certain amount, the plan may not accommodate it.

The type of debt. Generally speaking, debt management helps in the resolution of unsecured debt. Creditors of secured loans do not need to negotiate with borrowers. Their loans are backed by collateral.

The client's current financial situation. The client's circumstance must be considered holistically. In other words, it's not just about their unsecured debt dilemma. Other factors include their level of secured debt, their monthly budget, and the client's short and long-term financial goals.

Agencies often determine a minimum debt amount in order to enroll in a DMP. The debts generally must be unsecured although some agencies assist with other types of debt. Also, the client must show a level of monthly income sufficient to maintain the proposed payment plan.

BENEFITS TO THE CREDITOR

From the creditor's point of view, customers who enroll in debt management plans are doing something about their debt. Though they may be in default of a loan, the creditor is open to negotiation because, with a commitment to debt management, the customer in default has pro-actively taken the first step. Both creditor and borrower are linked in their desire to resolve the debt.

- A debt management plan is a cost effective alternative to the creditor selling a delinquent account to a collection agency often for as little as $.020 on the dollar. Instead, the creditor makes a fair share contribution to the credit counseling agency while recouping a larger percentage of the original debt.

- The debt management plan is also a viable alternative to bankruptcy for many delinquent borrowers. Unsecured creditors have less power than secured creditors when it comes to a default. There is no collateral to seize. Unsecured debts are usually wiped out in a Chapter 7 bankruptcy.

- Another benefit to the creditor is that participation in a DMP shows that the creditor is willing to work with consumers in financial trouble. It helps the creditor from a public relations standpoint.

RESPONSIBILITIES OF THE CLIENT

The Federal Trade Commission has recommended that clients participating in a debt management plan do the following:

Make regular, timely payments. Usually, clients can choose what time of the month their payment becomes due. They can also opt for an automatic deposit of their monthly payment.

Monitor your monthly statements. Clients should not relinquish their responsibility to check and read mailings from their creditors. Participation in a DMP does not mean you get to throw away you billing statements! Alert the agency immediately if the creditor is not receiving payments.

Inform the agency about any changes in your circumstance. Just as you would contact a creditor if you are having difficulty making a payment, clients need to let their counselors know when there is a problem. The agency can offer budget counseling or the plan may be adjusted for the client.

FREQUENTLY ASKED QUESTIONS

While it is important for counselors to assess the client's financial situation, it is also crucial that credit counselors provide answers to questions that clients will have regarding the process of debt management. Here are some of the more frequently asked questions fielded by counselors.

How can a debt management plan help me with my monthly budget?

By consolidating all your payment dates to one date that is most convenient, you will be able to set up a simpler, more efficient monthly budget.

Will a debt management plan stop collection letters and telephone calls?

Some creditors may continue to contact you until you establish a regular payment history. If you do experience collection activity after several on-time payments to the DMP, call the credit counseling agency's customer service.

How will I know that my payments are going to my creditors?

You will receive monthly statements listing the accounts on the plan.

If I enroll in a debt management plan, can I still use my credit cards?

Generally, accounts over a certain balance will be closed. The goal of the DMP is to get you out of debt as soon as possible. Incurring more debt will only prolong the process. In some cases, however, clients are allowed to maintain one card.

How does a debt management plan affect my credit report?

This depends on your current credit rating. If you have perfect credit, than participation in a DMP may have a negative effect. However, if your credit is already blemished from late payments or charge-offs, a DMP can have a positive effect. Some creditors report reduced payments as late or they may insert a line stating "payments administered by credit counseling agency." If, in the course of the DMP, accounts are re-aged, then the effect will be positive. Successfully completing a DMP will help in re-establishing credit.

What if I file bankruptcy?

That depends on whether you file a Chapter 7 or a Chapter 13. In a Chapter 7 bankruptcy, you may be required to surrender all assets not exempt in your state. You may receive a discharge where you debts are wiped out but the bankruptcy could remain on your credit report for up to 10 years. With a Chapter 13 bankruptcy, you get to keep your assets while paying into a re-payment plan that may last for up to 5 years. As with a Chapter 7, it may remain of your report for 10 years. Keep in mind that several types of debt are non-dischargeable through bankruptcy. These include child support, alimony, taxes and certain student loan obligations.

What's the difference between a debt management plan and a Chapter 13 bankruptcy?

Through a DMP, consumers maintain a positive relationship with their creditors. A Chapter 13 bankruptcy may discharge any unpaid portion of your debts at the end of the payment period. With a DMP, creditors are not forced to write off debts owed to them.

Will a DMP protect me from creditor legal action?

Creditors will retain the right to take you to court even if you are enrolled in debt management. In the event that a creditor notifies you of a legal action, the credit counseling agency can provide you with records of your payment history which can serve as evidence of your good faith effort to repay the debt.

Can I withdraw from a debt management plan at any time?

Participation in a DMP is completely voluntary. However, if you drop out of the program, you will lose the benefits of the agreement. Your monthly payments will no longer be consolidated and your overall monthly amounts will increase. Also, collection activity will resume.

A CLOSER LOOK A DEBT SETTLEMENT

Debt settlement offers a way to avoid bankruptcy for people with significant debt issues who have run out of options. What is debt settlement and how exactly does it work? Let's find out.

History

A debt settlement is an agreement between a creditor and a debtor to satisfy a debt for a reduced payoff amount. Since the debtor is unable to fully meet his/her debt obligations, the creditor agrees to reduce the debt and accept the agreed upon sum as full payment.

Although the practice of settling debts through a third party began soon after the invention of money, debt settlement as a business service is relatively new. Debt settlement developed in the late 1980s and early 1990s as bank deregulation, coupled with an economic recession, left many consumers facing financial hardships.

In the late 1980s, banks set up debt settlement departments to address the high number of charge-offs generated from cardholders defaulting on loans. Bank personnel were authorized to negotiate with consumers and settle outstanding balances for payments that ranged from 25% to 65% of the amount owed. From their standpoint, something was better than nothing.

By the early 1990s, independent agencies were established for the negotiation and settlement of consumer debt. Today, the debt settlement industry continues to grow as individuals and families find themselves in unresolved debt dilemmas.

THE DEBT SETTLEMENT PROCESS

Debt settlement is process wherein the debtor saves money earmarked for a particular creditor, a settlement amount is negotiated, and a lump-sum payment is made to the creditor. It is repeated for each outstanding account until all accounts are considered "settled-in-full."

There are essentially three steps to this process which involves three players -- the debtor, the creditor and the negotiator:

1. **Notifying the creditors.** The negotiator will contact each creditor and notify them that, due to financial hardship, the debtor cannot make payments on the account. Instead, the debtor is seeking a negotiated settlement to resolve the debt.

2. **Establishing a savings account.** A special savings account is established in the debtor's name into which monthly payments are accumulated. The funds remain in the account until a formal agreement to settle with one creditor is reached.

3. **Paying the creditor.** When the funds in the account are sufficient to settle the debt, the creditor is paid.

This process is repeated for each remaining creditor. Some accounts are settled with one lump-sum payment while others are paid through short-term installment payments depending on the debt amount and the creditor's policies.

THE DEBT SETTLEMENT CLIENT

Debt settlement is an alternative available for consumers who are facing bankruptcy but do not qualify for debt consolidation. Often they must choose between paying off bills and buying essentials such as groceries and heating fuel. Debt settlement offers to lower the amounts owed typically by 25 - 65% and therefore resolve debts faster.

To enroll in a debt settlement program, the consumer must have a substantial amount of unsecured debt. Usually, this amount is at least between $7,500 and $10,000 although some companies will work with smaller debt loads. Secured debts such as mortgage and car payments cannot be negotiated because the creditors can simply repossess the property that was purchased.

Clients are often advised to:

Communicate with creditors. If a creditor calls, it may be in order to inform you that an account has been moved by the creditor to a different agent or collector. Clients help the process by monitoring account changes and reporting them to the debt settlement company.

Utilize budget counseling. Many companies offer budget counseling or financial coaching to assist clients in the development of a viable spending plan that supports consistent payments to the savings account.

DEBT SETTLEMENT VS. DEBT MANAGEMENT

Though often confused as synonymous, debt settlement is very different from debt management plans (DMPs) serviced by the consumer credit counseling industry. With a DMP, credit counseling agencies work to lower the interest rate on a credit card account to lower monthly payments and ensure more funds are directed toward paying down the principal instead of interest charges. Since the debtor typically has more than one account, the debt accounts are consolidated into one payment to the credit counseling agency who is responsible for distributing the payments to each creditor based on a scheduled repayment plan. This usually lasts three to five years.

Debt settlement programs involve the debt settlement company negotiating with the creditor to lower the outstanding balance of the debt. Lower interest rates are usually not negotiated, and the companies do not distribute monthly payments to creditors. The debt settlement companies, typically through a third party payment processor, arrange for paying off debts once a reduced balance settlement is agreed upon. Though the client does make monthly deposits into their settlement fund, it is managed by an independent, third-party processor.

SUMMARY

1. Consumers experiencing debilitating debt have two primary options: resolving the debt or file bankruptcy.

2. Consumer options for resolving debt include credit counseling, debt settlement, and debt consolidation loans. Different financial circumstances require different plans of action.

3. Many consumers can benefit from budget counseling.

4. Paying off debt requires commitment.

1. Identify three options available to the consumer for resolving debt.

2. What is the difference between credit counseling and debt settlement?

3. Explain why consumers might benefit from getting outside help with their debt issues.

4. Describe the typical debt settlement client.

5. What are some creditor concessions that a client in credit counseling may receive?

Unit 22: Bankruptcy

- To determine the difference between Chapter 7 and 13 bankruptcies.
- To learn about Bankruptcy Abuse Prevention and Consumer Protection Act.
- To survey the guidelines for pre-bankruptcy counseling.
- To identify ways to avoid bankruptcy.

Bankruptcy filings have increased steadily since the early 1970s to over 1.4 million each year today. Among the reasons for this steady increase are a volatile job market, soaring medical costs, divorce, a lack of savings and high levels of consumer debt. When financial setbacks occur, the balancing act of living paycheck to paycheck falls like a house of cards. Bankruptcy is a legal proceeding that can offer consumers who cannot conceivably pay all that they owe a fresh start from which to improve their financial situation.

The Bankruptcy Abuse Prevention and Consumer Protection Act of 2005 ushered in the most comprehensive changes to the bankruptcy code since the Bankruptcy Reform Act of 1978. Whereas, in the past, the debtor was assumed to be well-intentioned but unlucky, the new law assumes abuse unless proven otherwise.

Consumers looking to file for bankruptcy are now required to pass a means test that determines eligibility. They are also required to receive credit counseling prior to filing either Chapter 7 or Chapter 13.

In this unit, we will explore the role of credit counselors as they interface with a new kind of client. The pre-bankruptcy client, for the most part, will be seeking to dissolve, not resolve, their debt. Also, their financial circumstance will be more severe than clients who are considering debt management.

CHAPTER 7

Sometimes referred to as a liquidation bankruptcy, Chapter 7 bankruptcy wipes out any debt filed under it. It is a last resort option for debtors who cannot pay back their creditors. It can provide a fresh start for consumers who are ready to rebuild their personal finances while avoiding past mistakes.

Filing bankruptcy is not free and it is not easy especially now that the new bankruptcy law has gone into effect. Bankruptcy is a process that takes about four to six months. Filing costs are now over $200. Attorney fees are much higher. Paperwork is extensive and must be accurate.

Eligibility

A debtor whose income exceeds the states median income for a family of the same size must pass a means test. This test is designed to ascertain whether or not the debtor, after paying for monthly living expenses, has enough disposable income to maintain a Chapter 13 repayment plan. If the debtor does not pass this test, a Chapter 13 may be ordered by the court.

Below is an outline of the process:

1. **The debtor files a petition with the court.** A Chapter 7 proceeding begins when a consumer submits a two-page petition to the court along with a series of forms that asks for:

   - your current income and its sources
   - your current monthly living expenses
   - a list of your property
   - a list of your debts
   - any property you are claiming as exempt by state law
   - property you owned and money you spent during the previous two years
   - property you sold or gave away during the previous two year
   - a certificate stating that you received credit counseling within the 180 days prior to filing

In the case of an emergency such as an impending foreclosure or eviction, the debtor can file just the two-page petition and file the rest of the paperwork within 15 days.

2. **The automatic stay is put into effect.** Once the petition has been filed, the automatic stay stops all creditor actions to collect what is owed. It is a temporary Order of Relief that stops garnishments, bank seizures, utility shut-offs and seizures of property.

3. **A creditors meeting is scheduled.** A week or two after the petition has been filed, the debtor receives a notice that a creditors meeting has been scheduled. This meeting is run by a court-appointed person called a bankruptcy trustee who swears in the debtor and asks questions concerning the case. The trustee reads over the forms and asks if the information is 100% accurate. Assets that can be sold to pay off the creditors are noted. In most cases, no assets are found. Also, it is very rare that the creditors attend this meeting which can take as little time as a minute or two.

4. Debts filed in the petition are discharged. Within 3 to 6 months after the creditors meeting, the debtor receives a court notice that states: All debts that qualified for discharge were discharged. The debtor no longer legally owes the creditors for any discharged debts. Also, the debtor is no longer under court supervision.

QUESTIONS AND ANSWERS ABOUT CHAPTER 7

There are several important points to consider before filing a Chapter 7. Below are the most important questions to ask.

What debts cannot be discharged in a Chapter 7 bankruptcy case?

Nondischargeable debts fall in two categories:

1. Debts that survive bankruptcy. These include child support obligations, tax debts and student loans.

2. Debts the court declares nondischargeable due to creditor objections. This could be debts incurred by fraud or malicious acts.

Are there limits to the automatic stay?

Yes. In some cases, the automatic stay will not stop actions by the IRS, lawsuits to collect child support or criminal proceedings.

What property is exempt in a Chapter 7 proceeding?

Exempt property is property that cannot be taken by the court to raise money to pay off creditors. What filers get to keep in a Chapter 7 bankruptcy varies from state to state. The following is a list of typical exemptions:

- Motor vehicles, to certain value
- A portion of the equity in a home
- Necessary household furnishings and appliances
- Tools necessary for employment
- Pensions
- Life insurance
- Public benefits such as welfare, Social Security and unemployment

Non-exempt property includes a second motor vehicle, a second home, cash, bank accounts, investments and family heirlooms.

What can happen if the information filed in the petition is less than 100% accurate?

Inaccurate or incomplete information could lead to dismissal of a case. Also, if the court finds that you are deliberately hiding assets, you can be penalized severely. Remember that when you submit papers to the court, you are swearing that everything is true under penalty of perjury.

How does Chapter 7 affect your credit rating?

A bankruptcy proceeding will appear as an item on a credit report for a period of 10 years. It will damage your credit rating, lower your FICO score, and make it difficult to obtain credit in the future. The worst effects of Chapter 7 can be mitigated by re-establishing credit with a secured credit card and consistently paying on time.

What is the waiting period if I filed previously?

Under the Bankruptcy Abuse Prevention and Consumer Protection Act, a debtor can file for a Chapter 7 eight years from the date of the first filing.

Can I file without an attorney?

You can but it is not advisable. Specialized knowledge is often needed concerning types of debts, exemptions, and state laws. In the case of a partnership or cooperation, an attorney is required.

Can I get free legal assistance?

Legal assistance is available for some who meet income guidelines. In some cases, a petition preparer is used to help create the filing forms. However, they are prohibited from giving legal advice or representing you in court.

Should I file separately or jointly with my spouse?

Whether you should file a joint petition or a separate one depends on several factors that involve the types of debt incurred, when they were incurred, property you own, and state laws. There are two types of marital property ownership -- community property and common law. Currently, nine states apply the community property rules while the other states follow common law rules. What rules your state follows and how they can affect your petition should be sorted out by a qualified bankruptcy attorney prior to filing.

Do I have to go through the pre-bankruptcy counseling?

Under the new law, you must complete a 90-minute counseling session within 180 days of filing. The counseling focuses on the availability of credit counseling and other alternatives to bankruptcy. A certificate of completion must be included in your petition. This requirement can be waived if the petitioner is disabled or on active duty in the military.

Do I have to obtain debtor education before my case is discharged?

As with the pre-filing counseling, this is one of the new requirements in the Bankruptcy Abuse Prevention and Consumer Protection Act. It states that a certificate must be filed with the court within 45 days of the creditors meeting or else the court will close the case without issuing a discharge.

What does the court require as far as wage statements?

Filers must include a statement of current monthly income with their petition. The court defines current monthly income to mean the average of the income you have received over the past six months. This is one of the requirements of the new bankruptcy law.

Why are there so many people filing bankruptcy?

Many factors contribute to the current level of bankruptcy filings. Unforeseen events such as loss of income or a medical emergency can devastate an individual or a family's financial situation particularly when there is no money set aside to deal with these events. Other contributing factors include destructive spending habits, high levels of consumer debt and poor use of credit.

How can bankruptcy be avoided?

Do not borrow more than your income can handle. Establish an emergency fund equal to 3 - 6 months of your current income. Use a spending plan to meet financial goals. Research and obtain medical insurance.

CHAPTER 13

Sometimes called the wage earner's plan, Chapter 13 is a reorganization bankruptcy whereby the debtor repays all or a portion of what is owed over a five year period. While the debtor is under court supervision, the court provides protection from creditor actions such as garnishments and seizures.

Eligibility

To be eligible for a Chapter 13 bankruptcy, you must show the court, through a repayment plan, how you will pay off your debts. You must have sufficient disposable income to maintain a monthly payment plan. Disposable income is that portion of income left over after meeting basic living expenses.

Here is a summary of a Chapter 13 bankruptcy proceeding.

A Chapter 13 proceeding begins when a debtor files a repayment plan with the court. Included are forms listing your assets, your income, your monthly expenses and the nature and amount of your debt.

Payments begin within 30 days of the filing. The debtor makes payments to the trustee who then distributes the money to the various creditors. In this way, Chapter 13 resembles a debt management plan. And like debt management, Chapter 13 requires a high level of commitment due to the extended time frame and the fact that on-going money pressures continue as always.

The debtor can have the case modified at any time. Life goes on. During a five year repayment plan, things happen. You may suddenly find yourself without a job. Whether temporary or permanent, the trustee has the discretion to modify your plan to accommodate your needs. Depending on the situation, the trustee may give you a grace period or reduce the monthly payment.

In the event that the bankruptcy court will not let your plan be modified, you have the right to convert to Chapter 7 or have the court dismiss your case.

Certain remaining debts at the end of the five year repayment plan are wiped out in a superdischarge. Under the new law, debts incurred through fraud, theft or malicious acts are no longer included in the superdischarge.

COMPARING CHAPTER 7 AND CHAPTER 13

While most people who file for bankruptcy file for Chapter 7, there are reasons to file for Chapter 13. Here are the primary considerations:

1. You filed a Chapter 7 already. If you filed for a Chapter 7 bankruptcy within the last eight years, you are still eligible for a Chapter 13 .

2. You want to protect nonexempt property. Another reason to file for Chapter 13 is that you may have valuable nonexempt property you want to keep. Under a Chapter 7, your valuable assets are liquidated to pay the creditors a portion of what you owe. Chapter 13 offers protections from creditor actions against your property.

3. You have delinquent secured debt. If you are behind on your mortgage payments or car loan, a Chapter 13 allows you to keep your property while you catch up through a reorganization plan. Under a Chapter 7, you may have to give up your property.

4. You want to protect your cosigner. In a Chapter 7, the creditors may go after a cosigner of a loan appearing in the petition. In other words, even though the debt is discharged, a cosigner is still responsible for the debt. Under a Chapter 13, you are solely responsible for the debts through your repayment plan.

5. You want to do "the right thing." Some people will not consider dissolving their debts. They feel it is their moral obligation to pay off their debts as best as they can. A Chapter 13 can make this possible.

Which type of bankruptcy is right for which circumstance depends on:

Eligibility. Filing for Chapter 7 under the new law requires that you take a means test. Your income and expenses are put through a series of calculations in a determination to find funds for a monthly repayment plan. If you show consistent money left over after living expenses, you may be ordered into a Chapter 13. To be eligible for a Chapter 13, you must have adequate income to cover your basic living expenses and be able to maintain a court supervised payment plan lasting 5 years.

Number of Years Between Filings

	Chapter 7	Chapter 13
Previous Chapter 7	8	6
Previous Chapter 13	6	2

The question of eligibility also depends on whether you have filed for bankruptcy in the past. The chart above provides an overview of filing time frames.

REASONS FOR FILING
Why are you filing bankruptcy? This list outlines some important distinctions.

Reason for Filing	Type of Bankruptcy
You want to stop bill collectors.	Neither. Under the FDCPA, you can stop collectors with a cease and desist letter.
You want to stop a foreclosure.	Chapter 13. You can include your arrears in your payment plan & receive court protections.
You want to protect nonexempt property.	Chapter 13. You keep all of your property. Under Chapter 7, you may have to give the fair market value of any nonexempt property.
You need relief from debts you cannot pay.	Chapter 7. This bankruptcy is designed to give people a fresh start when there is insufficient income to pay off debt.
Your debt problem involves cosigners.	Chapter 13. During the repayment plan, creditors are prohibited from seeking payment from a cosigner. With a Chapter 7, they can.
You want to get rid of high medical bills.	Chapter 7. Especially if the medical problem prevents you from working.
You owe debts from a divorce decree.	Chapter 13. Any unpaid balance at the end of the payment plan is wiped out in a superdischarge. Under Chapter 7, the ex-spouse could object to the discharge.
You owe non-dischargeable debts.	Neither. These debts must be paid in full or else you will continue to owe the balance even after a repayment plan.

The Bankruptcy Abuse Prevention and Consumer Protection Act (BAPCPA) went into effect on October 17, 2005 after a long and contentious debate in Congress. Whereas in the past, bankruptcy filers were seen as well-intentioned victims of circumstance, they are now considered to be abusing the system unless proven otherwise.

Its many provisions limit Chapter 7 eligibility, increase the paperwork and cost of filing, and diminish the benefits of a Chapter 13. The pendulum that swung in favor of debtors with the passage of the Bankruptcy Reform Act of 1978 has just swung in the opposite direction in favor of creditors.

As a counselor, it is important that you assess your attitude toward bankruptcy. Do you think debtors have a right to discharge debts they cannot pay? Do you think that the creditors are to blame for soliciting consumers to take on debt they can ill afford? Are millions of bankruptcy filers abusing the system each year?

Studies show that the primary causes of bankruptcy are job loss, health problems, and divorce. Others, however, point to credit-card debt and frivolous spending as the real culprits. However you view the subject of bankruptcy, it is essential that you, as a counselor, remain nonjudgmental toward clients who are considering this option.

We will now survey the most important changes ushered in by the new law.

CHANGES IN THE BANKRUPTCY LAW

1. **Limits Chapter 7 Eligibility.** Under BAPCPA, abuse is presumed if a debtor's income is above the state's median income for a family of the same size. The debtor, in this case, must prove there are no funds available to pay back the creditors.

   A means test is administered to determine whether or not a debtor can afford to pay at least $100 a month to the creditors. However, the means test does not use the debtor's actual income and expenses to make its calculations. The debtor's income is expressed as the average income of the last six months regardless of whether or not the debtor has experienced a job loss. Also, expenses are based on IRS rules that state what "reasonable" expenses are.

   Critics of the new law include consumer advocates and women's groups who see an essential financial safety net removed. If credit-card debt cannot be wiped out, that's less money that can go toward essential expenses such as child support. On the other hand, proponents of the law see the means test as the primary tool for reducing the epidemic numbers of bankruptcy filings.

Filers who do not pass the means test must file either a Chapter 13 and enter a five year repayment plan or slip further into debt.

2. Limits to Chapter 13. While many debtors who are ineligible for a Chapter 7 will presumably enter a Chapter 13 repayment plan, several changes in this type of bankruptcy make it less powerful:

- Many debts that were dischargeable in a superdischarge can no longer be discharged. These include debts resulting from theft, fraud, certain back taxes, and fines and damages.

- An auto lien can no longer be stripped whereby the debtor pays only the secured portion of the debt if the vehicle was purchased within 910 days of the filing.

- All repayment plans must last five years. In the past, some plans lasted only three years.

3. Mandatory credit counseling. All debtors must receive credit counseling from an approved budget and credit counseling agency either in an individual or group briefing within 180 days prior to filing bankruptcy.

There are exceptions to this requirement in the case of an emergency and the debtor could not receive credit counseling within five days or if the U.S. Trustee has determined that the approved agencies are not adequate to provide the required counseling. Any debt management plan that is developed must be filed with the court.

4. Limits on the automatic stay. The automatic stay no longer stops or postpones evictions, actions against a driver's license or professional license, lawsuits to establish paternity, child custody, or child support or divorce proceedings.

5. Increased time between filings. A Chapter 7 debtor cannot receive a discharge if a prior discharge was received within eight years as opposed to six years of the new filing.

6. Mandatory debtor education. A debtor can be denied a discharge if the debtor does not complete a course in personal financial management that is approved by the U.S. Trustee.

7. Limits to the discharge. Debts owed to a single creditor totaling more the $500 in luxury goods purchased within 90 days of filing are considered nondischargeable. Also, nondischargeable are cash advances totaling $750

within 70 days.

8. Increased paperwork. A case can be dismissed if the debtor fails to submit the following documents:

- List of creditors
- Schedules of assets and liabilities, income and expenses
- Certificate of credit counseling
- Evidence of payment from employers received 60 days prior to filing
- Statement of monthly net income and any anticipated increase in income or expenses after filing
- Tax returns or transcripts for the most recent tax year
- Tax returns filed during the case including tax returns for prior years that had not been filed when the case began
- A photo ID

9. Required verification by the attorney. Attorney fees are expected to rise substantially due to increased legal responsibility. Attorneys must verify and attest to the accuracy and completeness of a filer's petition. Numerous other provisions in the law address homestead exemptions, domestic support obligations, taxes, and student loans. The above list in no way should be consulted as a legal resource. Many provisions are extremely detailed such as the limits imposed on the automatic stay and how the means test is administered and interpreted.

In summary, filing bankruptcy after October 17, 2005 takes longer, costs more and offers fewer protections from creditors. New duties are imposed on debtors and their attorneys. The previous concept of the unfortunate debtor who is entitled to relief from debts has been replaced by the idea that the debtor is abusing the system unless proven otherwise.

THE BANKRUPTCY CLIENT

If you are an approved agency to provide the required pre-filing credit counseling or pre-discharge education, you will be interfacing with a different type of client than one who is seeking to resolve debts through debt management or budget counseling. The bankruptcy client will most likely be experiencing a more severe level of financial distress than the typical client who seeks credit counseling.

One important distinction is that the counseling is mandatory for the bankruptcy client. This client may view the required counseling as a pointless exercise and express their frustration, anxiety or even anger toward you.

As a result, the bankruptcy client may lack motivation to consider options other than filing. By the time the client contacts you, a decision has already been made to file bankruptcy. This may have been an extremely hard decision to make after a long period of time dealing with the effects of delinquent debt. Unlike a client who pro-actively contacts an agency, the bankruptcy client is not seeking to pay down debt. Instead, the client is seeking relief from debt.

Who is the bankruptcy client? Contrary to what you might think, the bankruptcy client is middle class, more likely to have attended college and more likely to own a home than the average American. This is not hard to believe once you consider that you need income to incur debts and that one of the reasons for filing bankruptcy is to protect assets.

A Harvard study conducted by Elizabeth Warren found that one half of all bankruptcies are triggered by sudden uninsured medical expenses. Other leading causes of bankruptcy are job loss and divorce.

PRE-BANKRUPTCY COUNSELING
One of the biggest changes in the bankruptcy law is the requirement for consumers who want to file for bankruptcy to complete a credit counseling briefing. It is the first time in history that credit counseling is mandatory.

GUIDELINES
The U.S. Trustee of the Department of Justice, which oversees various aspects of the new law, has drafted guidelines for the required counseling.

- The briefing must be at least 90 minutes long.
- It can be completed in either an individual or group setting.
- It should cost about $50. (Couples, in some cases, are charged $75.)
- The requirement can be waived for certain filers including those with disabilities and those on active duty in the military.

The counseling must consist of:

1. an analysis of the current financial situation.
2. a discussion of the factors that caused the current situation.
3. a discussion of all the options for resolving the debt.
4. guidance in developing a plan of action.

CLIENT EMOTIONS

Some authors writing on the subject of bankruptcy claim that the stigma of bankruptcy is a thing of the past. Others, including bankruptcy attorneys, report that creditorsmeetings are often very emotional occasions that can cause tears, embarrassment and shame.

As counselors, it is important to remain sensitive to the emotional side of bankruptcy. For many, filing bankruptcy is a sign of personal failure. Some may be hesitant to give sensitive information. Others will express confusion about the entire bankruptcy process.

What You Can Do?

How can counselors help quell the shame and guilt that often accompanies the decision to file bankruptcy? It is important for clients to know that many people from all walks of unexpectedly fall on hard times. A volatile job market, soaring medical costs and a culture of buy now pay later has left large numbers of Americans financially vulnerable.

If they take nothing else away with them after a pre-bankruptcy counseling session, it should be that they are not alone. In fact, you are in good company. Consider the following list of famous people who have filed bankruptcy:

- Rembrandt
- Mozart
- Thomas Jefferson
- James Whistler
- Mark Twain
- Oscar Wilde
- Henry Ford
- Charles Goodyear
- Walt Disney
- Donald Trump

Use verbal encouragement to draw out information from hesitant clients. Short responses such as "go on", "I see" and "yes" let the client know you are giving your undivided attention.

Demonstrate positive regard by addressing the client by name and focusing on the client's strengths and past successes.

Remain non-judgmental. Avoid judgmental reactions to client statements such as "That's terrible!" Instead, use objective responses such as "I see." Also, do not assign blame when examining past mistakes.

GUIDELINES IN DETAIL

The four components that are required under U.S. Trustee guidelines correlate with the problem-solving process outlined in Module III. Let's look at each one in comparison with the stages of counseling we discussed earlier.

1. **Analysis of the clients current financial condition.** Gathering all the facts while establishing and building rapport is the first step in the problem-solving process. It's finding out where the client is now. During this first stage, it is essential to view the credit report. If the client does not have a current copy, you can get a free copy by going to www.annualcreditreport.com. The report will help you identify the kinds and amounts of debts and to ascertain whether or not any court actions are listed. Also, it is important at this stage to check the report for accuracy. Any errors found can be contested under the Fair Credit Reporting Act.

2. **Discussion of the factors that caused the current condition.** This is the other side of gathering all the facts. While avoiding the blame game, you examine where the client is now in terms of on-going issues that may involve destructive spending habits, poor credit behavior, or conflicts over money. Other factors contributing to insolvency may include job loss, lack of medical insurance and divorce. Each factor should be discussed so that the underlying causes of debt can be addressed as well as the debt itself. Solutions are added to the action plan.

3. **Discussion of the alternatives to address the current condition.** This component correlates with the second step in the problem-solving process that tries to determine where the client wants to go. What is the preferred scenario? In this case, options are considered for resolving debt that may or may not necessitate filing for bankruptcy. Determining the right alternative depends on the client's level of debt and overall financial situation. The deeper a client is in debt, the fewer the options will be. Also, each option carries with it a human factor. Can this individual successfully follow through with the action plan? Are values compromised? Will the action plan cause stress in the household? Do destructive spending habits need to be addressed?

4. **Development of a plan of action.** The fourth step is often the trickiest. It correlates with the final step in the problem-solving process. How will the client reach the identified preferred scenario?

A good action plan will include specific measures of success and specific time frames. Obstacles for each action to be undertaken will need to be identified and overcome. Here is an example of an action plan.

Goal	Actions Needed	When
Pay off credit card debt	Call creditors Stop making charges Find 2nd job Create spending plan	Today In one week Within one month This weekend

Obstacles	Resources	Monitor Success
Childcare	Arrange for babysitting After school programs	Post balance reductions Child feedback
Back to school sales	Use cash from yard sale	School essentials checklist
Not sure how	Library, Internet, free counseling	Revise spending plan

Each goal will need a separate action plan. By identifying specific actions and anticipating the obstacles to the actions, clients will have a much better chance of actually accomplishing what they set out to do.

EVALUATING THE ALTERNATIVES

Let's explore Step Three of the guidelines by considering the options. Which debt-relief alternative is best for the client both financially *and* emotionally?

CONSUMER WORKOUT

Consumers should contact their creditors whenever they are having trouble making a payment. Generally, creditors will want to maintain a positive relationship with customers by allowing a temporary or permanent modification for repayment.

Financial side: Is the setback temporary? Will the consumer have regular income in the future? How long has the debt been delinquent? Is it in collections? In the best case scenario, a consumer should contact his or her creditor in anticipation of paying a bill late. However, if the consumer is late by a month or two, negotiation might work. Success is also contingent on the specific creditors involved and their policies concerning payments.

Human side: Negotiating with creditors can be time consuming and frustrating. A client should understand that this option requires assertiveness and perseverance.

CREDIT COUNSELING

Many people simply do not have the time or skills necessary to negotiate with all the creditors they owe money to. Credit counseling provides a liaison between consumers and lenders.

Financial side: A debt management plan is a viable option if the client can show money left over each month after paying for expenses. The income must be sufficient and regular enough to maintain the payment plan worked out.

Human side: Maintaining the plan, which could last from three to five years, takes commitment. Individuals in a debt management plan will need to change their spending habits and their use of credit.

DEBT CONSOLIDATION

This option could make sense for individuals who owe several creditors and wish to manage their debt by making one monthly payment.

Financial side: Taking out a loan only makes sense if the individual has a steady source of income and a fair to good credit rating. If the debtor is a homeowner, they might consider a home equity loan. Other types of consolidation such as 0% transfers come with severe penalties that could exacerbate the debt situation.

Human side: Taking on more debt, especially trading in unsecured debt for secured debt in the case of a home equity loan, can mean added financial stress. Unless the issues that caused the debt in the first place are addressed, this is probably not a good option.

CHAPTER 13

If the individual needs asset protection while paying off debts, this may be the best option. However, did you know that the vast majority of debtors who file for a Chapter 13 never complete their payment plan?

Financial side: As stated earlier in this chapter, a debtor must submit to the court a repayment plan that shows adequate money each month to maintain payments.

Human side: Like debt management, this option takes commitment. Also, you must also consider that, during the five-year plan, your finances are subject to court supervision.

DEBT SETTLEMENT

If you are deep in debt and wish to avoid bankruptcy, debt settlement could be a way to resolve delinquent debt by paying a reduced, negotiated portion of the debt.

Financial side: The debtor must raise funds to pay the negotiated amount. This could mean selling an asset or asking for help from a family member. Also, to be considered is the damaging effect this will have on the credit rating.

Human side: This option promises a quicker way of getting out from under debt and it may help some individuals avoid bankruptcy. However, creditor actions to collect what is owed will not stop until the reduced amount is paid.

CHAPTER 7

This is the last resort option as long as the debtor can pass the means test and does not have a previous Chapter 7 within the last eight years.

Financial side: After expense allowances, the debtor must show close to no disposable income for paying off debts. Also ask, "Will enough of my debts be discharged to make it worth doing?" and "Is there property I want to keep that I might have to forfeit?"

Human side: Consider how the client feels about bankruptcy. For some, the emotional toll may be too much.

Legal Advice: Working Definition

It is more important than ever to define legal advice and understand what you, as a counselor, can and cannot do. It is illegal for anyone other than an attorney to do the following:

- Interpret the law by explaining what a statute, regulation, or case means.
- Prepare legal documents or interpret any legal documents originating from a court or an attorney.
- Offer an opinion as to how a client's specific legal problem should be handled.

Counselors may not say, "I think you should file bankruptcy" or "If I were you, I would file a Chapter 7."

However, in developing a plan of action, the counselor can say, "It appears that bankruptcy may be an option" or "It looks like you may need an attorney."

PRE-DISCHARGE DEBTOR EDUCATION

Also mandated under the new law is a two-hour course in personal financial education. In order to be granted a discharge by the court, the debtor must complete the course within the 45 days following the creditors' meeting. According to the U.S. Trustee's Office, this course must include the following four components:

1. **Budget development.** This includes setting short and long-term financial goals and understanding the difference between fixed, variable and discretionary expenses.

2. **Money management.** Debtors would explore needs versus wants, the importance of savings and insurance, and effective shopping strategies.

3. **Using credit wisely.** This component would examine the types and availability of credit and loans, avoiding credit problems, and understanding credit reports and scores.

4. **Consumer resource information.** The course would include a survey of resources for the consumer such as assistance programs as well as consumer rights.

As with the pre-bankruptcy counseling, the course must be administered by an approved agency.

AFTER BANKRUPTCY

If the premise of bankruptcy is to provide a fresh start for consumers whose debt situation is truly debilitating, any counseling or education would be incomplete without providing guidance for a post-bankruptcy action plan.

Generally speaking, clients will want to re-establish their credit as soon as possible while at the same time, avoiding the past mistakes that may have contributed to the need to file bankruptcy. The debtor who has just come out of a bankruptcy should understand that there is nothing "forever" about credit. Althoug, a bankruptcy can stay on your credit report for up to 10 years, the effect it has on your credit score can be lessened through the responsible use of credit. The best strategies are:

Get your credit report and fix any errors. As you know, credit reports can contain mistakes that translate into more money out of your pocket. Make sure that any debts that were filed under the bankruptcy are not still listed as open and overdue. If they are still listed as overdue, the debtor must contact the credit bureaus and insist that the accounts be reported as included in bankruptcy. Also, check to make sure the correct type of bankruptcy is listed. If you filed a Chapter 13, make sure it does not report it as Chapter 7.

Apply for a secured credit card. Considering all the multiple bankruptcies filed in recent years, it is more than just possible to re-establish credit in a relatively short amount of time. You may not qualify for a regular credit card right away but you can get a secured credit card. This type of credit card draws money from an amount you deposit in the bank. By making charges on a secured card and making regular payments on time, you can get back in the credit game. Also, it is best not to charge more than 30% of your credit limit.

Three things to keep in mind:

1. Beware of secured cards that carry high application or annual fees.

2. Ascertain whether or not the card issuer reports to the three credit bureaus. If not, you won't be getting "credit" for your good use of credit.

3. After a 12 -- 18 month period of sound credit use, you should be able to upgrade the secured card to a regular card.

Apply for an installment loan. Establish that "healthy mix" that creditors like to see by getting an installment loan. If you have a student loan, make sure it is current and try to pay more than the minimum payment each month. Also, do not think you will not qualify for a mortgage. Typically, you could qualify for a Federal Housing Administration Loan in as little as six months after bankruptcy.

After bankruptcy discharge, consumers are often inundated with high-cost credit offers. These offers promise to "rebuild" your credit but, in reality, can derail your post-bankruptcy fresh start. It is important to choose new credit very carefully. Although, many consumers coming out of bankruptcy will be anxious to obtain credit again, it is best not to succumb to creditor solicitations and, instead, pro-actively seek the best credit options.

Whatever alternative the client chooses for dealing with debt, it is important that he or she create a spending plan that supports it. Only through a spending plan can money be allocated to resolve the debt while avoiding debt in the future.

Above all, it is important to remember that bankruptcy is not the end of the road but a chance for a new beginning.

SUMMARY

1. Chapter 7 bankruptcy wipes out any debt filed under it.

2. Chapter 13 bankruptcy reorganizes debt into a monthly payment plan and offers certain court protections from creditor actions.

3. Considering bankruptcy involves knowing which debts are dischargeable and what property you are allowed to keep.

4. The Bankruptcy Abuse Prevention and Consumer Protection Act is the most extensive revision of the bankruptcy code since the Bankruptcy Reform Act of 1978.

5. A means test is applied to determine bankruptcy eligibility.

6. New counseling and education is required for those filing bankruptcy. Consumers must receive counseling prior to filing bankruptcy and personal financial management education before receiving a discharge.

1. What is the difference between a Chapter 7 and a Chapter 13 bankruptcy?

2. List debts that cannot be discharged through a Chapter 7 bankruptcy.

3. List three or four provisions in the new bankruptcy law.

4. Describe the components of pre-bankruptcy counseling.

5. What are the alternatives to bankruptcy?

Congratulations! You have completed the Keys to Success Credit Counselor Certification Exam Study Course!

LINK TO REVIEW AND TESTING

Go to www.acecertificate.com to view Module Review Presentations, take the Practice Test and request the Certification Exam. If you have any questions, feel free to contact by telephone or email listed at the site.

Appendix A: Glossary

COUNSELING KEY WORDS

Active listening is a special form of undivided attention that counselors give to their clients. It is demonstrated through verbal and non-verbal techniques and behaviors.

Congruence -- What effective counselors say and how they feel are the same. What you see is what you get. There are no mixed messages.

Emotional spending is spending that involves ulterior motivations that go beyond the actual product or service purchased. It includes spending for approval, to alleviate stress or to exact revenge.

Empathy is the ability to understand what another individual is going through. You relate to another persons situation as if it were your own.

Enhancing statements are those that comment on some positive aspect or attitude about the client. They provide encouragement or support to the client.

Genuineness is the quality of being yourself with the client. Clients need to know they are talking to another human being as well as a trained professional.

The Human/Business Model is a way of looking at every day interactions as operating on two levels. The business level is where specific objectives are met. The human level is where an individual's needs are fulfilled. These include the need for attention, courteous treatment, respect and acceptance.

Immediacy is spontaneous communication, responding to things as they happen in the counseling session. Immediacy allows for communication that deviates from the prescribed counseling steps.

Life-cycle planning is the idea of planning being a lifelong process with goals shifting from phase to phase.

Locus of control determines whether you experience power over outside forces (internal locus) or you feel that outside forces have control over you (external locus).

Maslow's Hierachy of Needs categorizes human needs into successive levels. Each level of need must be met before the higher level can be addressed.

Money relationships describe how we perceive and interact with finances. Some people associate money with achievement while others use money to seek approval from others. Money relationships often fuel impulsive spending.

Nonreflective listening involves attentive silence along with short verbal responses that are objective such as "I see", "Yes" and "Okay."

Outcome goals are those goals that the client presents to the counselor. In the case of financial counseling, outcome goals involve personal finances.

Positive regard refers to showing respect for the client as an individual with inherent value and dignity regardless of any external factors the client may demonstrate. Positive regard is giving affirmation to the client.

Presenting concern is the issue that brought the client to counseling. The presenting concern initially defines the outcome goals of the counseling session although it may change or shift during the course of counseling.

The Problem-Management/Opportunity-Development Model describes the fundamental process utilized by helpers to address client needs. Optimum counseling for the financially stressed involves reducing debt and non-essential expenses (managing the problem) as well as discovering ways to increase income (developing opportunities).

Process goals work to create trust, respect, and rapport between client and counselor. When process goals are met, clients and counselors can collaborate productively to solve problems and discover opportunities.

Reflective listening gives clients non-judgmental feedback through clarifying, paraphrasing, summarizing and responding to feelings. It also lets clients know that what they have communicated has been accurately and objectively understood.

Reframing is a solution-focused technique whereby a negative situation is seen in a positive light.

Self-disclosure helps to convey genuineness by being open to personal questions the client may ask. Effective counselors answer these types of questions directly and briefly.

Self-efficacy is the belief that you have what it takes to accomplish a particular plan of action.

Spending personality refers to how a consumer behaves when making purchases. Spending personalities include the impulsive buyer, the fanatical shopper and the ulterior motive spender.

CREDIT KEY WORDS

Annual fee is a special fee charged once a year for the use of certain credit cards.

Annual percentage rate (APR) determines how much interest will be charged.

Balance computation methods are used by credit card issuers to determine interest that is applied to an account. Methods include the average daily balance, the adjusted balance and the previous balance.

Balloon payment is a single, lump-sum payment made at the end of a loan.

Budget is a financial statement of estimated income and expenses for an individual or family over a selected period of time. Also referred to as a spending plan, it is a way to plan with your money.

Budget analysis is the process used to determine how well resources are being allocated. Daily expense record tracks everyday expenses by listing exact amounts going out at the point of purchase.

Chapter 7 is a chapter of the bankruptcy code providing for liquidation of certain consumer debts.

Chapter 13 is a chapter in the bankruptcy code that provides for a court ordered repayment plan during which time the debtor is given certain protections from creditor actions.

Charge-off occurs when a lender transfers an account deemed uncollectable from the company's receivables to a loss.

Collection agencies are given authorization by the credit grantor to collect money owed on a commission basis. Generally, they keep 50% - 60% of all the funds collected -- not a percentage of the actual debt.

Consumer workouts occur when those who are having trouble paying their bills contact their creditors directly and attempt to negotiate an agreed upon arrangement for repayment.

Co-signer is a person who pledges in writing as part of a credit agreement to repay the debt if the primary borrower fails to repay it.

Credit counseling offers a debt management option where agencies negotiate with creditors on behalf of their clients and enroll clients in payment plans that involve one monthly payment.

Credit limit/line of credit refers to the maximum amount a borrower can draw from or the maximum amount that an account can show as outstanding.

Credit report is a confidential report on a consumer's payment habits as reported by their creditors to a consumer credit reporting agency. The agency provides the information to credit grantors who have a permissible purpose under the law to review the report.

Credit scoring is used by credit grantors to help them make lending decisions. A credit score helps evaluate the risk in granting a consumer credit. FICO scoring is the most common method in use today.

Creditworthiness is the general qualification for borrowing in the opinion of the lender as based on the borrower's credit history, ability to repay the loan and other factors such as amount of current assets.

Credit reports contain information about a consumer's credit history which includes credit transactions, payment patterns and legal actions if any.

Debt-to-income ratio is a percentage calculated by adding all monthly payments and dividing the sum by the monthly income.

Debt settlement works to settle debts with a reduced lump-sum payment that is negotiated and agreed upon with the creditors.

Deficiency balance is the portion of the loan still outstanding after the sale of property used as collateral. The amount from the sale is deducted from the total amount of the loan. The borrower is then responsible for paying off the difference.

Delinquent refers to accounts past due. These are generally classified by time -- 30, 60, 90 and 120 days past due. Special account classifications include charge-off, repossession and transferred.

Discharge is a court action to release a debtor from debts that were included in a bankruptcy petition.

Dispute is an action initiated by the consumer disputing credit report information believed to be in error. A dispute can also be about a creditor billing error.

Debt-to-income ratio is a percentage calculated by adding all monthly payments and dividing the sum by the monthly income.

Economizing is allocating spending so that it has the maximum benefit for everyone in the household.

Emotional spending is spending that involves ulterior motivations that go beyond the actual product or service purchased. It includes spending for approval, to alleviate stress or to exact revenge.

Finance charges are the amount of interest a consumer pays for the use of credit. It is based on the lender's annual percentage rate (APR).

Financial success means different things to different people. A general definition is: obtaining maximum benefits from financial resources.

Financial literacy is the state of being knowledgeable about personal financial management. This includes knowing how to balance a checkbook, read and interpret lending agreements and creating and maintaining a spending plan. Lack of financial literacy is one of the most prevalent sources of delinquent debt.

Fixed rate describes an APR that does not change.

Inquiries appear on a credit report any time a request is made to see the report. Too many inquiries can be a reason for denial of credit.

Nuisance fees are fees charged by credit issuers above and beyond finance charges. These include late fees, transaction fees, over-the-limit fees and annual membership fees.

Installment credit refers to accounts in which the debt is divided into amounts to be paid successively at specified intervals. Examples include a mortgage and an automobile loan.

Lawsuits are initiated by creditors of unsecured debt to collect on unpaid accounts. If the lender wins a court judgment, lawsuits can result in liens on property, wage garnishments and seizures of bank accounts.

Lien refers to a legal document used to create a security interest in another's property. A lien is often given as a security for the payment of a debt.

Mortgage workouts can help when clients are having trouble paying the mortgage. Sometimes an easier payment schedule can be negotiated either temporarily or permanently with the lender.

Negative amortization occurs when a consumer pays only the minimum required payment on a balance and this payment does not keep pace with growing finance charges and other fees so that the balance cannot be paid down or paid down in a reasonable amount of time.

Nuisance fees are fees charged by credit issuers above and beyond finance charges. These include late fees, transaction fees, over-the-limit fees and annual membership fees.

Obsolescence is the period oftime negative information remains on a credit report. Under the Fair Credit Reporting Act, the obsolescence period for a bankruptcy is 10 years while for all other negative items, it is 7 years.

Notice of Acceleration is the second step in the foreclosure process. This notice alerts the consumer that the total amount of the loan must be paid to avoid foreclosure.

Notice of Default is the first step in the foreclosure process. At this point, you have 90 days to cure the debt by making up all your missed payments plus late charges.

Notice to Quit (Notice to Vacate) is the notice the renter receives from the landlord as a first step in the eviction process.

Payment status reflects an account's history including any delinquencies or derogatory conditions occurring during the previous 7 years.

Personal information is a category in a credit report which may include any name variations, driver's license number, Social Security number, date of birth, spouse's name, employers, address and telephone number.

Personal statement is a special statement the consumer may request to be included in a credit report. It remains for 2 years.

Petition refers to a consumer's initial filing of a bankruptcy which has not yet been ruled upon by a judge.

Plaintiff is the party who initiates a legal action against another (defendant) seeking a court decision.

Re-age is to make an account current again after a period of default. Typically, an account is re-aged after a series of consistent payments.

Predatory lending exploits vulnerable consumers by extending high-cost loans that do not take into account the borrower's ability or inabilty to repay the loan.

Public record data is a category of information in a credit report containing items involving tax liens, lawsuits and judgments that relate to a consumer's debt obligations.

Repossession is a creditor's taking possession of property pledged as collateral on a loan agreement. Repossession usually occurs when the borrower is significantly behind in payments.

Revolving account describes credit that is automatically available up to a predetermined maximum limit so long as the consumer makes regular payments.

Secured credit is a loan for which some form of acceptable collateral such as a house or automobile has been pledged as part of the loan agreement.

Settle means to reach an agreement with a lender to repay only part of the original debt.

Terms refers to debt repayment terms of a loan agreement.

Tradeline describes the consumer's account status and activity. Tradeline information includes company names where the consumer has accounts, dates accounts were opened, credit limits, types of accounts, balances owed and payment history.

Transaction fees are fees charged for certain use of a consumer's credit line -- for example, to get a cash advance from an ATM.

Unsecured credit is credit for which no collateral has been pledged.

Universal default is a lending practice whereby penalty rates are applied by several creditors if you default on the loan agreement of just one.

Variable rate describes an APR that may change over time.

Victim Statement is a statement added to a credit report at the request of the consumer to alert credit grantors of fraudulent use of the consumer's identification for the purpose of obtaining credit. The statement requests that the credit grantor contact the consumer by telephone before issuing credit. It remains on file for 7 years unless the consumer requests that it be removed.

Appendix B: Consumer Protection Legislation

THE EQUAL CREDIT OPPORTUNITY ACT

The Equal Credit Opportunity Act (ECOA) ensures that all consumers are given an equal chance to obtain credit. This does not mean all consumers who apply for credit get it. Factors such as income, expenses, debt and credit history are considerations for creditworthiness.

The law protects you by barring banks and lenders from denying credit based on race, national origin, religion, age (except as a positive reflection), sex, job status rating, marital status, pregnancy, alimony/child support liability or information concerning a spouse's income. Some states bar discrimination based on mental or physical disabilities and sexual orientation.

Read more at:
[#http://ftc.gov/bcp/edu/pubs/consumer/credit/cre15.shtm~http://ftc.gov/bcp/edu/pubs/consumer/credit/cre15.shtm#]

THE TRUTH IN LENDING ACT

The Truth in Lending Act requires that all credit card issuers disclose their method of finance charge, annual percentage rate (APR), loan terms and conditions. This act also regulates the advertising of credit terms, prohibits card issuers from sending unrequested cards and limits a cardholder's responsibility for unauthorized used of a card to $50.

Read more at: www.truthinlendingact.uslegal.com/

THE FAIR CREDIT BILLING ACT

The Fair Credit Billing Act states that a consumer has 60 days after the receipt of a bill to dispute it in letter form. They must send it to the address of the customer service department usually located on the back of the billing statement. They must include their name, account number and why they believe the bill is in error. Copies of receipts of other purchases made within the period in question may be helpful in clarifying the billing error. As with all correspondence, keep a copy for your file.

Within 30 days, the creditor must respond with some explanation of the charge. The consumer cannot be reported to the credit bureau as delinquent until the dispute is settled. The creditor can, however, continue to add finance charges on the amount.

This act also allows consumers to withhold payment for faulty or defective goods or services that were bought with the credit card.

Read more at:
[#http://www.ftc.gov/bcp/edu/pubs/consumer/credit/cre16.shtm~http://www.ftc.gov/bcp/edu/pubs/consumer/credit/cre16.shtm#]

THE FAIR CREDIT REPORTING ACT

Under the Fair Credit Reporting Act, anyone obtaining or reading a consumer's credit report for reasons other than these listed may face heavy fines or imprisonment:

• Written permission for employment or other authorized reason
• Application for government license
• Application for business license
• Credit or insurance transaction
• Court subpoena from a federal grand jury
• Requirement for setting child support

The Fair Credit Reporting Act also requires disclosure to consumers of the name and address of any consumer reporting agency which supplied reports used to deny credit, insurance or employment. Within 60 days of denied credit, employment, insurance or housing a consumer may request a free copy of their report. Reports are issued free to consumers on welfare, or if there is a reason to suspect fraud. Also the act limits the amount of time certain information can remain in a credit report.

Read more at: http://www.ftc.gov/os/statutes/fcrajump.shtm

THE FAIR DEBT COLLECTION PRACTICES ACT

The Fair Debt Collection Practices Act (FDCPA) was passed in 1977 as a means to protect consumers and debtors from harassment or unfair treatment by debt collectors. In 1986, an amendment was made to include only those attorneys who collect debts as a regular part of their practice. Debt collectors must abide by FDCPA rules when attempting to collect delinquent debts.

Although this law has afforded debtors some protection, private collectors still resort to underhanded scare tactics. If the collector is from the original retailer or lending institution, the FDCPA holds no restriction to debt collection practices. In this case, complaints of excessive telephone calls within a short time period or threats which go beyond litigation are often hard to restrict.

Read more at:
[#http://www.ftc.gov/os/statutes/fdcpa/fdcpact.shtm~http://www.ftc.gov/os/statutes/fdcpa/fdcpact.shtm#]

THE SERVICEMEMBERS CIVIL RELIEF ACT

The Servicemembers Civil Relief Act (SCRA) offers protection for active duty personnel from legal proceedings and transactions that can have devastating effects on their finances. This includes protections from foreclosures, evictions, debt collection activities, and lawsuits. Also, under this act, lenders must generally reduce their interest fees on outstanding debts to no more than 6 percent. These protections are to remain in place until 90 days after discharge.

In most cases, these rights are NOT automatic. They must be requested to be granted. To find out more about the SCRA visit:
https://www.servicememberscivilreliefact.com/

THE UNIFORM DEBT MANAGEMENT SERVICES ACT

The Uniform Debt Management Services Act provides a uniform set of rules to govern the two primary services available for consumers in debt: credit counseling and debt settlement. The Act is a comprehensive statute requiring, among other things, registration requirements, bond requirements, certification requirements, disclosure requirements and penalties for non-compliance.

UDMSA may be divided into three basic parts: registration of services, service-debtor agreements and enforcement. Read more at: http://www.udmsa.org/

THE PENSION PROTECTION ACT OF 2006

This law states that a credit counseling organization shall not be exempt from tax under 501 (c)(3) unless such credit counseling organization is organized and operated in accordance with certain requirements which include:

1. The credit counseling organization must provide credit counseling services tailored to the specific needs and circumstances of consumers.

2. The credit counseling organization must not make loans to debtors (other than loans with no fees or interest) and must not negotiate the making of loans on behalf of debtors.

3. The credit counseling organization may provide services for the purpose of improving a consumer's credit record, credit history, or credit rating only to the extent that such services are incidental to providing credit counseling services.

4. The credit counseling organization must not charge any separately stated fee for services for the purpose of improving any consumer's credit record, credit history or credit rating.

5. The credit counseling organization must not refuse to provide credit counseling services to a consumer due to the ineligibility of the consumer for debt management plan enrollment or the unwillingness of the consumer to enroll in a debt management plan.

6. The credit counseling organization must establish and implement a fee policy which requires that any fees charged to a consumer for services are reasonable, and allows for the waiver of fees if the consumer is unable to pay.

7. The credit counseling organization must not receive any amount for providing referrals to others for debt management plan services, and must not pay any amount to others for obtaining referrals of consumers.

8. The credit counseling organization must not solicit contributions from consumers during the initial counseling process or while the consumer is receiving services from the organization.

Read more at: http://www.dol.gov/ebsa/pensionreform.html

THE CREDIT REPAIR ORGANIZATIONS ACT

Consumers have a vital interest in establishing and maintaining their creditworthiness and credit standing in order to obtain and use credit. As a result, consumers who have experienced credit problems may seek assistance from credit repair organizations which offer to improve the credit standing of such consumers.

Certain advertising and business practices of some companies engaged in the business of credit repair services have worked a financial hardship upon consumers, particularly those of limited economic means and who are inexperienced in credit matters.

The purpose of the Credit Repair Organizations Act is to ensure that prospective buyers of the services of credit repair organizations are provided with the information necessary to make an informed decision regarding the purchase of such services; and to protect the public from unfair or deceptive advertising and business practices by credit repair organizations.

Under this law, organizations are prohibited from making untrue or misleading statements or collecting fees in advance of services. Also, credit repair organizations must provide consumers with the following written statement before any contract or agreement is executed:

Consumer Credit File Rights Under State & Federal Law

You have a right to dispute inaccurate information in your credit report by contacting the credit bureau directly. However, neither you nor any credit repair company or credit repair organization has the right to have accurate, current, and verifiable information removed from your credit report. The credit bureau must remove accurate, negative information from your report only if it is over 7 years old. Bankruptcy information can be reported for 10 years.

You have a right to obtain a copy of your credit report from a credit bureau. You may be charged a reasonable fee. There is no fee, however, if you have been turned down for credit, employment, insurance, or a rental dwelling because of information in your credit report within the preceding 60 days. The credit bureau must provide someone to help you interpret the information in your credit file.

You are entitled to receive a free copy of your credit report if you are unemployed and intend to apply for employment in the next 60 days, if you are a recipient of public welfare assistance or if you have reason to believe that there is inaccurate information in your credit report due to fraud.

You have a right to sue a credit repair organization that violates the Credit Repair Organization Act. This law prohibits deceptive practices by credit repair organizations.

You have the right to cancel your contract with any credit repair organization for any reason within 3 business days from the date you signed it.

Credit bureaus are required to follow reasonable procedures to ensure that the information they report is accurate. However, mistakes may occur. You may, on your own, notify a credit bureau in writing that you dispute the accuracy of information in your credit file. The credit bureau must then re-investigate and modify or remove inaccurate or incomplete information. The credit bureau may not charge any fee for this service. Any pertinent information and copies of all documents you have concerning an error should be given to the credit bureau.

If the credit bureau's re-investigation does not resolve the dispute to your satisfaction, you may send a brief statement to the credit bureau, to be kept in your file, explaining why you think the record is inaccurate. The credit bureau must include a summary of your statement about disputed information with any report it issues about you.

The Federal Trade Commission regulates credit bureaus and credit repair organizations. For more information contact:

The Public Reference Branch
Federal Trade Commission
Washington, D.C. 20580

In addition, under the Credit Repair Organizations Act, consumers have the right to cancel any contract with a credit repair organization without penalty or obligation by notifying the credit repair organization of the consumer's intention to do so at any time before midnight of the 3rd business day which begins after the date on which the contract or agreement between consumer and credit repair organization is executed.

Read more at: http://www.ftc.gov/os/statutes/croa/croa.shtm

The Credit Card Accountability, Responsibility, and Disclosure Act of 2009 (CARD Act)

The Credit CARD Act is often called the Credit Cardholders Bill of Rights. Signed into law in May, 2009, many of its most significant provisions took effect in February, 2010. The law has two main purposes:

Fairness. Prohibit certain practices that are unfair or abusive such as hiking up the rate on an existing balance or allowing a consumer to go over the limit and then imposing an over-the-limit fee.

Transparency. Make the rates and fees on credit cards more transparent so consumers can understand how much they are paying for their credit card and can compare different cards.

As a result of this legislation, credit-card industry practices have changed in four significant ways:

- The long-standing practice of hiking interest rates on existing cardholder accounts has been dramatically curtailed.
- The amount of late fees consumers are paying has been substantially reduced.
- Over-the-limit fees have virtually disappeared in the credit card industry.
- Consumers report that their credit-card costs are clearer, but significant confusion remains.

See:
[#http://banking.senate.gov/public/_files/051909_CreditCardSummaryFinalPassa
ge.pdf~http://banking.senate.gov/public/_files/051909_CreditCardSummaryFinal
Passage.pdf#]

Appendix C: Consumer Resources

FEDERAL AGENCIES

Three federal agencies work to promote integrity within the credit counseling industry and help individuals obtain reliable high quality services. In doing so, each agency pursues its individual enforcement responsibilities.

• **The Internal Revenue Service (IRS)** ensures that credit counseling organizations holding themselves out to the public as tax-exempt charitable and educational organizations comply with the requirements for tax-exempt status. The IRS website provides resources for persons needing to verify the tax-exempt status of a credit counseling organization, and information about its initiative to ensure that credit counseling organizations comply with federal tax laws. It also highlights provisions of a new law that establishes standards an organization must satisfy to qualify for exemption under Internal Revenue Code section 501(c)(3) or 501(c)(4). http://www.irs.gov

• **The Federal Trade Commission (FTC)** The Federal Trade Commission is the agency responsible for the enforcement of consumer protecion laws. Contact information below includes a link to its website where you will can scroll to Bureau of Consumer Protection. Here you will find links to its seven regional offices which investigate concerns and complaints. http://www.ftc.gov

Federal Trade Commission
Pennsylvania Ave. and Sixth St., NW
Washington, DC 20580
202-326-2222
800-FTC - HELP

• **The U.S. Trustee Program (USTP)** at the Department of Justice approves credit counseling organizations to provide pre-bankruptcy counseling and pre-discharge debtor education as required under the Bankruptcy Abuse Prevention and Consumer Protection Act of 2005. The USTP's website provides information for consumers about the role of credit counseling organizations in personal bankruptcy proceedings, and offers links to assist consumers in selecting a credit counseling agency from the list of approved providers that fits the consumer's needs. These agencies provide educational resources that are helpful to both consumers and credit counseling organizations. http://www.justice.gov/ust

The various federal consumer credit laws are enforced by federal agencies. If you would like further information or have a particular credit problem that you would like addressed, you can contact the appropriate agencies. Addresses are listed below.

If your problem is with a retail department store, consumer finance company, all other creditors, and non-bank credit card issuers, credit bureaus or debt collectors, write to:
Division of Credit Practices
Federal Trade Commission
Washington, DC 20580

If you have a problem with a particular national bank, write to:

Office of the Comptroller of the Currency Deputy Comptroller for Customer and Community Programs Department of the Treasury
6th Floor L.Enfant Plaza
Washington, DC. 20219

If you have a problem with a particular state member bank, write to:

Federal Reserve Board Division of Consumer and Community Affairs
20th and C Streets, NW
Washington, DC 20551

If you have a problem with a particular nonmember insured bank, or if you are uncertain of your bank's charter (state or national), write to:

Federal Deposit Insurance Corporation Office of Consumer Compliance Programs
550 17th St., NW
Washington, DC 20429

If you have a problem with a particular savings institution insured by the Federal Savings and Loan Insurance Corporation and a member of the Federal Home Loan Bank System, write to:

Federal Home Loan Bank Board Department of Consumer
and Civil Rights Office of Examination and Supervision
Washington, DC 20522

If you have a problem with a federal credit union, write to:

National Credit Union Administration Office of Consumer Affairs
1776 G St., NW
Washington, DC 20456

Many of these federal agencies have regional offices.

CONSUMER EDUCATION & ADVOCACY

Consumer Federation of America is a nonprofit association of over 250 pro-consumer groups with a combined membership of 50 million. Its members advance consumer interest through advocacy and education.
http://www.consumerfed.org

Better Business Bureau is a nonprofit organization focused on advancing marketplace trust. It provides free business reliability reviews at the request of consumers. The BBB consists of 116 independently-incorporated local BBB organizations in the United States and Canada, coordinated under the Council of Better Business Bureaus (CBBB) in Washington, D.C.
http://www.bbb.org/

Other resources for consumer education and/or advocacy
http://www.consumer-action.org/
http://www.consumeraffairs.com/
http://www.consumer.org/
http://www.consumerlaw.org/
http://www.cbpp.org/
http://www.asec.org/
http://www.mymoney.gov/
http://www.firstgov.gov/
http://www.consumer.gov/
http://www.nolo.com/

CONSUMER TOOLS
These sites offer tools such as free budget calculators, repayment calculators as well as cost-cutting tips.

FREE CALCULATORS
http://www.mymoney.gov/
http://www.bankrate.com/
http://www.kiplinger.com/tools/budget/
[#http://mappingyourfuture.org/money/budgetcalculator.htm~http://mappingyourfuture.org/money/budgetcalculator.htm#]
[#http://www.calculatorweb.com/calculators/budgetcalc/~http://www.calculatorweb.com/calculators/budgetcalc/#]
FREE COST CUTTING IDEAS
http://www.savingsnut.com/
http://familybudgetideas.blogspot.com/
[#http://www.moneymanagementtips.com/budgeting.htm~http://www.moneymana

gementtips.com/budgeting.htm#]
[#http://www.personal-budget-planning-saving-money.com/~http://www.personal-budget-planning-saving-money.com/#]

FREE CONSUMER QUIZZES/ASSESSMENTS
http://consumerman.com/quizzes.htm
http://www.nca.ie/nca/games-quizzes
[#http://www.funtrivia.com/quizzes/world/business_world/consumer_protection.html~http://www.funtrivia.com/quizzes/world/business_world/consumer_protection.html#]
[#http://ago.mo.gov/cgi-bin/ConsumerCorner/quizzes/credit.cgi~http://ago.mo.gov/cgi-bin/ConsumerCorner/quizzes/credit.cgi#]
http://www.consumercredit.com/card-act-quiz.php
http://www.creditscorequiz.org/

CREDIT CARDS
These websites provide guidance and options for obtaining credit products.
http://www.cardtrak.com/
http://www.bankrate.com/
http://www.creditcardguide.com/
http://www.indexcreditcards.com/
[#https://www.billshrink.com/credit-cards/cards.html~https://www.billshrink.com/credit-cards/cards.html#]
http://www.cardhub.com/
http://www.cardratings.com/
http://www.credit.com/
http://www.lowcards.com/
http://www.nerdwallet.com/

CREDIT REPORTS
Below is a list of reputable links where you can order a copy of your credit report.
www.equifax.com
www.transunion.com
www.experian.com
www.myfico.com
www.fairisaac.com
www.annualcreditreport.com
http://www.credit.com/

BANKRUPTCY
http://www.usdoj.gov/ust
http://www.abiworld.org
http://www.ftc.gov

IDENTITY THEFT
[#http://www.ftc.gov/bcp/edu/microsites/idtheft2012/~http://www.ftc.gov/bcp/edu/microsites/idtheft2012/#]
http://www.idtheftcenter.org/

ASSISTANCE PROGRAMS
http://www.benefits.gov/
http://www.nutrition.gov/
http://www.fns.usda.gov/
http://www.rentassistance.us/

STUDENT LOANS
http://www.loanconsolidation.ed.gov/
http://www.salliemae.com/
http://www.youngmoney.com/
http://www.fastweb.com/

EMPLOYMENT
http://www.careerbuilder.com/
http://www.jobweb.com/

HOUSING
http://www.hud.gov/
http://www.freddiemac.com
http://www.homepath.com/
www.renters-rights.com/
http://www.tenant.net/
http://www.homefair.com/

HEALTH CARE
http://www.hrsa.gov/
http://helpwithmedicalcosts.com/
http://www.needhelppayingbills.com

MARITAL ISSUES
www.divorcestopper.com
www.marriagematters.com
www.marriagesuccess.com

CHILD SUPPORT
http://www.acf.hhs.gov
http://www.supportkids.com
http://www.supportguidelines.com
http://www.childsupportlawyer.com

FATHER'S RIGHTS
http://www.dadsrights.com
http://fatherhood.about.com

STRESS MANAGEMENT
http://www.mindtools.com
http://www.stress-management-isma.org

RECOVERY & REFERRAL
http://www.debtorsanonymous.org
http://www.gamblersanonymous.org
http://www.drugabuse.gov
http://www.drug-rehab.com
http://www.aa.org
http://www.healthyplace.com
http://www.counseling.org
http://www.apa.org
http://www.suicideassessment.com
http://www.befrienders.org
http://www.findtreatment.samhsa.gov

References

Alessandra, Tony, PH.D. & Hunsaker, Phil, PH.D. (1993). Communicating at Work. New York, NY: Simon & Schuster.

Bachman, John Phd. (2002) http://www.CreditCollectionsworld.com ; Thomas Corporation

Bank Rate. (2003). http://www.bankrate.com

Bassano, Anselm (2001) in John Bachman, PhD (Ed.) The Psychology of Debt. http://www.CreditCollectionsworld.com; Thomas Corporation.

Becvar, Dorothy Stroh, & Becvar, Raphael J. (1996). Family Therapy: A Systemic Integration (3rd ed.). Needham Heights, MA: Allyn and Bacon.

Berg, Stacie Z. (1999). The Unofficial Guide to Managing Your Personal Finances. New York, NY: Macmillan, Inc.

Borck, Leslie E., PH.D. & Fawcett, Stephen B., PH.D. (1982). Learning Counseling and Problem-Solving Skills. New York, NY: The Haworth Press.

British Standards Institute. Consumer Credit Counseling Agencies Code of Practice.

Consumer Aid. http://www.Consumeraid.org

Cook, Frank. (2004). You're Not Buying That House Are You?. Chicago, IL: Dearborn.

Cook, Marshall J. (1993). Slow Down and Get More Done. Cincinnati, OH: Betterway Books.

Cooke, Robert A. (1998). Personal Finance For Busy People. New York, NY: McGraw-Hill.

Corey, G. Theory and Practices of Counseling and Psychotherapy. 3rd ed

Cudney, Milton R., PH.D., & Hardy, Robert E., ED.D. (1991). Self-Defeating Behaviors. New York, NY: Harper Collins Publishers.

Davidoff, L. Introduction to Psychology. 2nd ed

Detweiler, Gerri. (1997). The Ultimate Credit Handbook: How to Double Your Credit, Cut Your Debt, and Have a Lifetime of Great Credit. New York, New York: Plume Books.

Diaz-Lefebvre, René. Coloring Outside the Lines

Echelman, R. The New Rules of Money. Harper Collins Publishers.

Dominguez, Joe, & Robin, Vicki. (1992). Your Money Or Your Life. New York, NY: Viking.

Egan, Gerard. (1994). Exercises in Helping Skills: A Manual to Accompany The Skilled Helper (5th ed.). Pacific Grove, CA: Brooks/Cole Publishing Company.

Egan, Gerard. (1994). The Skilled Helper: A Problem-Management Approach to Helping (5th ed.). Belmont, CA: Brooks/Cole Publishing Company.

Egan, G. The Skilled Helper. 2nd ed

Ellis, Albert, Ph.D., & Hunter, Patricia A., Psy. D. (1991). Why Am I Always

Broke?: How to be Sane about Money. New York, NY: Carol Publishing Group.

Equifax. (2003). http://www.equifax.com

Experian. (2003). http://www.experian.com

Fair, Isaac. Understanding Your Credit Score. www.myfico.com

Fannie Mae Foundation. (2003). www.fanniemae.com

Federal Trade Commission (FTC) Bureau of Economics. (2003). Retrieved 2003, from http://www.ftc.gov

Forward, Susan, Dr., & Burk, Craig. (1994). Money Demons: Keeping Them from Sabotaging Your Relationships and Your Life. New York, New York: Bantam Books.

French, Scott. (1988). Credit: The Cutting Edge. Boulder, CO: Paladin Press.

Gazzaniga, M.S. (1987). The Social Brain. Fremont, CA: Alex Chis Books.

Garner, R. et al. Personal Financial Planning Guide. Ernst & Young, P.F.P.G.

Glanz, Barbara A. (1993). The Creative Communicator. McGraw-Hill.

Glossbrenner, Alfred, & Glossbrenner, Emily. (1998). Smart Guide To Managing Personal Finance. New York, NY: John Urley & Sons, Inc.

Goodman, Jordan Z. (2002). Everyone's Money Book (on Credit). Chicago, IL: Dearborn Trade Publishing.

Gronlund, Norman E. (1998). Assessment of Student Achievement (6th ed.). Needham Heights, MA: Allyn & Bacon.

Hackney, Harold L., & Cormier, Sherilyn L. (1996). The Professional Counselor: A Process Guide to Helping (3rd ed.). Needham Heights, MA: Allyn & Bacon.

Halberstam, Joshua. (1993). Everyday Ethics: Inspired Solutions to Real-Life Dilemmas. New York, NY: Viking Penguin.

Hammond, Bob. (2000). Life After Debt: Free Yourself from the Burden of Money Worries Once and for All (3rd ed.). Franklin Lakes, NJ: Career Press.

Feinberg, Andrew. (1993). Downsize Your Debt: How to Take Control of Your Personal Finances. New York, NY: Penguin Books.

Ferrell, O.C., & Gardiner, Gareth. (1991). In Pursuit of Ethics: Tough Choices in the World of Work. Springfield, IL: Smith Collins Company.

Hibbert, Jeffery R., Auburn University; Beutler, Ivan F., Brigham Young University. The Effects of Financial Behaviors on the Quality of Family Life: Evidence from Adolescent Perceptions. School of Family Life, Brigham Young University.

Howard, Clark & Meltzer, Mark. (1998). Consumer Survival Kit III. Marietta, GA: Longstreet Press, Inc.

Irwin, Robert. (2000). Buy You First Home, Chicago, IL: Dearborn.

Janik, Carolyn. (1998). Homeology. Wahsington, D. C.: Kiplinger Books.

Klein, Gary, Loonin, Deanne, & Sheldon, Jonathan. (1999). Surviving Debt: A Guide for Consumers (3rd ed.). Boston, MA: National Consumer Law Center, Inc.

Knuckey, Deborah. (2001). The Ms Spent Money Guide: Get more of What you Want with What You Earn. New York, NY: John Wiley & Sons, Inc.

Kobliner, B. Get a Financial Life.

Kramer, C. S. Extension Specialist at Kansas State University. Untitled Manuscript. North Carolina Cooperative Extension Service, North Carolina State University, Raleigh, NC.

Lawrence, Judy. (2001). The Budget Kit: The Common Cents Money Management Workbook (3rd ed.). Chicago, IL: Dearborn Trade Publishing.

Leonard, Robin. (1996). Money Troubles: Legal Strategies to Cope with Your Debts (4th ed.). Berkeley, CA: Nolo Press.

Leonard R. Take Control of Your Student Loan Debt.

Leonard, R. Credit Repair. 4th ed.

Locke, E. A. & Latham, G. P. (2002). Building a Practically Useful Theory of Goal Setting and Task Motivation, 57 (9), 705-717.

Marks, Lawrence I. (1998). Deconstructing Locus of Control: Implications for Practitioners. Journal of Counseling & Development. (Vol.76 No.3). 251-260.

McKinley, Robert & Robinson, Marc. (2000). Management Credit. New York, NY: DK Publisher.

McNaughton, Deborah. (1999). All About Credit: Questions (and Answers) About the Most Common Credit Problems. Chicago, IL: Dearborn Financial Publishing, Inc.

McNaughton, Deborah. (1998). The Insider's Guide To Managing Your Credit: How to Establish, Maintain, Repair, and Protect Your Credit. Chicago, IL: Dearborn Financial Publishing, Inc.

Miller, Scott D., & Berg, Insoo Kim. (1995). The Miracle Method. New York, NY: W.W. Norton & Company, Inc.

Morris, Kenneth M., & Morris, Virginia B. (2000). Guide to Understanding Personal Finance. New York, NY: Lightbulb Press, Inc.

Mundis, J. (1990).How to Get Out of Debt, Stay Out of Debt, and Live Prosperously., New York, N.Y.: Bantam Books.

Myers, Isabel Briggs & Peter B. (1992). Gifts Differing. Consulting Psychologists Press, Inc.

National Consumer Law Center. (1999). Surviving Debt: A Guide for Consumers. Boston, MA: National Consumer Law Center, Inc.

O'Neill, Barbara. (2001). Predatory Lending Practices and Sub Prime Credit: What Financial Counselors and Educators Need to Know. Proceedings of the Association for Financial Counseling and Planning Education.

Ormon, Suze. (2000). The 9 Steps to Financial Freedom. New York, NY: Three Rivers Press.

Pond, Jonathan D. (1993). The New Century Family Money Book. New York, NY: Dell Publishing.

Pulvino, Charles J., Ph.D., & Lee, James L., Ph.D. (1991). Financial

Counseling: A Strategic Approach. Madison, WI: Instructional Enterprises.

Ram Research Group. http://www.ramresearch.com

Ramsey, Karen (1999). Everything You Know About Money Is Wrong: Overcome the Financial Myths from the Life that You Want. New York, NY: Regan Books.

Seligman, Martin E.P., PH.D. (1990). Learned Optimism. New York: Alfred A. Knoph, Inc.

Steinback, Robert. (1989). Out of Debt: How to Clean Up Your Credit and Balance Your Budget While Avoiding Bankruptcy. Holbrook, MA: Adams Media Corporation.

Tieger, Paul D. & Barbara Barron. (1998). The Art of Speed-reading people. Boston: Little, Brown & Company.

TransUnion. (2003). http://www.transunion.com

Webb, Martha. (1998). Finding Home: Buying The House That's Right for You. New York, N.Y: Three Rivers Press.

Weinrach, S.G., Ellis, A., MacLaren, C., DiGiuseppe, R., Vernon, A., Wolfe, J., Malkinson, R., & Backx, W. (2001). Rational Emotive Behavior Therapy Successes and Failures: Eight Personal Perspectives. Journal of Counseling & Development. (Vol.79 No.3). 259-268

Made in the USA
Monee, IL
22 March 2022